THE CHICAGO GUIDE TO **Fact-Checking**

Chicago Guides
to *Writing*, Editing*s*
and Publishing

The Chicago Guide to
FACT-CHECKING

Brooke Borel

Second Edition

THE UNIVERSITY OF CHICAGO PRESS   Chicago and London

The University of Chicago Press, Chicago 60637

The University of Chicago Press, Ltd., London

Published 2023

Printed in the United States of America

32 31 30 29 28 27 26 25 24 23   1 2 3 4 5

ISBN-13: 978-0-226-81789-7 (paper)

ISBN-13: 978-0-226-81790-3 (e-book)

DOI: https://doi.org/10.7208/chicago/9780226817903.001.0001

Library of Congress Cataloging-in-Publication Data

Names: Borel, Brooke, author.

Title: The Chicago guide to fact-checking / Brooke Borel.

Other titles: Chicago guides to writing, editing, and publishing.

Description: Second edition. | Chicago : The University of Chicago Press, 2023. | Series: Chicago guides to writing, editing, and publishing | Includes bibliographical references and index.

Identifiers: LCCN 2022044586 | ISBN 9780226817897 (paperback) | ISBN 9780226817903 (ebook)

Subjects: LCSH: Research—Handbooks, manuals, etc. | Internet research—Handbooks, manuals, etc.

Classification: LCC ZA3075 B67 2023 | DDC 001.4/202854678—dc23

LC record available at https://lccn.loc.gov/2022044586

♾ This paper meets the requirements of ANSI/NISO Z39.48-1992 (Permanence of Paper).

Contents

Introduction

As I was reporting and editing the first edition of *The Chicago Guide to Fact-Checking* from 2014 to 2016, many fact-checkers, journalists, family members, and friends offered more or less this sentiment: *There's never been a better time to write about fact-checking.* They were referencing several high-profile journalism scandals: *Rolling Stone*'s inaccurate 2014 story about a rape at a University of Virginia fraternity; the 2015 revelations that NBC's *Nightly News* anchor, Brian Williams, had fabricated his experience of a rocket-propelled grenade attack while reporting in Iraq, among other things; and the 2016 disclosure of the deceptions of an *Intercept* reporter, Juan Thompson, who invented a source and fabricated quotes in his coverage of the mass murderer Dylann Roof. Many other outlets picked up Thompson's false report, including the *New York Daily News*, the *New York Post*, *New York Magazine*, *The Root*, and the *Toronto Sun*.

I said it then and I'll say it again now: the idea that there has never been a better time to write an editorial fact-checking guide could just as easily apply to most eras in journalism—or in any nonfiction media, for that matter. Looking back: in 2012 it was Jonah Lehrer, a wunderkind science writer who fabricated Bob Dylan quotes in his book *Imagine*, among other transgressions. In 2003 Jayson Blair was caught making up stories and plagiarizing while Judith Miller was publishing inaccurate articles about Saddam Hussein's capacity to build weapons of mass destruction, both while writing for the *New York Times*. In 1998 the Pulitzer finalist Patricia Smith admitted she made up sources to give her *Boston Globe* column a kick, and in the same year a young journalist named Stephen Glass was caught in many elaborate frauds, including making up entire stories, for the *New Republic* and other publications. And in 1981 it was Janet Cooke, who had published a made-up story in the *Washington Post* about an eight-year-old heroin addict named Jimmy the previous year. We could probably go back in time to the birth of the printing press and beyond to find cringeworthy examples of stolen words, biased assumptions, or outright lies.

In between the time that the first edition of this book published, in September 2016, and as I write these words now in early 2022, well, I guess we could say a lot has happened. There have been plenty of new journalism scandals, from the accusations of inaccuracies and plagiarism in Jill Abramson's book *Merchants of Truth* to the fabrications of Claas Relotius at the German weekly magazine *Der Spiegel*. Trouble has also been brewing more broadly: democracies around the world have gone through tumultuous times under populists and alleged autocrats, many of whom have shown open disdain for truth—and for journalism in general. The American public, too, has shown a waning trust in journalism and many other institutions. According to Gallup, which has tracked the public's confidence in several U.S. institutions since 1972, trust in the media dipped to the second-lowest point in 2021; the lowest was 2016.

Since the first edition of the book, we have also endured the accelerating upheavals of climate change—floods, wildfires, droughts, extreme weather, and more—as well as a deadly pandemic. Both crises have been fertile ground for the proliferation of misinformation, disinformation, conspiracy theories, and propaganda. For instance, politicians and partisan websites have pushed claims that wildfires are the work of everyone from environmentalists to antifa rather than a result of a rapidly changing climate, while lies surrounding vaccine safety have intensified with COVID-19. And falsehoods have surged in ways that I certainly didn't predict five years ago. So have the profiles of conspiracy theorists, like Alex Jones at Infowars. While Jones has long had a sizable following, his influence shifted around 2015, when Donald Trump, then a presidential candidate, gave a live interview on Jones's website. (Although Jones's empire took a major blow in 2022, when he was found liable for more than a billion dollars for spreading lies about the 2012 shooting at Sandy Hook Elementary School.)

Who knows how the landscape of false information will morph over the coming years. The only thing I *do* know is that if I'm given the opportunity to write this introduction again in the coming years, I'll have a whole new list of concerns and elements that fact-checkers will need to grapple with.

So, the claim that *there's never been a better time to write about fact-checking* isn't quite right. A more accurate assertion: *It is always a good time to write about fact-checking.* And, for that matter, to talk about it, post about it on social media, discuss it with friends and family, and apply it to our journalism. In truth, no matter the era or the media—whether print or online or audio or video—fact-checking is relevant, and not only for flagrant examples of journalistic misconduct and correcting the lies of powerful politicians and conspiracy theorists but also for smaller errors. Misspellings. Sloppy descriptions. Poor sourcing. If journalism is a cornerstone of democracy, then fact-checking is its building inspector, ensuring that the structure of a piece of writing is sound.

Many journalists never learn about the process of editorial fact-checking—that is, a line-by-line reality check performed by an independent person who was not involved in a story's creation. That's because the process isn't always taught in journalism school or used in every newsroom. That's not to say that journalism professors and newsroom editors aren't pushing their students and staff to verify information—that's an intrinsic part of the gig. But many newsrooms simply aren't able to have a dedicated staff member double-check every single story (in these cases, the editorial teams use other verification processes to help catch errors, which I will discuss in this book, an approach that is also largely taught in journalism schools). Still, every journalist will benefit from understanding how editorial fact-checking functions in the newsrooms that use it—even if they never get a chance to work with a fact-checker directly.

To understand the fact-checker's job, it's also helpful to make a clear distinction between different types of fact-checkers. Throughout this book, unless otherwise noted, I am talking about editorial fact-checkers, who are hired by a publication and double-check articles before publication. This is different from political fact-checkers, who check the claims of politicians and other public figures. To confuse matters more, journalists often do political fact-checking at places like PolitiFact or the Fact Checker column at the *Washington Post.*

And to understand the role of the editorial fact-checker, it is helpful to know about other key editorial roles—in particular, the writer, editor, and copy editor—and how they all fit together. While there is some overlap of responsibilities, each person also has a unique role in crafting a story. Those roles can sometimes even be in conflict.

The goal of any writer of nonfiction—whether you want to call that writer a journalist, a reporter, or something else entirely—is to build a story out of facts. The first step is to ask a question, which will be central to the story. For instance: *What really happened the night of a particular crime? Does scientific research support a current health trend? Who is behind the latest dance trend on TikTok?* The next step is to gather facts to help answer that question—and maybe refine it—which may come from interviews, written reports, data sets, and more. The writer must sift through these facts and figure out how they connect to each other, and then use this scaffolding to inform the structure of their story. How should they introduce the reader to the information? How and where will they support each claim? If the story is a long narrative, what are the main threads and how will the writer braid them together? What is the conclusion of the story, and how will the writer pare it down to a pithy or insightful kicker? From a blank page, the writer must stitch their reporting into a cohesive piece.

The editor has several jobs. For one, they must take a piece and evaluate the story for clarity and flow. Maybe, for example, the writer's structure is too complicated for a reader to follow, and the editor decides to streamline it by changing the opening scene and the order of the following sections—a convoluted piece that jumps forward and backward in time may become a straightforward, chronological account. The editor also looks for holes in the story, from leaps in logic to missing pieces of key information, and may send the writer to hunt for more facts to fill these in and connect the dots. Good editors, too, will push back on the writer if something sounds too simple to be true or if the sourcing appears inadequate. And the copy editor takes a story and polishes, zooming in on individual sentences to make sure they meet the outlet's standards. (Traditionally, the editor and the copy editor are not the same person, although as budgets have tightened and lines have blurred, these days some editors do have to take on copyediting duties.)

After a story goes back and forth between a writer and an editor, often many times—and maybe even to a separate editor for a fresh set of eyes—they get it into nearly final form. Then, ideally, it will land on the desk of a fact-checker. It is the editorial fact-checker's job to unbraid the pieces of the story and examine each strand, testing its strength and probing for weak points; in the process, fact-checking also attempts to uncover whether any vital pieces of the story are missing. The fact-checker takes a hard look at the writer's sources to assess if they are trustworthy; decides whether the writer used the facts fairly and accurately to build the story; and pushes back against the writer and editor—who are now invested in the story and its structure—if the evidence doesn't support the way the story is written. "Even the best writing is really not good enough," says John Banta, global research director at Condé Nast, in describing why fact-checkers are needed. (Banta previously headed the fact-checking team at *Vanity Fair*.) "We provide a service where we go in and we take everything apart," he adds. "We take the engine out of the car, throw the parts on the floor, and put it back together again."

There is certainly overlap in the skill sets required of a fact-checker and a journalist. Learning how to fact-check helps journalists become better at reporting, because in a way fact-checking is reporting in reverse. Knowing how a fact-checker might pick a story apart helps a writer learn to think twice before relying on a questionable source. Journalists and other nonfiction writers also benefit from understanding the fact-checking process, even if they will never have the chance to do it themselves, particularly if they work for outlets that require it. Going through a fact-check can be nerve-racking, but it teaches writers to organize their source material and think about its quality: some outlets that use fact-checkers will require a writer to provide an annotated copy of their story that footnotes the sources they used for each and every fact. Knowing how to fact-check will help writers when they are working for places that forgo the process. It's nearly impossible to truly fact-check one's own work—we tend to trust our judgment too much, assuming our reporting is solid even when it's shaky—but taking a step back from a piece and giving it the most critical read possible can save a writer from embarrassing mistakes.

In some newsrooms, there is some overlap between the roles of fact-checker and editor. In the course of fact-checking, for instance, the fact-checker may find that the structure of a piece isn't sound—and make suggestions on how it could be rewritten in order to be more accurate (though the editor usually has the final say over any changes). And there are also some similarities between the work of the fact-checker and that of the copy editor. Both may be concerned with issues such as the correct spelling of names and other basic facts. But copy editors are focused on style and grammar, and they typically are not responsible for verifying the broader factual accuracy of a story (at some outlets, though, and particularly those with small teams, the fact-checker and the copy editor are the same person).

Historically, editorial fact-checking was most common at print magazines, first at publications including the *New Yorker* and *Time* and then spreading to others. This may be because magazines had the time to invest in fact-checking, particularly compared to newspapers or nightly news shows, which were more ephemeral, a flash replaced the next day by new stories or updates. Because of this speed, newspapers have not typically employed fact-checkers, instead relying on their journalists and editors to take extra care in verifying their information (that's not to say that a magazine writer doesn't do the same, but that there are different checks and balances in place to catch errors). The speed of daily news also meant that corrections could come faster—if a journalist made a mistake, they could correct the record with the next newspaper or broadcast. Magazine editors, on the other hand, had to wait a month or two to print a correction, so it made sense to employ fact-checkers to get it right the first time around.

Today, both print and digital publications are investing in fact-checking. In 2018, with support from the Knight Science Journalism Program at MIT, I led a research project to explore this landscape in science journalism, which is the journalistic niche where I have spent most of my career. We surveyed around 300 people and interviewed 91—including fact-checkers, journalists, editors, and professors and directors from journalism programs—and found just about the same percentage of digital publications and print publications were investing in editorial fact-checking. Based on our interviews, many outlets were also applying fact-checking to their stories in new ways, a shift from what I observed when I worked on the first edition of *The Chicago Guide to Fact-Checking*. In particular, some outlets are investing in the longer, more expensive magazine approach to fact-checking for long-form, investigative work, and stories of any length that are legally sensitive. These same publications are taking the newspaper approach—that is, relying on the journalist to verify their own work, with the assistance of their editor and, in some cases, a copy editor—for breaking news and other timely pieces, as well as for short items that are relatively straightforward.

In this book, I will outline the magazine model, the newspaper model, and this hybrid model that uses a bit of both. And since fact-checkers are increasingly working in other media such as podcasts, documentaries, and nonfiction books, I will also provide tips and tricks that are unique to these different forms of storytelling. (Worth noting: nonfiction books aren't typically fact-checked, at least by the publisher. Some book authors hire fact-checkers on their own, paying them out of often small advances, and others fact-check their own work despite the pitfalls of this practice.)

| | |

For decades, the fact-checking trade has, for the most part, been passed down apprenticeship-style—we learn on the job. Accordingly, the advice presented in this book draws heavily from firsthand experience. My first job in journalism, which served as my journalism school, was as a fact-checker and, later, a research editor at a magazine called *Science Illustrated*—an unusual fact-checking experience, as the magazine publishes in Danish and, during my tenure, was translated into English and then fact-checked and repackaged for an American audience. I've also worked as a fact-checker at

Quanta Magazine, an online publication that runs articles about complex science and mathematics. For several years, I've also taught courses on fact-checking to writers and others interested in learning this skill; run workshops for newsrooms; and consulted with publications starting new fact-checking departments. After writing my first nonfiction book, I fact-checked it myself, although I think the task is truly better off in the hands of a third party whenever possible. And from 2019 to 2022, I was a project lead at the Fact-Checking Project at the Knight Science Journalism program, where we created free resources for journalists, from a database of fact-checkers who are available for work to online modules for professors and teachers, to various fact-checking guidelines for editors who are trying to start up new fact-checking teams.

To supplement my own experience and widen the range of perspectives included in the book, for the first edition I conducted a survey of 234 current or former journalists, writers, fact-checkers, and research heads, and I interviewed dozens of experts (some who responded to the survey, and some whom I found later on). The outlets they've worked for include *The Atlantic, Audubon*, CBS, *Discover, Entertainment Weekly, GQ, InStyle, Laptop Magazine, Men's Journal, More, Mother Jones, National Geographic, The Nation*, National Geographic Channel, the *New Republic*, the *New York Times Magazine*, the *New Yorker, Outside, Playboy, Popular Mechanics, Popular Science, Radiolab*, Retro Report, *Saveur*, the Smithsonian Channel, *Der Spiegel, Sports Illustrated, This American Life, Time, Vanity Fair, Vice*, the *Village Voice, Vogue*, and *Wired*. Some of the checkers have also worked on best-selling nonfiction books. Their tales from the field appear throughout the book, and their advice informs my discussion even where it isn't specifically quoted. For this second edition, I've kept the advice that was still apt and relevant; contacted anyone who was quoted in the first book in order to give them a chance to update their thoughts on fact-checking; added about half a dozen new voices; and pulled information from the interviews and surveys from the 2018 Knight Science Journalism fact-checking report.

| | |

Although its very name implies a rigid objectivity, fact-checking is rarely cut-and-dried. Truths and facts can be more slippery than most want to admit, particularly when you move from the basics, like the spelling of a person's name, to the fuzzier realms of argument building or narrative pacing. Fact-checking, too, is not a static practice. It changes from one publication to another and even from one type of story to another. "The degree of fact-checking that's needed is so dictated by the contents, first and foremost," says Yvonne Rolzhausen, research chief at *The Atlantic*. A "highly sensitive, litigious subject," she adds, will get "the highest level of fact-checking we have with the most experienced fact-checkers." Newsier pieces that need to get out fast will receive a lighter touch. At many publications, the readers' expectations on a story matter, too; the stakes in a celebrity profile, for example, aren't the same as those in a 30,000-word investigation into environmental toxins or campaign fraud, and the accompanying reality check is similarly different. Because fact-checking ideals change from one publication to the next and even one story to the next, you may find fact-checkers who disagree with portions of this book—surely even among the people I've interviewed.

Working as a fact-checker is often a humbling experience. The task often seems unattainable: How do you decide if the facts you've found and confirmed amount to a story that is *true*, when that seemingly objective term isn't actually solid at all? Whose truth? Whose perception of reality? "Fact" and "truth" may seem synonymous, but the words are distinct. A fact is something you can't argue your way out of, like the dimensions of this page you're reading or the fact that this sentence started with the words "a fact." Truth is a fact or set of facts in context: it includes not just the facts on the page, but the information that surrounds it, as well as the unavoidable perspectives that are baked in from the people who were interviewed for the story—and different perspectives from those who were not. It is also shaped by the curatorial styles of the editorial team.

In other words, while the facts are indisputable, the truth a writer builds from them is a matter of interpretation. Even if the facts don't change, the order in which you place them can shift the meaning of a piece: give two journalists the same assignment, and each will write a different story. Give them identical source material to build their story, and each will still come up with something unique to their sensibilities. In fact, in 2019, the NPR podcast *Invisibilia* did just that: two journalists cut together two different stories using the same tape. The tape was from an interview with a man who had formerly identified as an incel, or involuntary celibate, which is a person who can't seem to succeed with romantic or sexual relationships. Incels are usually men, and they typically blame their lack of success on both their own physical shortcomings and the targets of their affection—usually women. The results of the podcast experiment were wildly different. The first journalist, Hanna Rosin, used an empathetic framing to try to understand the man's story; the second, a producer and reporter named Lina Misitzis, added in broader context about the incel subculture, which often promotes violence against women and has even led to some high-profile murders, as well as the perspective of women who have been in abusive relationships. (The episode is called "The End of Empathy" and it is worth a listen.)

Despite the challenges in accurately reflecting and contextualizing the facts in a story, a good fact-checker forges on, aiming for truth even when reaching it is impossible, critically examining the premise of the words in a story, and holding those words up to every possible light.

Because of these and other obstacles to uncovering facts

and discerning truth, you will find that even the most thoroughly fact-checked writing may have errors or fudges. No matter the medium, pulling together a story is an act of deciding what to include and what to leave out. Every step of the way, a journalist, editor, or fact-checker is making decisions as to what bits are important to get the basics of the story across, all within the constraints of word limit (or airtime) and deadlines—and with a goal of producing compelling material. A story that includes a fact-checker's every hedge, clarification, and lengthy contextual explanation won't just run over in terms of word counts or time slots; it will also be a snooze, more of an encyclopedia entry than a story that convinces the reader or listener to stay until the end. Knowing how to get the information right while keeping the heart and soul—and yes, truth—of a story intact is an art.

And it's key to remember that while we may strive toward something like objectivity in journalism, it isn't actually possible in reality. Journalists, editors, and fact-checkers are human, and with that come inevitable failures. We're complex creatures with messy psychologies and faulty memories. In every story we write or edit or fact-check, we are dealing with deadlines, interpersonal politics, and our own unavoidable biases. Given that, the examples of mistakes or corrections I use in this book aren't intended to shame those who made them, but to serve as a warning of what can go wrong even in the most prestigious publications operating with the most earnest intentions.

Even this guide will have errors—at least in someone's interpretation—despite the surreal meta-experience of hiring a fact-checker to fact-check a fact-checking book, and then another fact-checker to fact-check the updates for this new edition, and I cringe in anticipation at the delight that readers will surely take in pointing out my own errors for years to come. (*Aren't you the person who wrote the fact-checking book? Shouldn't you always get everything right?!*)

Well, it's more complicated than that. Through this book, I hope to show you why. I also hope to convince you that fact-checking is a vital part of the journalistic process.

| | |

This book has two big themes: it is part guide, to help you work as a fact-checker or attempt to check your own writing, and part overview of fact-checking in today's media, to offer context for the settings in which the work of checking takes place.

Chapter 1, "Why We Fact-Check," offers a more thorough explanation of the underlying need for fact-checking than you've experienced in these short introductory pages. The chapter also provides cautionary tales where fact-checking or reporting went wrong, as well as what a fact-checker might look for to prevent similar debacles from happening under their watch. Here, I also go through some of the legal implications for getting facts wrong, although if you find yourself in a legal quandary, you'd definitely be better off contacting a trained media attorney than relying on advice from this book. So would I, for that matter.

A short version of chapter 2, "What We Fact-Check," might read: "everything." But it isn't enough to say that and expect someone to know what it actually entails. The chapter lays out the sorts of information that a fact-checker should check. Beginning here, you'll find occasional "Think Like a Fact-Checker" sections that invite you to try your hand at some fact-checking skills. The questions are open-ended, and there are no answers provided, but the goal is to encourage reflection on the issues raised and let you experience the complexity of what it means to fact-check.

Chapter 3, "How We Fact-Check," gets into the process of fact-checking. The chapter is a good reference for when you are new to fact-checking and you aren't sure where to start or how to keep track of the facts in a story (or how to get along with your editor or writer). Here, I break down the magazine model, the newspaper model, and the hybrid model. I also show how fact-checking can be applied to media beyond the written word, including audio and video, both of which have unique considerations. You'll also find tips on collaborating with writers, editors, and producers, as well as suggestions on how to find fact-checking gigs. And while fact-checking your own work is seen as impossible by many folks, the chapter also provides tips on how to double-check your own story if you are working without a fact-checker. Here you will also begin encountering boxed features labeled "Quick Guide," which summarize key sections of the text for easy reference, and "Pro Tip," which offer more detailed or specialized information on issues discussed in the text.

While the previous chapter walks you through the process, chapter 4, "Checking Different Types of Facts," is a reference guide that explains how to check specific categories of facts, from descriptions to statistics to polls to summaries of a scientific study. The chapter also gives tips on special considerations for working on sensitive topics, such as trauma and abuse.

The quality of a fact-check depends on the quality of the source materials. Chapter 5, "Sourcing," explains the difference between primary and secondary sources and explores how to judge a source, whether it is one that you've found on your own or something a writer has offered in their backup material for a piece. The chapter also provides advice on how to contact people who are sources, as well as how to interact with them.

Chapter 6, "Record Keeping," is a brief chapter offering suggestions on how to organize and store your documents and explaining why this is important from both legal and practical perspectives.

In chapter 7, "Test Your Skills," you will find two exercises. In the first, you'll try to count all of the facts in a short piece of writing, which is much more difficult than it sounds. In the second, you'll examine a list of sources and try to figure out whether they are primary or secondary. You'll also need to rate these in terms of their quality. The answer keys for both exercises are in appendix 1.

The conclusion offers some final thoughts about fact-checking in a world that is increasingly digital and overrun with misinformation, disinformation, and other lies and misrepresentations. The internet, of course, has allowed false information to spread faster than ever before, intensifying the challenges for fact-checking. But I also do my best to look toward the future, by discussing other technologies that may affect fact-checking (and journalism as a whole), from the latest in machine learning to blockchain to deepfakes to the metaverse. If you don't know what any of that means, don't worry. I'll walk you through it.

If, after all this, you want to learn even more about fact-checking, you'll find additional books, articles, and radio programs on the topic in appendix 2.

When writers present a piece as nonfiction, they create a contract with the reader. This is true whether the piece in question is a newspaper article, a magazine feature, or the script for a documentary or nonfiction podcast. The writer is saying, *this happened.* To bolster their account, they present evidence including, though certainly not limited to, quotes from experts, data, and eyewitness reports. Together, these sources give the story a foundation. The overarching argument that the writer builds on top of this foundation is important, too: it tells the reader *not only did this happen,* but *here is the context in which you should consider what happened.*

Journalists should do the hard work of making sure they keep up their end of the contract, both to protect their reputations and to keep readers' trust. In other words, journalists must vet "content appropriately so that it stands up," says Luke Zaleski, the legal affairs editor at Condé Nast. "That is how you earn your credibility and that's how you become a person in this space that can be believable."

But somewhere between all the reading, interviewing, and thinking, the foundation of a story may crack and crumble. Maybe the problem is minimal—a simple misunderstanding or copy error, like flubbing a person's official title or inadvertently transposing the digits in a number. If the crack is small and the remaining sources are solid, the story could survive. Still, it's a crack, and an observant reader starts to wonder about the rest of the structure. Take, for example, a 2012 *Vogue* profile of Chelsea Clinton in which Daniel Baer, who at the time was the deputy assistant secretary for the Bureau of

Democracy, Human Rights, and Labor at the U.S. Department of State, was identified as an interior designer. Or a 2016 piece on NPR that said Donald Trump's running mate for the coming presidential election was Hillary Clinton. On the surface, flubbing a job title or mixing up a name is a relatively small misunderstanding. But knowing these particular flubs, do you trust the rest of the information in these stories?

Then there are the more glaring problems that shake a story's foundation: explanations oversimplified to the point that they are wrong, credulous sources, and gross misunderstandings of an event and its context. In 2012, for instance, after a Supreme Court ruling on the Affordable Care Act, both CNN and Fox News briefly reported that a controversial and key piece—the individual mandate—had been struck when in fact it had not. Or consider a 2015 article by *New York Times* tech writer Nick Bilton, which suggested that wearable technologies are as bad for your health as smoking cigarettes. Science writers criticized the story, pointing out that Bilton cherry-picked a handful of studies that tried to link cell phones to cancer—ignoring an abundance of research that said otherwise—and also quoted a controversial alternative medicine proponent as an expert. The mistake ultimately resulted in a response from the newspaper's public editor at the time, Margaret Sullivan, and the online version later included a 200-word addendum.

Even worse are full-blown earthquakes where the writer commits plagiarism or publishes outright alterations or fabrications of quotes, or other lies. For examples of journalistic misconduct, look no further than Jayson Blair, who plagiarized and fabricated stories for the *New York Times* including a series on the Washington Sniper in 2002; Patricia Smith, who fabricated pieces of her *Boston Globe* column; Jonah Lehrer, who self-plagiarized several posts for the *New Yorker* blog and made up several Bob Dylan quotes in his book *Imagine*; Stephen Glass, who fabricated not only stories but also his fact-checking notes and sources while working for the *New*

Republic; Judith Miller, who relied on inaccurate sources in her coverage leading up to the Iraq War; Michael Finkel, who made up a composite character, along with other fabrications, for a *New York Times Magazine* profile in 2001; or Claas Relotius, a star writer for *Der Spiegel* who fabricated many stories at the German news magazine during his seven-year career before he was caught, in 2018. All of these writers committed these journalistic sins in order to tell a good yarn or make a persuasive argument.

In other cases, writers may twist the ground rules with a source in order to use or attribute material that wasn't agreed on. Usually, writers and their sources will be clear about whether the source's comments are on the record, which means their identity may be included in the story, or on background, in which it may not (for definitions and further discussion, see chapter 4). Writers should honor these and other rules of source attribution, but a look at their interview notes and recordings may reveal that they, in fact, have not.

There are also grayer areas that fall between simple errors and intentional rule breaking. A writer's own biases may sneak into the work. Writers and editors, too, while crafting a compelling and page-turning narrative, may shuffle a few facts to help with the story's flow. And when a writer has spent weeks, months, or even years on a piece, it is difficult, if not impossible, to step outside to catch these mistakes. A blind spot will probably continue to be a blind spot. Further, each newspaper, book publisher, magazine, podcast, and more has a unique worldview, and the stories it shares will reflect that, which adds another layer of perspective on how a story is told.

Independent fact-checkers—people who are not involved in the story's creation—temper these gray areas and catch the more obvious and easy mistakes. "Fact-checkers, we're like the janitors, the custodians. We clean up after everybody," says Beatrice Hogan, a longtime fact-checker who has worked at *More* magazine, *The Atlantic*, and *MIT Technology Review* and also teaches fact-checking at New York University. Indeed, a good fact-checker goes through a story both word by word and from a big-picture view, zooming in to examine each individual fact or statement and then zooming out to see whether the story's premise is sound. The fact-checker's presence does not absolve the writer and the editor from their mistakes; the responsibility is on everyone to deliver the most accurate story possible. Still, the fact-checker will likely feel the weight of a mistake the most, particularly if it was an oversight on their part or the insertion of an error where there was none before, and not an error the team made collectively. The fact-checker is indeed like a janitor—an especially meticulous and skeptical one.

It's also worth noting that a fact-checking department is only as good as its outlet allows it to be. If everyone involved in a story, from the writer to the editors to the art department, respects the craft of fact-checking, this support only furthers the cause. If the staff doesn't care about the fact-checking process, or if checkers feel that they can't speak up when they see a story's foundation crumbling, the entire process is doomed.

Fact-checking is vital when it comes to working online, in terms of both how we find and use sources and how we consume digital media. This was true when I wrote the first edition of this book, when hoaxes were regularly making it into national news reports unchecked. Since then, how we consider online information has become even more important, as misinformation, disinformation, propaganda, and conspiracy theories cascade across social media and play increasingly big roles in national and international politics. (By the way, *mis*information and *dis*information aren't interchangeable—the former refers to false information that may be spread unwittingly, while the latter is spread intentionally.)

There is nothing inherently bad about online information, and its potential for falsehoods isn't entirely unique from a historical perspective. Hoaxes, sensationalism, and other wildly inaccurate accounts were around long before we went digital. Take, for example, the Great Moon Hoax, published in *The Sun* in 1835, which claimed that a (real) astronomer had discovered, among other things, (fake) bat-winged creatures living on the moon; or consider the yellow journalism of the 1890s, like the time William Randolph Hearst used his newspapers to fan the flames of the Spanish-American War. And both mis- and disinformation campaigns have been around a long time, too. I'm not sure we can really pinpoint the world's first example, but one possible early candidate dates to the Roman Empire. Around 44 BCE, Octavian distributed coins printed with propaganda about his political rival Marc Antony. According to researchers at the International Center for Journalists, the coins "painted Antony as a womanizer and a drunk, implying he had become Cleopatra's puppet, having been corrupted by his affair with her." Octavian's antics may have helped him become the first Roman emperor.

The difference between our modern digital era and the past isn't so much the medium, but how it functions. "Journalists tend to glorify earlier eras of journalism as more accurate, as having had more integrity," says Adrienne LaFrance, executive editor at *The Atlantic*. "And I think that's flawed." Painting print journalism as good and digital as bad, she adds, "would be foolish and shortsighted."

Still, of course, there are several key differences between past and present media. The first is that, previously, not everyone had a printing press—or the resources to make coins with lies about their enemies. The means of producing information were in the hands of the few. The digital age flipped that, making it possible for virtually anyone with an internet connection to publish anything they want. As such, everyone contributes to the second key difference between the past and now: we collectively and constantly circulate a glut of information—some of it great, some of it mediocre, some of it terrible, and some of it written with the sole intention of misleading the reader or viewer. While the internet has democratized journalism and publishing, making it more accessible to people who previously weren't able to participate in it, it's also led to a virtual avalanche that is hard to sift. For each of the countless stories we see, we have to ask: Is that piece of information actually fake news? And who is calling it that? It's exhausting.

Another key difference between the past and the present is that not only are we now all publishers, we also have the tools to be savvy marketers. Anyone is able to amplify any story— true or false—by pushing it on Twitter, Facebook, WhatsApp, Instagram, TikTok, or any other social media platform. It's so easy to "like" or republish a headline—even without reading the relevant story—or circulate a claim, we're collectively bombarded with inaccurate stories, whether intentionally so or because of honest mistakes.

Although some social media companies have tried to curb false information in recent years, these efforts have been like a Band-Aid on a knife wound. Facebook launched a third-party fact-checking system in December 2016, after facing accusations that its platform had played a role in spreading fake news surrounding the 2016 U.S. presidential election. But the program faced fierce criticism, which, as of this writing, continues. Some users, particularly those who were sharing false information to begin with, claimed the move was a form of censorship, while activists and critics of big tech said the fact-checkers simply didn't have the resources to address the sheer volume of fake or misleading posts. Even some of the journalists who worked as fact-checkers for Facebook's third-party groups pushed back, saying, as *The Guardian* reported in 2018, that "the company has ignored their concerns and failed to use their expertise to combat misinformation."

Twitter has faced similar problems. Early in the COVID-19 pandemic, the tech company announced a new initiative to promote accurate information about the coronavirus on its platform. But the approach didn't automatically filter out false information, so lies still got through; to name one example, researchers at Ryerson University (recently renamed Toronto Metropolitan University) traced the range of posts with COVID-related misinformation attached to a specific hashtag (#FilmYourHospital), which published after the company's initiative went into effect. The purpose of the hashtag was to spread disinformation claiming that the pandemic was a hoax, encouraging users to post photographs and videos of empty hospitals. The researchers found that the hashtag had 79,736 interactions among 41,903 Twitter users (a small percentage were bots, or fake accounts). In December 2020, Twitter launched a new policy to label coronavirus misinformation and suspend or ban related accounts, although it didn't stop false claims about the pandemic—or other topics, for that matter. YouTube, owned by Google, has similarly tried to remove false videos from its site, with mixed results. And in 2020 and 2021, executives from Twitter, Facebook, and Google were subject to congressional hearings, in part because of the companies' role in spreading lies.

Internet fact failures take many forms. In one category, legacy news outlets and newer media sites alike post stories without fact-checking them, essentially publishing hoaxes or misinformation as news. This phenomenon is, in part, an unfortunate result of aggregation, in which online outlets pick up stories from one another without adding any original reporting. Take this example from 2013, when bored Americans celebrating Thanksgiving were riveted by a drama unfolding on several news websites. A man named Elan Gale was live-tweeting an apparent feud with a woman named Diane on a US Airways flight. Gale claimed he had seen Diane act rudely to a flight attendant and proceeded to send her alcoholic drinks and notes essentially telling her to lighten up. She wrote back. Gale took photos of the notes and broadcast the images to his Twitter followers, which ballooned from a reported 35,000 to 140,000 following the exchange. The story hit its climax after the plane landed, when Diane approached Gale in the airport and slapped him. Many news outlets picked up the story, including ABC, Business Insider, BuzzFeed, CBC, Fox, and the *New York Daily News*.

But the story wasn't true. Gale—who had previously mostly posted jokes on Twitter—made it up in order to entertain his followers during the holiday travel. In a follow-up interview with ABC, Gale reportedly said of the initial media coverage: "My thought was I can't believe anyone is taking this seriously. I thought, 'Why isn't anyone doing any fact checking?' Then I saw it was on the evening news in Sacramento and it became this totally absurd thing."

Publishing a hoax weakens readers' trust in an outlet's ability to report the news, which is a problem on its own. But publishing incorrect information in more dire circumstances has even more harmful consequences. Take the media frenzy during Hurricane Sandy in 2012, the Boston Marathon bombing in 2013, or any other catastrophic event that has unfolded in the age of social media. In these cases especially, outlets are under pressure to publish—and publish fast. And it means that a lot of that published information ends up being wrong. During Hurricane Sandy, for example, Reuters picked up a rumor circulating on Twitter that nineteen Con Edison workers were trapped in a power station, surely an upsetting report for anyone with family or friends who worked for the utility. And after the Boston Marathon bombing, reporters from outlets including CBS and BuzzFeed retweeted a message that said: "Police on scanner identify the names of #BostonMarathon suspects in gunfight, Suspect 1: Mike Mulugeta. Suspect 2: Sunil Tripathi." The trouble was neither man was actually a suspect, and there is no evidence that the Boston police even mentioned the latter's name. Tripathi, a Brown University student, not only had nothing to do with the bombing—he had been missing for a month and his family had been frantically searching for him. The false accusations were painful on their own, but, worse, he was later found dead from an apparent, and unrelated, suicide.

Another case where the pressure to publish breaking news played an unfortunate role was in the aftermath of a 2011 shooting in Tucson, Arizona, where a gunman opened fire on a crowd, hitting eighteen people, including U.S. Representative Gabrielle Giffords. Six people died. Early reports claimed Giffords was one of them, from outlets including CBS, CNN, Fox, the *Huffington Post*, the *New York Times*, NPR, and Reuters. In fact, Giffords wasn't dead but had been shot in the head and was rushed into surgery. The false news and Twitter announcements made an already frightening and sobering situation all the more difficult for Representative Giffords's family and constituents, as well as the nation as a whole.

A year after the Arizona shooting, journalist Craig Silverman—who at the time covered errors, corrections, fact-checking, and verification at the Poynter Institute blog *Regret the Error* and has a book by the same name—recounted the debacle: "Twitter gave me a window into the captivating mixture of urgency, confusion and information that emerges when major news breaks and the story takes off." Indeed, this process used to happen in the newsroom as reporters decided how and when to report breaking news. In the internet era, the often-messy aspects are aired in the open, which is unfortunate because this is where readers can access the information and assume it is true. As Silverman notes in the same post, local Arizona news outlets got the Giffords story right. This provides insight on how to judge news when you're tweeting from a distance: look for publications as geographically close to the story as possible, because they have the best vantage point (for more tips, see Silverman's *Verification Handbook: A Definitive Guide to Verifying Digital Content for Emergency Coverage.*)

More recently, the media ecosystem has gotten even more confusing, between old-fashioned hoaxes, journalistic errors, and all of the mis- and disinformation. And when traditional

 **NPR News** ✓
@nprnews

☼

BREAKING: Rep. Giffords (D-AZ), 6 others killed by gunman in Tucson
http://n.pr/fjnZW5

↩ ⇄ ★ ❨ •••

RETWEETS FAVORITES
592 18

🞅 🌱🞅🞅🞕🞙🞅🞈🞅

1:12 PM - 8 Jan 2011

Figure 1. NPR News was one of many outlets that falsely reported the death of Representative Gabrielle Giffords in the aftermath of a chaotic shooting.

media publishes a hoax or makes other errors, we may be helping false information to thrive, since those errors give ammunition to those who call real journalism "fake news." "If news organizations do make genuine mistakes, the stakes are a lot higher," says Carl Zimmer, a science writer and columnist for the *New York Times* who worked as a fact-checker for *Discover* magazine early in his career. "Because even a small number of errors—some people will see that as validation of their distrust."

Although breaking-news outlets have systems in place for verifying information, it's not common for them to employ independent fact-checkers, partly because of time constraints; television and web reporters who are covering these sorts of stories have to rely on their own sourcing because they're on short deadline. Still, examining where stories like this can go wrong is instructive: look for the potential weak spots to see how you would have checked it, if you had the opportunity. In the Gale Thanksgiving hoax, a fact-checker might have confirmed the story not just with Gale, but also with the airline and, if possible, "Diane." In the stories about Hurricane Sandy, the Boston Marathon, and the Arizona shooting, a checker should know that a rumor circulating on Twitter must be confirmed before it is repeated or put in a story—this could have been accomplished through a phone call to Con Ed, the Boston Police Department, or Tucson-area hospitals, respectively.

| | |

Beyond these philosophical and practical reasons for fact-checking, there are also the legal incentives. If a story is wrong, it damages not only the writer's reputation but also that of the editorial staff and the publisher, particularly for controversial or investigative pieces where the stakes are high. Factual errors may open a journalist or outlet to lawsuits, which can run into damages worth millions of dollars. Fact-checkers should be aware of several areas of law—including defamation, copyright, and invasion of privacy—and be especially vigilant with relevant sources. Necessary disclaimer: what follows is not intended as legal advice; if you're unsure about whether your work opens you or your publication to lawsuits, consult an attorney.

Defamation comes in two flavors: slander, which is spoken, and libel, which is written (although, confusingly, defamation in news broadcasts and the like is usually considered libel). In either case, defamation involves making a false statement about a person or company—one that is done so with fault and damages a reputation. Usually, a plaintiff—the person bringing the suit—has to prove the information was indeed inaccurate and that it harmed them in some tangible way, such as causing them to lose a job or anything else that can be connected to money (although the injury could also be the emotional stress that results from a damaged reputation).

Defamation laws are different for public and private citizens. Public figures include celebrities, government officials, politicians, and more, all of whom lose some of their expectations for privacy when they enter the public sphere. In order to successfully sue for defamation, a public figure must prove that the information was published or spoken with actual malice. This doesn't mean the publisher or speaker harbored actual ill will against the public figure, but that they knew the information was incorrect and published it anyway. It's up to the plaintiff to prove actual malice.

Here's one example: in 2011 former Chicago Bulls player Scottie Pippen sued NBC Universal Media LLC and CBS Interactive Inc. because of an inaccurate story that suggested he had filed for bankruptcy. But although the reporter had documentation proving a Scottie Pippen had declared bankruptcy, it turned out that it was not the basketball player but a different man. The U.S. Supreme Court ultimately declined to hear the case, while a lower court dismissed it, because Pippen could not prove that the publications knew they had the wrong person and thus had no evidence of actual malice. Of course, even though the case was dismissed, it would have been better to avoid it to begin with. If faced with a story like this, a fact-checker would want better confirmation that the Scottie Pippen on the bankruptcy documents was indeed the basketball player, perhaps by comparing addresses and other identifying information in those documents, or by contacting the athlete through his booking agent or other representative.

The court case that established actual malice in public figure defamation is a famous one, and it's worth mentioning: *New York Times Co. v. L. B. Sullivan*, which went before the U.S. Supreme Court in 1964. L. B. Sullivan, the public safety commissioner in Montgomery, Alabama, sued the *Times* for libel in state court after the paper published an advertisement seeking money to defend Martin Luther King Jr. in a 1960 indictment. The ad included a few errors—it said, for example, that Alabama police had arrested King seven times, when it had been four—and although Sullivan wasn't specifically named, he felt the information was defamatory. An Alabama state court awarded him half a million dollars. But the case got bumped to the Supreme Court, which unanimously ruled for the newspaper. Under the First and Fourteenth Amendments, the court said, a state can't award damages to public figures unless they can prove actual malice, defined as a statement "made with knowledge of its falsity or with reckless disregard of whether it was true or false." Despite the outcome, this case underscores the importance of checking even seemingly small facts, like the number of times an event happened—in this case, King's arrests.

In another famous libel case, this one starting in 1984 and lasting a decade, the psychoanalyst Jeffrey Masson sued the *New Yorker* and affiliates for $10 million after Janet Malcolm, a writer for the magazine at the time, wrote a lengthy and juicy profile about him. The suit alleged that Malcolm had fabricated quotes and other information and, at one point during the long case, pulled the fact-checker into the conversation. Masson said he had raised points of inaccuracy with the checker, Nancy Franklin, and that she had brushed him off. In one of many rulings, an appeals court that sent the case back to a trial jury suggested that because the *New Yorker* employed a fact-checking process that uncovered questions about some of the details in Malcolm's article, the magazine was open to greater scrutiny than if it had no process. Ultimately, the court let Malcolm off the hook, concluding that although the quotes might be false, they needed more evidence to prove it. The *New Yorker* has a famously robust fact-checking team, so it's hard to know whether there was something more Franklin could have done, particularly in this case, where the subject of a negative story had so much incentive to sue. It's still a good reminder that as a fact-checker, your work may be scrutinized by a court.

The law shields private figures from the public eye, which makes it easier to prove defamation. Specifically, private individuals only have to prove that a publisher or broadcaster was negligent, meaning they failed to follow the reasonable journalistic steps required to figure out if a piece of information is true or false. Of course, private individuals still have to prove that the statement was indeed false and that it caused them injury. The key Supreme Court case establishing rules for private figures is *Gertz v. Robert Welch, Inc.*, in which a lawyer, Elmer Gertz, sued Robert Welch, the owner of the John Birch Society's *American Opinion*. The publication had run a story in 1969 about a Chicago police officer who had shot a man dead and was subsequently convicted of second-degree murder. Gertz had represented the dead man's family in a separate civil case, and *American Opinion* claimed that the lawyer was a "communist-fronter" and "Leninist," among other things. Welch tried to invoke *New York Times v. Sullivan*, but the Supreme Court's decision pointed out that Gertz was a private individual and therefore had greater protection against defamation. For any fact-checker, it is important to consider whether a person in a story is a public or a private figure, particularly if that person is depicted in a negative light, and take extra care in fact-checking such claims.

Defamation laws vary greatly from one country to another. In the United Kingdom, for example, it used to be far easier to sue for slander or libel than in the United States. In one famous case that began in 2008, the writer Simon Singh published a column in *The Guardian* criticizing chiropractic therapy, an alternative medicine. The British Chiropractic Association sued Singh, and a court battle ensued that lasted two years. Eventually the BCA withdrew their suit. The laws in the U.K. have changed a bit since then. The country's Defamation Act 2013 declared, among other things, that in order to bring a defamation suit, a person had to prove that they suffered "serious harm" to their reputation. The law also allowed defendants to present evidence that "the statement complained of was, or formed part of, a statement on a matter of public interest," and that "the defendant reasonably believed that publishing the statement complained of was in the public interest," a provision that, arguably, Singh's case may have fallen under, had the law existed back then. Still, all writers and fact-checkers should be aware of defamation laws in the countries in which their stories will appear.

Unlike defamation, invasion of privacy can include statements that are true. The definition here is knotty, but the concept basically means that a person is allowed a reasonable expectation of privacy. A reporter or publication, for example, can't record someone in their home without their knowledge or consent and then publish quotes or other information that came from those recordings. Publications often can't reveal intimate or private facts such as sexual practices or particularly sensitive illnesses, or use a person's name or likeness without their permission. In one famous invasion of privacy case, the father of a soldier who died in Iraq sued *Harper's Magazine* for publishing a photograph from the soldier's open-casket funeral. An Oklahoma district court sided with the photographer and *Harper's*, because the funeral was public and the story was a matter of public interest. Had the photograph shown a private citizen at a closed funeral, however, the case may have had legs. These are the sorts of details a fact-checker should confirm.

There is also the matter of copyright infringement, in which an author uses intellectual property that belongs to someone else without permission. This may include not only text but also images, song lyrics, music, audio, or video. The responsibility for most of these cases will fall to either the editorial team or the art department, but it's still helpful for the fact-checker to be aware of the rules and look out for possible slips. (Copyright infringement shouldn't be confused with plagiarism. According to Rob Bertsche, a Boston media and First Amendment attorney at the law firm Klaris Law, a very broad generalization is that the former is the unapproved use of someone's creative expression, while the latter is use without attribution.)

For journalists, there are important exceptions from copyright infringement: ideas and facts. These are free and legal for *anyone* to use; it's *how* the ideas are expressed that is protected by copyright. In other words, you can use the same basic facts as another writer, but you can't imitate how that writer presents those facts. And in some cases, even the use of a specific expression may be defended by what is called fair use, a complicated calculus that may determine that the use of the material is allowed.

Such legal matters may be hard for the layperson to parse, and so some publications employ a media-savvy lawyer to look over stories before they publish. The lawyer will typically go through a story to look for any potentially damaging statements, and then ask how they were sourced, possibly requesting to see the backup material. If the sourcing is sound but the wording still opens the publication to suit, the lawyer may suggest changes to the text that offer better protection. A fact-checker isn't the only person responsible for bringing potential legal problems to the lawyer's attention—this mainly falls to the editors and research directors—but a fact-checker should still be familiar with media ethics and look out for potentially damning statements.

With all this in mind, why isn't independent fact-checking more common in the media? Part of the reason, as already noted, is that it simply isn't possible in fast-paced daily newsrooms or on 24-hour news cycles—instead, verification is primarily the responsibility of the journalist, who isn't working with the safety net of a fact-checker (although good editors and copy editors can help fill holes in the reporting). For many online publications, which often pay writers less compared to print magazines, there isn't a budget for a fact-checking team. "It's heartbreaking to see fact-checking get treated like an outmoded luxury that old-fashioned journalism indulged in along with three-martini lunches," says the science writer Carl Zimmer. "I understand that online journalism has to be a torrent of words to succeed financially, but allowing material to flow online without checking it corrupts our shared understanding of the history we're living."

Fact-checking shouldn't be a luxury in journalism or any work of nonfiction. But some traditional publications have smaller or stagnant budgets for fact-checking staff, or are using fewer checkers on tighter schedules, and some new publications fail to incorporate editorial fact-checking into their routines. Still, it's not all bleak. In 2018, I led a team of researchers from the Knight Science Journalism Program at MIT on a project to understand how fact-checking fared in one small slice of journalism (the final report is titled *The State of Fact-Checking in Science Journalism*). We found that there are actually a fair number of publications that are doing editorial fact-checking in some form, particularly on long or complex pieces, or on those that are legally sensitive. Just over a third of the outlets that responded to our survey assign fact-checking work to designated fact-checkers, and 15 percent assign it to their copy editors. The remainder rely on a combination of journalists and editors to verify information, rather than having a separate person fact-check each story. Independent fact-checking has worked its way into other media, too, from documentary films put out by the National Geographic Channel to podcasts including *This American Life* and *Radiolab* to the documentary publisher Retro Report. Even the comedy news show *Last Week Tonight with John Oliver* has employed researchers to double-check its segments.

Writers can also apply the tools of fact-checking to their own work. While it isn't a perfect solution, it is at least a chance to ask: Did this happen the way I think it happened? Why do I think so? Where did I find each of these facts, and are my sources trustworthy? And ultimately: How do I know this is true?

The opening scene of the short film *FCU: Fact Checkers Unit*, a 2008 Sundance Film Festival selection, will be familiar and funny to most fact-checkers. In the scene, an editor at the fictional *Dictum* magazine, played by Kristen Schaal, stands over a team of two fact-checkers, played by Peter Karinen and Brian Sacca. The checkers fly through a list of facts she's assigned to them, finish, and proudly hand her their report.

"Oh, you missed one," the editor says, pointing to a piece of paper that has fallen on the floor.

One of the checkers picks it up and reads aloud:

"Celebrity sleeping tips: If you're having trouble sleeping, just drink a glass of warm milk before you go to bed, like Bill Murray."

"Where did they find that?" the other checker asks.

"I think Wikipedia," the editor says.

In a panic, the checkers sputter:

"That is a user-generated site!"

"That could have been written by a seven-year-old!"

"I think we're gonna need some time on this one."

Instead, the editor gives them the near-impossible deadline of *tomorrow*. The checkers pray to a portrait of Alex Trebek of *Jeopardy!* fame and then—spoiler alert—set to work, ultimately tracking down Murray's address, breaking into his apartment, and getting caught once they're there. Instead of kicking the fact-checkers out, Murray asks them to stay, and in a montage that flits through several hours, the trio watches *M*A*S*H*, drinks martinis, reads, plays checkers and catch, and jams out an interpretive version of chopsticks at the piano. Then, just after midnight, Murray yawns and one of the checkers pours him a glass of warm 2 percent milk. As the checkers watch him drift to sleep in his bed, they say to one another: "Fact, checked."

It's a silly example, but the film's exaggeration hints at the great lengths a checker may take in order to prove a fact. Of course, in the real world, a phone call with Bill Murray's publicist, or at the very least some solid secondary sourcing, such as an interview in which he discloses his love for warm milk before bed, would be preferable to breaking and entering. But traveling great distances to a source isn't necessarily outlandish for a fact-checker. Cynthia Cotts, a journalist and researcher with more than twenty-five years of experience who has been a staff research editor for the *New York Times Magazine* since 2017, recalls an all-expenses-paid trip from New York to Los Angeles to access source materials for a *New Yorker* story in 1995. The story was an excerpt from Norman Mailer's book *Oswald's Tale: An American Mystery*, which covered, among other things, Lee Harvey Oswald's experiences in the Soviet Union. The source material was at the home of Mailer's colleague, the movie producer Lawrence Schiller, who didn't want the papers to leave his sight because they had been difficult to procure. And so Cotts and a colleague traveled to Schiller and spent three or four days sifting through original documents, including pieces from the Russian intelligence agencies.

Comedy and intrigue aside, when a fact-checker asks what they need to check, the answer is: everything. Even if the fact is a celebrity's sleep tip, and especially if the original source came from Wikipedia or any other source compiled by anonymous sources (for more on sourcing, including when and how Wikipedia is useful, see chapter 4).

What is *everything*? To give a nonexhaustive list of examples:

- The spelling of names and places
- Physical descriptions of people, places, and things
- Dates
- Ages
- Pronouns
- Quotes
- Numbers
- Measurements and conversions
- Geographic locations and descriptions
- Scientific or technical explanations
- Titles, job descriptions, and affiliations
- Details about products including prices, specifications, and descriptions
- Quotes from movies or other well-known media
- Historical quotes or stories, even those that are widely assumed to be true
- Illustrations and photos, including the captions
- Definitions and word choices
- Overarching arguments
- Even things that aren't on this list
- Even the thing you just checked last week
- Even things you think you know are true

This last category—things you think you already know are true—is especially difficult, because it's tempting to skip familiar information. A thorough checker does not give in to this temptation, according to Corinne Cummings, who has worked as a fact-checker for *Rolling Stone* and *Playboy* and freelanced for various other outlets. "One thing I do think that fact-checkers should keep in mind is to be more sensitive when you know a subject well," she says. "That is when you can get caught up in reading and think: *Of course I know that that's true.*" One way to get around your own knowledge bias is to force yourself to identify a source for each fact, whether that source comes from the writer or from your own research. You'll need this documentation for your records, anyway (see chapter 6), so you might as well read it carefully and make sure whatever knowledge you think you have is indeed correct.

Finally, a good checker must also look for what is missing from the story. Are there any possible sources or perspectives that, by omission, make the story wrong? The best checkers will doggedly pursue each fact as well as these gaps, and those who try the hardest and longest to confirm each piece of information are those who will be the most successful at the job. It isn't a matter of being a genius researcher, but of being tireless and resourceful.

While each individual fact may be relatively easy to identify as something the checker needs to confirm, there are also the grayer areas discussed in the previous chapter—the arguments that stand on the writer's fact-based foundation. As a checker, it is vital that you consider these, too, no matter how difficult. "We should constantly ask questions of ourselves, of the journalist, and of the expert: How do you know this? How are you in a position to know this? Were you there when it happened? Did you talk to people who were there?" says Yvonne Rolzhausen, research chief at *The Atlantic*. "You constantly turn over those stones to say 'why,' and if you continue to do that, you will ultimately be fine in terms of checking. In my mind, checking is such a combination of the small and the large—the trees and the forest. Do all of the trees match up to the forest? So if every fact is a tree, if you start lopping off the trees left, right, and center, do you still have a forest?"

To identify which pieces of a story are facts and need to be confirmed, a fact-checker must be diligent, patient, and tenacious. If you're unsure whether a specific part of a story is a fact, think about what steps you would need to do in order to confirm it. If those steps exist, it goes on the fact-checking list.

. . . .

Think Like a Fact-Checker

When you finish this chapter, get a pencil or pen and then read it again. Underline the facts that you would check if you were fact-checking these pages.

. . . .

Now let's go back to the fictional Bill Murray example in *FCU: Fact Checkers Unit.* If you were fact-checking this in real life, how would you do it? If the checker literally hands Murray a glass of warm milk and then puts the actor to bed, does that truly show us that this is something Murray would have done otherwise? Just as important as identifying each fact, if not more so, is *how* a checker proceeds through the fact-check—and whether those facts really amount to the truth.

THREE ||| How We Fact-Check

Now that you understand the why and the what, *how* exactly do you fact-check? On a broad level, it's helpful to know how fact-checking typically happens at different kinds of media outlets. When my team at the Knight Science Journalism Program at MIT put together our 2018 fact-checking report, we saw a pattern emerge from our interviews and surveys. Some outlets use what we call the magazine model, which is essentially the independent fact-checking that I described briefly in the first pages of this book. Other outlets are on the newspaper model, where verification is mainly the responsibility of the journalist. And still others use a hybrid model, applying the magazine approach to long, complex, or legally sensitive pieces and reserving the quicker, newspaper approach for breaking news or short items. What follows in this chapter is a general description of each of these models and how they function for written stories (that is, stories that are primarily text based). After that, I'll address other media, including audio and video. Details on how to check certain types of facts, as well as how to source those facts, appear in the following chapters.

It's also helpful to understand where fact-checkers fit in an editorial staff and process, which differs from one outlet to the next. In some cases, a research director or managing editor takes care of hiring and supervising staff or freelance fact-checkers; for smaller staffs or publications that need help on a one-off assignment, the checkers may be hired directly by individual editors. Either way, a fact-checker may work on several articles at once; those with less experience will more likely check shorter pieces, while more seasoned checkers take on complex narratives or other substantial features. Each story will typically have a writer (or, in some cases, a team of writers) and one main editor, usually the person who assigned the story (sometimes called, unsurprisingly, the assigning editor). Depending on the size of the staff, other editors, often those who are higher on the outlet's masthead, may read the story as it gets closer to its final state. For each story, depending on the outlet, the fact-checker may interact with only the assigning editor, only the writer, or a little bit of both. The fact-checker receives the story after the writer and editor have gotten it to a near-final draft, which makes it easier to fact-check, since the editing process usually deletes entire swaths of facts and creates new ones as sentences are removed, shifted, or added.

As a fact-checker, the actual process of double-checking stories against their source materials isn't your only important role. You'll have to do this while navigating your relationships with writers and editors (and sources, but we'll get to that in chapter 5). Sometimes, these relationships will be smooth and supportive, but other times you will be suggesting changes that may make these folks bristle. How you deliver your message will make a big difference in whether your changes are ultimately accepted. This chapter also provides suggestions on how to handle yourself while working with your team.

THE MAGAZINE MODEL
Step 1: Read

The first step, always, is to read the story you are checking. Your job is to familiarize yourself with it, but with a skeptical eye: no matter how great the writer or how seasoned the editor, don't trust everything they've said. You may eventually undo some of their lovely prose, clunking up the sentences to make them more accurate. Prepare yourself.

After you've read the story once, and if you have time, which many checkers won't, try to find a few articles on the same topic from reliable publications—think the *New York Times* rather than an anonymous personal blog. Don't use these as sources or even guidance, but to see other angles and representations. Maybe your writer is taking a provocative stance, or maybe previous stories have been wrong or incomplete. Or maybe the piece you need to check makes assertions that go beyond what one can logically draw from the facts or is missing a vital perspective. Whatever the case, you should try to get a sense of where your story fits in the subject's broader ecosystem. In addition to checking the black-and-white facts, you'll need to consider grayer, more subjective areas.

Indeed, think about the facts that are missing as well as the facts that are there. Are there any holes in the story? Is it inaccurate because of what's been left out?

"To say that we're just checking facts—like the spelling of names or people's ages—isn't quite right," says Michelle Ciarrocca, a senior associate editor at *The Atlantic* and a former fact-checker at *Vanity Fair*. "We are really digging in, reading the backstory, reading the context, and making sure that the tone is right and the sources are getting a fair shake."

Step 2: Identify the Sources

Contact the writer (or the editor, if you don't have a direct line to the writer) early on and ask for the source materials for the story, which may include notes, transcripts, interview recordings, reports, books, and contact information for key sources. Ask—delicately—if there are any parts of the story that either the writer or editor is worried about, or sources that are difficult to work with, which might help you identify sections that need extra attention.

The fact-checker's dream writer will also provide an annotated copy of the story. This means that within the electronic document—whether it exists in Microsoft Word, Google Drive, or other word-processing software—specific words, sentences, or even entire paragraphs will have comments, footnotes, or endnotes listing the relevant sources.

This won't always happen. Some writers will send a list of contacts and a folder of audio files, none of which have been transcribed. Some will send links to Wikipedia and unverified blog posts. Others will send nothing at all and will conveniently take off on a reporting trip, only to be reached in case of emergency via satellite phone at odd hours of the day during which they will be grumpy. Whatever the case, if you don't have the backup you need, talk to your editor and sort out a way to get better source lists from the writer. If this doesn't work, you may have to find your own sources (see chapter 4 for sourcing tips).

Step 3: Mark the Facts

For people who like to work on paper, print a copy of the story—double-spaced with extra-wide margins is best, to leave room for notes (if you prefer working on a digital draft, see p. 55). Arm yourself with your writing tools of choice and read the story again, marking each word or phrase that contains a fact. And yes, this may mean that you'll mark the entire document (if you didn't underline nearly every word in the previous chapter as part of the "Think Like a Fact-Checker" exercise there, go back and rethink your approach). Minimalists may prefer a single shade of pen or highlighter, while the sort of people who daydream about spreadsheets or enjoy diagramming sentences may use a system that is far more complex, with a different color for each type of fact—say, pink for quotes, yellow for proper nouns, green for the subjective murkiness that may creep into a writer's claims. Others prefer to use a different color per source.

The longer the story, the greater the need for a good fact-tracking system, says David Zweig, a former checker at *Vogue* and the former research head at the now-defunct *Radar*. For long features, Zweig recalls color-coding not only types of information and the source where he found it, but using a

Medical crowdfunding isn't new, of course. GoFundMe, the most popular platform for raising money for health care, says it hosts around 250,000 medical campaigns every year. Before Covid-19, most were for people who needed help paying astronomical medical bills. Now that the pandemic is here, plenty of GoFundMe campaigns follow the same trend. But there are also new types of medical fundraisers — for everything from masks and intensive care equipment to food and coffee for frontline hospital staff. Then there's the new wave of campaigns for small offices like South Slope Pediatrics. They're happening across the country, from pediatricians in California to family doctors in Texas. From optometrists in Maine, Indiana, and New Jersey, to dentists, and more.

Commented [TJ1]: Based on the sourcing that follows this paragraph

Commented [TJ2]: See interview transcripts/reordings Snyder, Woolhandler, Kenworthy

Commented [TJ3]: This is the number GoFundMe provides. See also **Himmelstein ed 2019.pdf** (citing the GoFundMe numbers)

Commented [TJ4]: Snyder and Kenworthy interviews

Commented [TJ5]: If you do a covid-19 + doctor searc on GoFundMe you'll likely see a TON of this sort of stuf

Commented [TJ6]: I collected links and brief descript at **GoFundMe campaign links.docx**

Figure 2. One way a writer may annotate a story is with comments. Each sentence or group of sentences should be highlighted with a comment, and the source information should be written clearly in that comment.

Medical crowdfunding isn't new, of course.[1] GoFundMe, the most popular platform for raising money for health care,[2] says it hosts around 250,000 medical campaigns every year.[3] Before Covid-19, most were for people who needed help paying astronomical medical bills.[4] Now that the pandemic is here, plenty of GoFundMe campaigns follow the same trend. But there are also new types of medical fundraisers — for everything from masks and intensive care equipment to food and coffee for frontlin hospital staff.[5] Then there's the new wave of campaigns for small offices like South Slope Pediatrics. They're happening across the country, from pediatricians in California to family doctors in Texas. Fro optometrists in Maine, Indiana, and New Jersey, to dentists, and more.[6]

---

[1] Based on the sourcing that follows in this paragraph
[2] See interview transcripts/reordings for Snyder, Woolhandler, Kenworthy
[3] This is the number GoFundMe provides. See also **Himmelstein ed 2019.pdf** (citing the GoFundMe numbers)
[4] Snyder and Kenworthy interviews
[5] If you do a covid-19 + doctor search on GoFundMe you'll likely see a TON of this sort of stuff
[6] I collected links and brief descriptions at **GoFundMe campaign links.docx**

Figure 3. Writers may also choose to annotate with either footnotes or endnotes.

number system to link a specific fact to its source—perhaps by writing the number next to the fact in the story as well as on top of a printed copy of the source.

In other words, there are many ways to organize our fact-checking, and none are necessarily right or wrong. Whatever system works for you is the best one, as long as it is thorough, consistent, and helps you track all of the information.

Step 4: Triage the Facts

What you do next depends on the story and how much time you have—some facts will be as wriggly as a freshwater eel, impossible to hold in your bare hands, while others will seemingly only be cleared from the mouth of someone who is currently meditating in a secluded mountaintop shack with no Wi-Fi. This is especially true when you have to speak with actual living, breathing people, each with their own schedules and priorities, to verify facts. Talking to you might not be a priority at all, as they may have already spent hours going through interviews with the writer or handing over documents and other materials. Contact these sources early—before you start fact-checking other sections that can be accomplished by reading printed or otherwise recorded source material, which you can work on in between source interviews—to make sure you can get through in time for your deadline. It may be helpful to collect all of the sources' contact information in one place, whether it's a Post-it note or a document saved on your desktop for easy access later on.

Not everyone likes a cold call, so, when possible, use email to set up a time to talk, unless otherwise directed (you may also need to track people down through text messages, social media, and any other way you can find). If you are dealing with a person you think will be hard to reach—a celebrity, CEO, or university department head, for example—find the email address for their publicist, assistant, or press department and include it on the message. Explain who you are, why you are writing, and how long you'll need to speak with the source. Also include your deadline.

While you're waiting to hear back from these sources, make a list of questions for each one so that you're ready for the interview. How you structure the questions will depend on the source and the type of story. If the source is, say, a scientist or technology expert, you may want to pull some of the language from the story into the questions to make sure it's precise— words that pop up in science may have completely different meanings than in everyday use. On the other hand, if there is sensitive material that may cause the source to balk if they hear it out loud, try asking as many neutral questions as you can to prompt them to talk about the same topic.

If the story includes personal or traumatic accounts, you might want to begin your conversation with the source by acknowledging that. You might say, for instance: *I know you've already spoken about this with the writer and that it may be difficult to go into the topic again. I really appreciate that you are giving us your time, which will help make sure we get the story right.* And no matter the source or the content, before you start your interview, it may also help to explain *why* you are doing a fact-check: it isn't because you don't trust the writer or because they are likely to have made a mistake, or that your team doesn't trust the source. Instead, you might say, the fact-check gives your team a chance to catch any inadvertent errors or misunderstandings.

Pay attention to how you word your questions. Although a simple yes-or-no format will work in some cases, sources may slide through these and answer incorrectly. Rather than spelling their name and asking if it is correct, word the question so that they have to spell it. Rather than offering a date and asking if it's right, ask them for the date. Of course, the more complicated the question or concept, the harder it will be to avoid a yes-or-no question. Try to think of follow-up questions to double-check that the source is paying attention.

Once the questions are ready, go back to the story and work through the facts that don't require an interview. Some checkers do this line by line, while others—usually the ardent color-coders—clump the fact-check into specific categories of facts, or facts from the same type of source.

Pro Tip: How to Contact Sources

When you email a source, be polite, brief, and specific. You may want to say your deadline is earlier than it actually is, to allow for the occasional and unavoidable rescheduling. Here's a sample email:

From: Vicky Verity <factchecker@magazine.com>
To: Professor Fancy-Pants <prof@universityx.edu>
Cc: University X Media <media@universityx.edu>
Subject: Important Magazine fact-check re: campaign donations (time-sensitive)

Professor Fancy-Pants,

I am a fact-checker at *Important Magazine*, and I am checking Jane Press's story on the legal limits for individual campaign donations. Ms. Press interviewed you for the piece, and I'd like to go over information that came from your conversations to confirm a few details. Do you have time for a brief phone call or video chat? I expect it will last around 20 minutes, and I need to speak to you by next Friday in order to meet our printing deadline. If you don't have time for a call, please confirm that you'll be able to answer the questions by email.

Thanks very much,
Vicky Verity

As you work through the story, you may find facts that aren't directly attributed to a person, but nonetheless would be easier to check by asking an expert than by deciphering reams of source material—particularly if the concepts are complex. In such a case, check the list of people whom you're already planning to interview to see if any might be able to answer these questions. If so, add the questions to the list that you plan to work through once you get a chance to talk to those experts on the phone or video chat. For example, let's say the writer interviewed one of the sources about a new type of motor for an electric car, and you have a list of questions surrounding that. When you go through the story again, you might notice some other facts about general car technology that you don't have a good source for—if you add these to the question list for the electric car expert, even if they don't know the answers, they may be able to direct you to the right information or to someone with relevant expertise. If you don't have an obvious expert on your list for the facts in question, try to find one on your own (more on this in chapter 5).

For some sources, you will have only a few easy questions. To save time, you may want to simply include these in your

---

Quick Guide: Triage Your Facts

Some facts will be more difficult to confirm than others. As you're reading through an assigned story, note which facts you think will be more difficult to find—such as those coming from a specific person, who may be traveling or otherwise hard to reach—as well as those that are easier, such as numbers from a study or dates when well-known events took place. Here's one way to organize your steps:

1. Contact each source ASAP to set up a phone or video interview.
2. Prepare the questions you'd like to ask each source (a separate document per source usually works best).
3. While you're waiting for sources to respond—or if you've already scheduled calls but have downtime to fill—check the easy facts that are based on documents or other tangible sources.

Quick Guide: Email vs. Phone Interviews
Fact-checkers are divided on which format is best for interviewing sources: email or phone/video. Email provides a written and accessible record and can be helpful for simple questions or for situations when a source can't be easily reached by phone. But phone or video interviews allow for follow-up questions and may tease out factual mistakes and nuance that are easily missed in an email exchange.

original email. But beware. A phone call or video chat may allow you to detect tone changes in the source's voice, which won't come across in an email; these cues could lead you to dig further into a question and get more accurate details. It is also easier to ask follow-up questions, such as when a yes-or-no question is inevitable, but you want to double-check that the source is paying attention, so you rephrase the question and ask again. And in some cases, a phone call or video chat may uncover even more information that email will not. Take this example from *More*, provided by Beatrice Hogan. She once checked a story about Martha McSally, a congresswoman and former U.S. Air Force pilot who sued the Department of Defense to get rid of a rule that required women pilots to wear an abaya, a loose overgarment, when traveling off base in Saudi Arabia. The story's original structure indicated that the rule was overturned because of that lawsuit. In a phone call for the fact-check, McSally's chief of staff volunteered that the rule actually changed because Congress passed a law about it, a fact that Hogan says she would have missed if she had used basic questions laid out in an email.

If you have a recorder, consider using it to keep an accurate record of your conversation with the source. Be sure to double-check the laws in your state: in some places, it's illegal to record someone without their consent. Even in places where it's legal, it's a better—and nicer—practice to simply tell the source you are recording the call to make sure you catch everything. If they object, explain that the recording isn't for broadcast, but for your notes and backup materials.

Step 5: Track and Document

When a fact checks out, mark the relevant word or words—a check mark, an X, or a line through the word all work well—and write the source in the margin, right next to the sentence. Yes, it can get messy. If you have a lot of sources, you may want to make a numbered list in a separate document so that you need only write the appropriate numbers in the margin.

If you need to make a correction, use common copyediting symbols to add suggested changes to the story. Most of these symbols, like a caret (^) to insert a word or letter or a ~~strikethrough~~ for deletions, may be familiar from the essays your teacher marked up in high school. But there are three common marks that may be new. Two of these may appear in the original draft that you receive from the writer. One is "TK," and it is the fact-checker's enemy; the other is "CK," and it is neutral. The third new mark is one that will appear throughout the fact-checking process: this is "stet," and although it can be frustrating, it may also be your friend.

The first two mark usually work like this. When a writer doesn't have a fact to bolster a sentence, they may insert "TK" in its place. This is old printing shorthand for "to come" and it's supposed to suggest that the writer is still working to find the information. Since "TK" isn't an actual word or proper spelling, it provides a red flag to let printers, designers, and editors know that the text isn't final, so that the letters don't accidentally appear in the final printed story.

"TK" may literally *mean* "to come," but some writers take a looser interpretation. Maybe the writer has given up; maybe they are lazy and decided to leave it for the fact-checker to fill in a statistic that supports whatever claim they've made. Either way, finding a good source will be up to you, but beware: the facts might not exist, so the sentence may simply need to be cut. Can't lie: this may give you pleasure.

Occasionally, you may see "CK." This isn't a misspelling of "TK." Instead, it means "check." Of course, you should always check everything anyway. But "CK," usually written in parentheses after the fact in question, means the writer is especially unsure of this specific fact or based it on memory with no identifiable source.

As for "stet," it is Latin for "let it stand," and it is used when

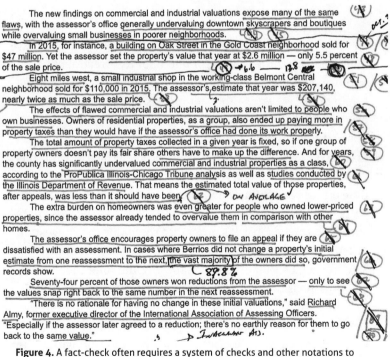

Figure 4. A fact-check often requires a system of checks and other notations to track each fact and its source. Here, investigative journalist Jason Grotto, working on the newspaper model, fact-checks his own story. Courtesy of ProPublica.

Symbol	Definition	Example
∧	Insert	Insert a or a missing ltter.
⟍	Delete	Delete delete an extra or inaccurate word or letterz.
∿	Transpose	Swap the words order of or parts of a sentence.
/	Lowercase	Change a letter from Uppercase to lowercase.
⹀	Uppercase	Capitalize a word, such as white house.
stet	Let it stand	Reverts an altered stet edited sentence back to its original.
TK	To come	The average story has TK of these.
CK	Check	The hippo is the largest land animal in Africa (CK)

Figure 5. Common copyediting symbols that may come in handy for a fact-checker.

an edit is made and then overturned. For example, you may find what you think is an error and offer a correction, but the editor may decide that you are being too picky and that the original text is better—the stet reverts the story back to that original text. The stet may occasionally frustrate you, particularly if it overturns a fact that you think is essential. But in order to get stets to work in your favor, keep track of who stets which facts in your story. If an editor or writer decides to ignore one of your factual changes, you should have a written record. You'll need this later if you were right and the story runs with an error, because it's proof that you made the suggestion but it wasn't accepted.

When a fact is incorrect, explain why and offer the most elegant fix possible. Sometimes it's a matter of adding a qualifier or softening a claim. See the difference, for example, between "we will each have our own robot butler within the next decade" and "robot butlers may be common within the next decade." Keep your fix to roughly the same word count as the original sentence. This is especially important for print magazines—the number of pages and layout design limit how many words will fit. Of course, straightforward changes, such as dates or spelling, don't require an explanation.

Step 6: Report Your Findings

Once you've finished the first round of fact-checking, you'll need to tell the writer or editor what's wrong with the story. And there will always be *something* wrong, or at least portions that could be clearer or more tempered. Be diplomatic and kind. This is true even if the writer sourced the entire piece with Wikipedia and then took off on a phone-free vacation the morning you started your fact-check. Diplomacy is important for three reasons. First, you might be wrong. The writer may have a better source that they forgot to send you, or new information may have unfolded in a breaking story. Second, even if you aren't working directly with a writer, you never know whether your words will make it back to them, and even the most seasoned or hardened writer might not take criticism well. Writers work hard on each story, maybe for months or even years, and you should respect that effort. And you may have to work together again. Third, and related, is that you have to convince both the writer and the editor that your changes make the story better. If you start that process as a confrontation, it'll only make your job harder.

In order to share fact-check changes, most publications will require a fact-check report, although its format will depend on both you and your team. One common approach is to save the original electronic copy of the story as a new document. Use "track changes" to show each suggested edit as well as the information you've deleted. Include your source and any extra explanation in a comment, footnote, or endnote. Before you start changing things directly in the story, though, check with your editor: some may prefer that you keep the suggestions as footnotes or annotations, while others may want a list of corrections in a new document.

Separately, make a list prioritizing your changes that only you will see. Start the list with those that you feel are absolutely necessary—without them the story will be inaccurate or may even open the publication to a lawsuit. After you've written down all of the must-haves, put the changes that fall into the gray area—that nebulous collection of words imbued with different meanings depending on who you are and how you are reading the story. The writer or editor may stet these, and that is fine so long as you raised the points. Put the smallest quibbles last—maybe the way the writer describes a style of music, for example, or the use of a common name rather than a formal one. Pick your list wisely, because in truth any sentence could be indefinitely tweaked for accuracy. There must be a compromise between your interpretation of the facts, the weight of those facts, and the reality of producing a compelling and readable story on deadline.

Step 7: Check Each Version

Fact-checkers who work at a print magazine will eventually see the story in layout, which is how it will look, more or less, in its final physical form, in which the magazine's art department stylizes it and includes graphics, photos, and special fonts. As a story goes through final fact-checking and edits, it is usually printed on extra-large paper with wide margins, where you can write corrections and notes. These paper copies are usually called "proofs." Magazines usually go through about three rounds of proofs per story. You should read each proof carefully to make sure your changes have made it from one round to the next. Also look closely for new text or other alterations. Editors love to sneak in sexy sentences to liven up a story, but they don't always source the changes. If this happens, ask the editor where these new facts came from, as well as for backup citations (tactfully point out that you need the information for record keeping). And finally, double-check the information that the art team has added to the headers and footers of

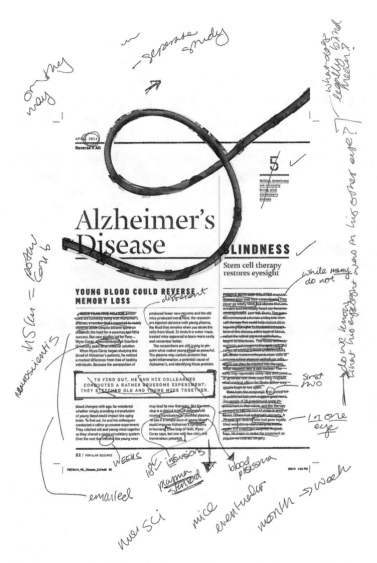

Figure 6. An example of a fact-checker's proof at a magazine. Courtesy of *Popular Science.*

the story, including the name of the magazine, the date it will publish, and the page numbers, as well as the information in the gutter (the middle seam where the pages will meet, which usually includes photo credit information and the like).

Some magazines publish on the internet rather than in print, and for these publications, you won't see printed proofs. Still, fact-checkers at online outlets will also likely see a story before it goes live. As with a printed proof, read the draft carefully against your original fact-checking report to make sure your agreed-on changes made it in; verify that the photographs and other images are correct; and look for new changes that the editor or writer introduced after the fact-check.

. . . .

Think Like a Fact-Checker

Find a story from your favorite magazine or online publication and identify all the facts, experimenting with whatever pen-and-highlighter combination is right for you, if you're working on paper. *Bonus:* Look up each fact and see if you can spot any mistakes. (Do not call or email people who appear in the story; you will confuse them. Only check facts that don't require a conversation with a person.)

. . . .

THE NEWSPAPER MODEL

If you are working solely as a fact-checker you won't likely come across the newspaper model. Still, it's helpful to know how it works. And a lot of fact-checkers—especially freelancers—also work as journalists or editors, which means you may have some clients or employers who use this model. Always double-check with your team to make sure you're clear on which system they use.

In the newspaper model, the journalist who reported and wrote the story will be the primary person responsible for

Pro Tip: How to Adapt the Fact-Check Process Using Electronic Documents

Hate paper? Love trees? Or are you working remotely without a printer? A paper-based fact-check isn't always practical or preferable. The process listed for the basic magazine fact-check is still in play, but with significant changes to step 3 and step 5. Here's how to approach these steps:

MODIFIED STEP 3: MARK THE FACTS

Make a separate copy of the story file and rename it. Then, using your software tools, either highlight or apply boldface to the entire text.

MODIFIED STEP 5: TRACK AND DOCUMENT

As you go through the story and confirm each fact, remove the highlight or boldface from the relevant words or sentences—this trick will both track the information you've already checked and provide a visual on how much more you need to do. Or, if you prefer, use "strikethrough" on the lines you've checked, crossing them out as you would on a printout. List the source for each fact as a comment, footnote, or endnote.

If you need to fix an error, make sure to use "track changes" to show what has been deleted and what has been added. If appropriate, leave a brief and polite explanation for the change in the comment, footnote, or endnote, as well as the source information. When are you are finished, the document can serve as your fact-checking report.

Pro Tip: Checking Letters to the Editor
Even letters to the editor need to be fact-checked in magazines that print them. First, the fact-checker needs to confirm that the letter is authentic and that the person who signed it indeed wrote it. The letters are also usually edited for clarity, length, and house style, which will need to be relayed to the letter writer. Also check that the writer's name, title, location, and any other personal information are accurate. And finally, verify that the information in the letter is true—if it is an attempt to point out an inaccuracy or oversight in a story, make sure that there is indeed a mistake. If the story was correct and the letter is wrong, the letter shouldn't be printed. Not only do you not want to print an inaccuracy, your media outlet is responsible for any potential defamatory claims in a letter.

fact-checking it, while the editor and, when applicable, copy editor will act as backup. In order to do this well, each member of the team has to read the draft with the facts in mind. The journalist should take care to double-check each fact before it goes into a story, and then keep a clear record of the source. The editor should think about fact-checking at every stage, from the assignment to the final read, asking tough questions. In particular, if the story contains big claims, the editor should ask: Where did you get this information? If, once provided, the sourcing is too thin, the editor should send the journalist out for more. And the copy editor should read the story with not only style and grammar in mind but also the facts. While copy editors don't often have the time to do an in-depth fact-check like you'd see in the magazine model, they may double-check bits that are relatively easy to look up, such as basic statistics or the spelling of places and names.

Some reporters go to great lengths to double-check their own stories. Jason Grotto, a senior reporter on the investigative reporting team at Bloomberg News, for instance, describes underlining every single fact in his stories much like a fact-checker would, numbering each fact, and then entering the numbers into a column in a spreadsheet. In another column in that spreadsheet, he marks whether the fact is correct; if it isn't, he adds the reasoning behind the correction in yet another column. The process was self-taught, he says, and inspired by wanting to be sure that any colleague could pick up where he left off if needed. "I kind of had this idea when I started, if I were ever hit by a bus right after a story ran, someone could go back and find out where every fact from the story came from, in case someone tried to take potshots at me or something," he says. "Which is sort of a weird, paranoid way of doing everything." It's worth noting that, from my experience, most reporters and fact-checkers are just as paranoid about getting their stories right. I've heard from many colleagues who have had fact-checking nightmares right before a story goes live.

Finally, although it isn't always easy to find the time, the team should figure the fact-check into their publishing schedule. In other words, the editor should give the journalist time to check through their story line by line—much as an independent fact-checker would in the magazine model—to confirm each fact and its sources. Grotto, for instance, notes that he does his underlining and spreadsheeting ideally after his story has already gone through final edits, which means he has had to negotiate with his editors to leave time for this process. (Freelance writers take note: ask your editor *early* in the writing and editing process for extra time for the fact-check, so you don't run into problems with their outlet's internal scheduling.)

THE HYBRID MODEL

In the hybrid model, an editorial team may switch how they fact-check from one story to another, to save both time and money. They may, for instance, want to stay nimble in some cases, using the newspaper model for stories that are very time sensitive, such as breaking news or a hot tip from a source who has been reliable many times in the past. They may also use the newspaper model for relatively straightforward pieces that don't necessarily need a deep dig—and the time and money it requires—such as a quick explainer, a basic news story by a beat reporter, or a news round-up. The same outlet may want to use the magazine model for complex stories, which typically go through many rounds of edits and present more opportunities for errors to sneak in, including long-form, legally sensitive stories of any length and package features, which usually have many shorter elements—from brief articles to infographics to Q&As—on one main topic. (For freelance fact-checkers and writers: if any of your clients are on the hybrid model, be sure you know which style of fact-checking a given story will go through so it is clear who is responsible for double-checking the work.)

FACT-CHECKING OTHER MEDIA

Stories take many forms beyond a magazine or web article, of course. As such, there are unique considerations for checking other nonfiction media, including radio pieces, television segments, podcasts, and documentaries, as well as genres such as memoir or even poetry.

Audio and Video

Historically, neither audio nor video pieces were typically fact-checked under the magazine model. But the practice has become fairly common for narrative radio shows and podcasts such as *This American Life, Serial,* and *Radiolab*. A handful of outlets that produce videos have independent fact-checkers, too. One example is Retro Report, which makes short web documentaries that look at past media stories—some many decades old—and explores how they've held up over time. Another is the National Geographic Channel, which requires all in-house and contract producers to submit to a fact-check.

For both audio and video pieces, the basic steps for fact-checking are similar to what you've already seen for a magazine or web story. The main differences are the documents you work with (scripts and audio or video cuts rather than articles), some of the people involved (hosts, reporters, producers, and editors, rather than writers and editors), and the time frame (sometimes tight turnarounds compared to a written feature).

Both audio and video teams work from scripts. The exact roles may vary, but in general: A reporter pulls all of the source material together, including recorded interviews and other audio clips (often, a producer oversees that work). The producer and editor then work to get the audio into the right order, and may send the reporter out to get additional material. Eventually, the audio gets turned into a script, and the reporter writes in the introduction and transitions, which may eventually be recorded by the host or a reporter. (On some shows, the same person might fill multiple roles—for instance, a host or a producer may also report.) Depending on the outlet, either the editor or the producer will make the final call on what the script should include and what might need to change.

A fact-checker will likely get a script that is close to its final form. The reporter or producer for the piece should hand over source materials just like in a magazine fact-check, and the checker should follow the same steps. Scripts and edited cuts, however, are often living documents that may change even within the hour before they air. Because of this, the fact-checker must work closely with the team and follow changes up to the point that the piece is live.

While checking a script may more or less follow the same

process as checking a written story, audio adds another dimension, as well as unique challenges. In a written story, for instance, a writer can include context wherever they choose, from a caveat to a source link. Audio can be trickier because "one thing that's very common is to have a character come in and narrate a sequence of events," says Wudan Yan, an independent journalist who has fact-checked investigative and narrative podcasts including *Drilled* and *This Land.* "But maybe their memory is fuzzy or maybe something suggests that they're not a reliable narrator. So you have to triangulate the same way that you do an investigative story." And if that narrator says something false right in the middle of a key sound bite, it can be more difficult to find a smooth way to acknowledge this in the final piece without mucking up the flow of the audio.

Journalists working with audio are just as committed to getting things right as those working with text. But because of the limitations with audio, many podcasts and radio pieces may need to prioritize storytelling over minor inaccuracies. That doesn't mean the shows will present an outright misrepresentation of a fact just to tell a good story. Still, in some cases, decisions may be made to keep minor factual inaccuracies, because there isn't a way to nod to them while keeping a cohesive and compelling piece of audio for the listener—and there isn't a way to go back and rerecord the original audio. For example: consider a situation where a source in a story says one small thing that is incorrect within the context of a larger quote—and the quote is vital to the story. Maybe, for instance, the source gets a minor statistic a few percentage points off or, during a retelling of a low-stakes story, recalls that an event happened on a Tuesday when it was really a Wednesday. And let's say the fact-checker doesn't notice this slip until the last stages of sound mixing and edits. For a written story, there might be an easier solution: you could paraphrase some or all of the quote, for example, or swap in material from elsewhere in the interview. But for audio, it's not always easy to do that. Together, the team will have to weigh the importance of the quote and the severity of the error. If the few percentage points or the day of the week makes a big difference to the story, maybe the host will add in some context by recording a quick aside, even if it disrupts the story's flow, or the team will get the interviewee back in the studio to rerecord. If the small error doesn't make much of a difference or harm anyone and it's not possible to rerecord, the team may opt to leave the quote as is.

Fact-checking videos can also be complex, since they have both an audio and a visual dimension. In addition to double-checking the accuracy of each image on its own, photographs and figures that appear on the screen during a television segment or documentary should accurately support what the news anchor or voice-over is saying. Also pay close attention to clips from other audio or video used to highlight an argument. Were the quotes or segments taken out of context? A checker should go back to the original source and listen to or watch the entire piece—or at least a good chunk of time before and after the quote appears—to make sure the clip is represented fairly.

And finally, when you're working with documentaries, keep in mind that even filmmakers don't agree on whether they're journalists, storytellers, or a mixture of both. This type of audio or video piece will be strikingly different from a straightforward news story or reported feature, and fact-checking will require balancing the filmmaker's point of view or goals with reality. Take, for example, the popular 2015 HBO documentary *The Jinx*, the true crime story about New York real estate heir Robert Durst, who, among other things, was at the time accused of murdering his friend Susan Berman in 2000 (in 1982, Berman had given an alibi for Durst when he was suspected of killing his wife, Kathleen McCormack Durst). The documentary, which won several awards, including two Emmys and a Peabody, was eerily compelling, but after the finale aired—

and after Durst was arrested, just one day earlier—critics began questioning the timeline and information it presented. Certain details, they said, may have been held or shifted in order to make the story more dramatic. In particular, the series ended with Durst mumbling to himself during a trip to the bathroom. His mic was hot, and it appeared to catch a confession: "What the hell did I do? Killed them all, of course." But later it became clear that the editors had manipulated the footage, pulling these lines from a longer recording and placing them out of order. In 2019, Durst's legal team said that they planned to use the manipulation as part of the defense in his murder trial. For what it's worth, the tactic didn't work: in September 2021, Durst was found guilty of Berman's murder. Six weeks later, he was indicted in McCormack Durst's murder. (As he awaited trial, Robert Durst died in early 2022 of natural causes, according to his lawyer.)

. . . .

Think Like a Fact-Checker

Watch a nightly newscast and pay attention to how the words that the anchor is saying link up to the graphic elements, including maps, photographs, boxes of text, and information that may run in a ticker at the bottom of the screen. Can you catch any moments where the graphics and verbal reportage don't align? If you had been fact-checking the piece, what changes would you have suggested?

. . . .

Books

NONFICTION

Every so often, a book author gets skewered in the media due to embarrassing missteps in a high-profile book. In 2019, these errors may have had a banner year: a former executive editor of the *New York Times*, Jill Abramson, was accused of both plagiarism and errors in her book *Merchants of Truth*, an account of the modern news business; the Pulitzer Prize–winning author Jared Diamond drew critiques for his book *Upheaval*, of which one reviewer wrote, "Before long, the first mistake caught my eye; soon, the 10th. Then graver ones. Errors, along with generalizations, blind spots and oversights, that called into question the choice to publish"; and a BBC interviewer uncovered that the writer Naomi Wolf had misinterpreted key historical documents in her book *Outrages*, to the point that it threatened her entire thesis, which dealt with the criminalization of homosexuality in the Victorian era. (In 2021, a revised edition of Wolf's book also came under fire; in a separate instance of spreading falsehoods that year, Twitter suspended her for posting misinformation about the coronavirus vaccine.)

It may surprise the average reader to learn that most publishers of nonfiction books don't do a formal fact-check. The publisher may have a lawyer look over the book to flag potentially libelous content, but beyond that, it is up to the author to make sure the book is accurate. While this may have changed at some publishing houses, there is still a "need to nudge the publishing giants on that one," says Emily Krieger, a writer and researcher, even as it is "probably a tough sell[,] because they don't want to be on the hook for fact-checking costs. Right now, authors pay for it." If fact-checking became standard at book publishers, Krieger adds, the cost could shift to the publisher, just as it already does with other key steps in book publishing, such as editing.

Without more industry support, the responsibility for fact-checking will continue to fall on the author. Some authors approach fact-checking by ignoring the process entirely. Others hire an independent fact-checker, do the fact-check themselves as best as they can, or pursue a combination of both in which a fact-checker only takes on specific parts of the manuscript. Usually, the choice to forgo a full independent fact-check is a matter of financial constraint: book advances are often too modest to support the cost of a checker, which means the author must pay out of pocket. But let's say you land a great book-checking gig. A book manuscript may be 80,000 or 100,000 words or more, many times that of even the heftiest narrative magazine feature. How do you begin?

Even before you start fact-checking, you should talk to the author about expectations, timing, and budgets, says Krieger, who has fact-checked popular science books, including the critically acclaimed *Spillover: Animal Infections and the Next Human Pandemic*, by David Quammen, along with online and print articles. Book fact-checking work will most likely be freelance, and it's better to sort out the hourly rate and estimated time frame before you start. This process will help to avoid sticker shock over your invoice and will also help you and the author identify which sections or types of facts need the most attention.

During the initial conversation, you should also ask what research materials you'll have access to, as well as whether the manuscript is footnoted or otherwise annotated (ask to see a sample chapter). If the manuscript has no annotations or you can't get your hands on the research material, your job will be much harder and take longer, which may become cost prohibitive for the author.

If you move forward with the project, you may get portions of the manuscript relatively early on in the writing stage—maybe one chapter at a time, rather than the complete document—and the amount of time you will have to work on the project will depend entirely on the author's deadline with the publisher. However you get the pages, don't think of the project as fact-checking a sweeping book. Instead, break it into smaller chunks. Work one chapter at a time and follow the same fact-checking process that you would with a magazine article, with the caveat that you should only check the types of facts or sections of the book that the writer asked for (this may range from checking everything to focusing on lighter facts like numbers and spelling).

If you need to interview people who appear in the book—or experts who were interviewed but aren't specifically mentioned—and you don't have the full manuscript yet, ask the author whether these sources appear in multiple chapters. If so, you might want to wait until you've seen all of the relevant sections before making contact to set up a fact-checking interview.

As you work through the book, periodically check in with the author with updates on how much time you've spent, adjusting your price and timing estimates as needed (for information on hourly rates for fact-checking, see p. 78). When you are finished, prepare a fact-checking report like you would for a magazine piece.

. . . .

Think Like a Fact-Checker

The next time you read a nonfiction book, choose a page and underline each verifiable fact. Make a list of the sources you would use to check each fact. Bonus: Take the next step and fact-check the section (but again, don't contact any of the people who appear in the story). Did you find any errors?

. . . .

MEMOIR

If nonfiction books don't usually go through a fact-check, then memoir is even further removed from the process. Memoir is autobiographical, a person's own account of their life based on their memory. This genre can slide into dicey territory from a fact-checking perspective. Our memories are faulty both because of our neurological limitations and because we see ourselves from an undeniably biased perspective.

Still, a wildly inaccurate memoir can get a writer or a publisher in trouble. Just ask James Frey, the author of *A Million Little Pieces*, which was published in 2003. Frey marketed the book as a true story about his drug addiction and rehabilitation. It was a best seller thanks, in part, to rave reviews by Oprah Winfrey. But a lengthy investigation by the website the Smoking Gun found that Frey fabricated much of the account, including his own alleged police records.

Your chances of getting hired to fact-check a memoir are probably slim. But if given the opportunity, you should start by asking about the publisher's goal. Do they want you to check straightforward facts, like names, dates, and timelines, to make sure they match the author's memory? Or do they need a more investigative take, like double-checking police reports and school graduation records, or speaking with friends or family members to see if their memory of an event aligns with the author's? Or are they worried about libel, which could result from a writer making inaccurate statements about their family and friends?

FICTION

Now we're in even slipperier territory: by definition, fiction doesn't claim to be factual. Look no further than the disclaimer at the beginning of a novel or movie, which usually says something like this: "The following work is fiction. Names, characters, places, and events are either products of the author's imagination or used fictitiously. Any resemblance to actual events or locales or persons, living or dead, is entirely coincidental." Still, a lot of great works of fiction are rooted in real worlds—or at least believable ones—and making sure certain details are correct can help bolster these backdrops.

While it's not typical for a piece of fiction to go through a formal fact-check, some book editors or copy editors may flag inaccuracies that don't support the world that the author is trying to build. Examples may include anachronism, such as referencing a technology that didn't exist at the time the story takes place. If this is a science fiction novel, then the reference may be intentional. If it is historical fiction, it may be an oversight. Or, perhaps, the author inadvertently put a real landmark on the wrong side of a city, or misspelled the name of an actual political figure. Regardless, a good editor or copy editor will point out these inconsistencies to help make the fictional world as rich with accurate details as possible.

Reviews, Criticism, Columns, and Opinion Pieces

Reviews and criticism may cover anything from a book to a movie to an album to a play to an exhibit at a museum. Whatever the object of the review, the fact-checker should look into it—read the book, watch the movie, listen to the album, go to the play, visit the museum (or get on the phone with the curator, if it's in another city). The most important part will be checking to make sure the details that the reviewer references are accurate. The rest of the review will likely be opinion based on the reviewer's expertise—presumably, that's why the publication asked this specific person to write it. It's tough to fact-check these more subjective aspects, but if there are any assertions that ring entirely untrue based on what you have seen or watched or heard, bring up your concerns to the editor.

Columns vary from one outlet to another, but in general, they attempt to teach the reader about something new and are infused with the author's own opinion and voice. The facts within a column need to be right, but a checker won't have much control over the conclusions a columnist draws from these facts. Check what you can and give your editor a heads-up on opinions or claims that seem outlandish, particularly those that could draw legal action.

The point of a more traditional opinion piece is to state a thesis or argument and then present facts and other material to try to convince the reader to agree. Opinions may appear as written essays or op-eds in print or digital outlets; come up in statements during segments on broadcast or internet shows;

or provide the basis for an interview podcast, in which the host and their guest talk about any number of subjects. The author—or, in the case of a show, the host or their guests—can argue whatever case they want, but that point should still be supported by real facts. Fact-checkers who work on an opinion piece need to make sure it doesn't stretch the truth, mischaracterize research, egregiously cherry-pick material, or downright tell a lie. If it does, the piece shouldn't run. "People are allowed to have their opinions," says Michelle Harris, a podcast fact-checker for Opinion Audio at the *New York Times*. "But if the foundational framework—the facts' foundational framework—isn't there, we're not going to be able to air that."

Miscellaneous

The list of items that may be fact-checked is near infinite—if a piece of writing exists, you can probably find *something* about it that can be double-checked. In addition to various news media or books, there is also poetry, advertising, cartoons, and more. For the most part, a fact-checker won't encounter these unusual cases, but in the rare times that you do, you can tailor the fact-checking process regardless of the format. Poetry, for example, may reference real-life events, and if there is an error, it's important to consider whether the author purposely twisted the information to make a point or slipped up by accident. Advertising—especially for products that make claims related to health or medicine, as in the pharmaceutical industry—may require in-house checkers to pore over supporting studies. If a brand says their products are scientifically proven to smooth your wrinkles, they have to have evidence or risk unwanted attention from the Federal Trade Commission, which penalizes companies for false advertising.

As for cartoons, Carolyn Kormann, a staff writer at the *New Yorker* who was the former deputy head of fact-checking for the print magazine and former head of fact-checking for NewYorker.com, has some good tips. Kormann says to ask yourself: Do you understand the joke? Are spellings and meanings of words correct, particularly those in languages other than English? Do the representations of specific animals or individuals make sense—e.g., is Superman's "S" right? Do the descriptive details of a place match reality—e.g., does the North Pole inaccurately show penguins, which actually only live in the Southern Hemisphere? Are all logos and mascots depicted correctly? And are sartorial details appropriate—e.g., the placement of the buttons on a men's versus a women's dress shirt?

In one example from the *New Yorker*, Kormann recalls a Harry Bliss cartoon that showed the "Here's Johnny" scene from *The Shining*, with Jack Nicholson's ax replaced with a fluffy white dandelion blowball. Shelley Duvall, who plays Nicholson's wife in the movie, holds a box of tissues instead of a knife, and the caption reads: "Here's Pollen." Trouble is, says Kormann, dandelion blowballs don't carry any pollen. Bliss redrew the image using a flowering dandelion instead.

. . . .

Think Like a Fact-Checker

Pick whatever media you're consuming at the moment—whether it's a novel, a podcast, or a television documentary—and select a short section (maybe a page for a printed work or a minute for audio or video). As you read, listen, or watch, make a list of the facts. *Bonus:* Look up each fact and see if you can spot any mistakes. (Do not call or email any real people who appear in the story. It will confuse them.)

. . . .

NAVIGATING RELATIONSHIPS WITH EDITORS, WRITERS, AND PRODUCERS

Knowing the steps required to fact-check a story is only part of the job. In fact, even if you are an expert researcher and can do these steps in your sleep, you will get nowhere as a checker if you don't learn how to approach relationships with the people you need to work with—namely, editors, writers, and producers.

As with many relationships, diplomacy is key. No matter how wrong you think the writer and editor are for including a bad fact in a story, keeping calm will help you accomplish your job. And if they still don't cooperate with you, hey, you tried. Just make sure to keep a good record—either paper, electronic, or both—of your interactions so you can point to them if the story ends up needing a correction.

Writers—or reporters and producers, if you're working with audio or video—will likely feel closer to the story than anyone else, and changes may be especially difficult for them. Approach these people respectfully. Let them know you liked the story (even if you didn't, try to find something positive to say). Rather than bluntly pointing out mistakes, tell them you found sources with conflicting information and ask if they have anything else that supports what the story says. "Sometimes fact-checkers want to find the flaws in the story, and that's what you're doing," says Mark McClusky, a former head of operations at *Wired* and a former fact-checker at *Sports Illustrated*. "But the point is not to play 'gotcha' with award-winning writers—it's to make them look as good as possible."

And although you should be kind and diplomatic, it doesn't hurt to be direct with your team when you've found a mistake. You can do this by creating clear and well-sourced fact-checking reports. It's important for a team to see how a story has improved thanks to a fact-check, particularly if you've saved them from an especially embarrassing or litigious mistake. It also helps for an outlet's management to know how fact-checking works, because it underscores the worth of the process, says journalist Tekendra Parmar, who helped set up the fact-checking process at *Rest of World*, a publication that covers technology and culture. Parmer says it was vital to "open up what my checkers were doing and give insights to my

Pro Tip: How Writers and Producers Can Work with Fact-Checkers

Having another person double-check your work can be anxiety inducing. And, yeah, depending on the situation, it might even be a little annoying. But it doesn't have to be that way if you reframe your thinking. Rather than considering the fact-checker as someone who is trying to catch you in a mistake, try seeing them as a key member in a collaborative process with the same goal: to publish an accurate, fair, compelling story. From that perspective, the fact-checker is there to help save you from your mistakes. Not every journalist has the opportunity to work with this sort of safety net, so find a way to appreciate the process.

To make the fact-check go as smoothly as it can, be sure to keep your notes and source material organized. Clearly annotate your story so that it's easy for the fact-checker to follow along. And if the checker digs up a potential error, be diplomatic as you negotiate how—and whether—to correct the piece. You are on the same team.

bosses, to show them that these checkers have caught this many changes in the piece. And this is why the process is essential."

If you do think there needs to be a change, have a solution at the ready. Talk through it with the writer if appropriate, but if you find that conflict is unavoidable, tell the editor, who is ultimately the one in charge.

Editors want every story to be right, but they are also preoccupied with many stories that are publishing simultaneously as well as juggling early drafts for next month's magazine or tomorrow's web posts or next month's narrative podcast episode. For audio or video stories, producers and editors will be

Pro Tip: How Editors Can Work with Fact-Checkers

It may not always feel like it, but if you're the editor, you're the boss. Or at least, you are *a* boss. Use your power wisely to help make fact-checking work smoothly:

(1) Make sure your team knows how the stories at your outlet make it through the editorial process. Fact-checkers should know when they are needed, and you'll help them greatly by letting writers know how and when the fact-check will happen.

(2) Provide clear guidelines to your fact-checkers. For instance, do you want them to check quotes against a transcript or a recording? Or with the source?

(3) Make sure that your team knows that you respect the fact-checkers—and that they should, too. If no one takes fact-checking seriously, or if you let some writers bend the rules, the process will break down.

(4) Be kind to both your fact-checker and your writer when you have to collectively negotiate new language for a story (and also be kind when someone inevitably makes a mistake, because someday that someone may be you).

(5) Consider your role in fact-checking before a story ever gets to that stage. For instance, kick the tires on a story before you assign it, as well as each time you read a draft. If something doesn't sound right, or if you get the sense your writer doesn't have the sourcing to back up a claim, push them toward accuracy.

(6) Designate a staff member to oversee the fact-checking team, to help keep the process moving efficiently.

similarly busy. Don't come to these people each time you hit a small problem; rather, work through as much of the piece as possible, make a list of outstanding issues, and schedule a time to go through them. And again, if you've found a problem, have a suggestion on how to fix it (keep in mind the new material will need to fit into the same amount of space for a magazine or time for a video or radio piece). Caveat: if you run into a very big problem, like a key source refusing to cooperate or evidence of plagiarism, tell your boss as soon as possible.

· ·

Think Like a Fact-Checker

The next time you find yourself poised to argue with a friend or family member over a point of fact—say, in a friendly debate over the health care system or what happened last night on your favorite television show—find a way to calmly and diplomatically present your evidence and see whether you can persuade them to change their mind. (Disclaimer: research suggests it's incredibly hard to change people's minds even with hard empirical evidence, but it's good practice for adjusting your tone and your tact in the workplace.)

· ·

FACT-CHECKING ON A BUDGET

There is no way around it: fact-checking is tedious. It takes time. It takes money. It takes resources. Depending on where you work, you may not be able to read the story multiple times, mark it up like a Day-Glo rainbow, and find primary sources for every fact. So, what should you do if you're asked to fact-check under these circumstances?

It's not the best approach, but it's better than nothing. Print a copy of the story, take a pen, and mark two types of facts: first and most important are the potential legal liabilities; second and on the opposite end of the seriousness spectrum are the basic facts that are both easy to mess up and easy to double-check. These may include proper nouns, unusual spellings, places, prices, dates, and so on (if you can't print, or don't want to, do the same by highlighting these sections or words in an electronic document).

The controversial bits should check out based on the writer's sources, but you still may need to talk to the editor to see if the publication should consult a lawyer. If you don't have access to a lawyer and you can't confirm the information based on what the writer has provided, here are a few suggestions: (1) ask that the story's publication be held while you track down appropriate confirmations, (2) soften the language so that it doesn't open the publication to a lawsuit, (3) cut the most outrageous claims, or (4) kill the story. If the editor doesn't agree with your take, you've done your due diligence in bringing it up. Just be sure to keep a written record as to who made the decision and when.

For the simpler facts, like spelling and prices, work your way through the fact-checking process laid out in the previous pages. You might have to rely on more online sources than actual people—say, for example, double-checking a price with a website instead of a publicist—but at the very least find the official online representation of a person or product to confirm information.

. . . .

Think Like a Fact-Checker

Find a short blog post or news story and identify all the facts you would ideally check, but give yourself ten minutes to check the most important ones. Did you find any mistakes? If so, where do you think the author went wrong while sourcing the story?

. . . .

FACT-CHECKING YOUR OWN WRITING

Many writers will never work with a fact-checker or research desk, particularly newspaper reporters, bloggers, newsletter writers, and nonfiction book authors. If that's you, how can you apply the rigor of fact-checking to your own work?

It's not easy, and many checkers will even say it's impossible or bad practice. A fact-checker brings an outside eye to a story, catching leaps of logic the author may have taken in order to build an interesting piece. When it's just you, there is no way to step outside your brain, which is rife with its own assumptions and blind spots.

Still, there are outlets that don't employ fact-checkers, and both time and money often limit hiring one independently. In cases like this, there are ways to distance yourself from your work in order to fact-check it as best as you can. For starters, don't move too quickly, says Jason Grotto at Bloomberg. "Sometimes when you're trying to get a story done, you're just rushed," he says. "It's really important to try to slow down and try to be mindful about what is on the page—and not get distracted." Always build time into your deadline so that you can step away from the story before it goes to your editor (or before it publishes, if you're writing without an editor). Ideally, you'll be able to pad the deadline with days or even weeks. In reality, especially when publishing online, this may only be an hour or two. Whatever your time frame, put the story aside for as long as you can and come back to it with fresh eyes. Try to look at it from the perspective of a skeptical fact-checker who doesn't necessarily trust your sources or claims, or an antagonistic reader looking for something to challenge. If you have time, print a copy out and follow the fact-checking process as though you were checking someone else's work. Make sure you keep your sources organized so that it is easy to go back to them (some writers annotate their stories as they work, dropping in footnotes with website links, source names, or report titles, while others use software

---

Tips and Tricks: Checking Your Own Writing

- Step away from the story for as long as you can to read it with fresh eyes.
- Change the story's font so it seems like you're reading something new.
- Print the story and read it away from your desk to get a different perspective.
- Read the story through the eyes of a skeptical reader or angry commenter. What mistakes would they catch?
- Consider the story from the perspective of each source. You shouldn't change anything just to please them, but this may help catch mistakes.
- Fact-check starting at the last sentence and work backward, so you don't get caught up reading the story and thus missing the facts.

---

such as Scrivener, which help organize and track research materials).

During the fact-check, also think about the sources you've used. Are they solid? Are there any facts that need extra backup—especially those that might be controversial or open you to a lawsuit? If so, consider finding additional sourcing to confirm the information.

Another way to fact-check the work is to run the entire story by an expert. This shouldn't be someone who is in the story. Instead, find a person who is knowledgeable about the topic and has no stake in how it turns out—this gets easier if you have a regular beat and have built a solid network of sources you trust. Having an outside source isn't the same as a fact-check and shouldn't replace it, but it will help identify potential holes in the story, as well as questionable claims. (Caveat: if you're working with an editor, confirm with them that it is okay to send copy to an outside source; some outlets prohibit the practice.)

For longer projects such as a book, try a combination of these approaches. Send sections of the book to appropriate experts, but also go through the entire manuscript sentence by sentence and double-check it against your original sources. As you check, reconsider the quality of those sources.

. . . .

Think Like a Fact-Checker
Pick a short article you've published or a section of a longer piece. Print it out and work through the fact-checking steps. Did you find any mistakes? How did it feel to double-check your own work? If you were to publish the story now, are there changes you would make?

. . . .

HOW TO GET A FACT-CHECKING JOB

So you want to be a fact-checker. How do you start? While some publications still have staff fact-checkers and researchers, many rely on freelancers. And when it comes to freelance gigs, many are filled behind the scenes. An editor, for example, may just ask around for recommendations from colleagues, contact a few promising candidates, and hire whoever seems like the best fit. And since the role is often freelance-based, replacing a fact-checker who isn't working out is often just a matter of not giving them new assignments.

This is unfortunate, because fact-checking can be a great gig, both for journalists who prefer to stay on the research side of things and for those who are just starting out and need a good job to help build their reporting foundation. For freelance journalists, a regular fact-checking gig can also be a lifeline, bringing in steady money amid the uncertain timelines and pay schedules that come with contract-based writing assignments. In my work with the Knight Science Journalism Program at MIT, we're aiming to help bring the profession out in the open a bit more: as of this writing, we have a public searchable database of about 200 fact-checkers who are available for work, and that list is growing. This is a way to help connect people who are interested in fact-checking work with editors and authors who otherwise wouldn't find them through their own limited professional connections. (The list is available at https://ksjfactcheck.org/find-a-fact-checker/.)

Of course, one relatively small list isn't enough to keep all the current and potential fact-checkers employed. So how do you find fact-checking work—particularly if you're just starting out?

If you are already working in journalism in some capacity, tap into your network. Do you have a friend or colleague who works at a publication that uses fact-checkers? If so, let them know you are interested in and available for fact-checking projects. Are you already freelancing for publications? If so, and the publications use fact-checkers, ask your editor if they are looking for additional help. If you did a good job reporting and writing for them, they're more apt to consider you for a fact-checking gig—even if you don't have fact-checking experience.

Finally, and importantly, how much are freelance fact-checkers typically paid? Like many jobs in journalism, the answer varies wildly but mostly falls under the category of *not enough*, especially considering how difficult the job can be. In *The State of Fact-Checking in Science Journalism*, released in 2018, my team observed, based on our interviews, that the average hourly rate was $27.76 according to editors and $34.27 according to fact-checkers. Some fact-checkers were able to get much higher rates—$75 or even $100 per hour—if they had a unique area of expertise, or could work well with a particularly difficult writer. Our reporting was just anecdotal, but the results reflect findings at other organizations; the Economic Research Institute, for instance, says that editorial fact-checking typically pays about $30 an hour. And in a 2020 survey from the Editorial Freelancers Association, members said that for fact-checking and research, their median pay was typically between $46 and $50 an hour.

FOUR ||| Checking Different Types of Facts

Now that you know the basic fact-checking process, how should you actually check each fact? There are tricks for checking different kinds—confirming a quote, for example, may require subtle skills that aren't needed to double-check the spelling of a state capital or the price of an iPhone. Here are tips for checking the major categories of facts that you'll likely encounter in your work, organized from the most common and (generally) straightforward to the murky and troubling. As you read, consider how Peter Canby, the former head of the checking department at the *New Yorker*, defines fact-checking: it is simply "elevated common sense."

BASIC FACTS

Every story you check will have elemental information including proper names, spelling, dates, and geographical locations. Always use a primary source for these when possible; if not, fact-checking departments often suggest two or three high-quality secondary sources per fact (see chapter 5 for the distinction between primary and secondary).

When confirming spelling, draw a diagonal line through each letter of the word as you read through the source material and keep an eye out for accents and other symbols. Double-check trademarked names, which may use unusual spelling or capitalization (think Kleenex and iPhone). If there is a reference to the timing of an event ("last month"), make sure it will still be accurate whenever the story will publish. Similarly, always double-check a person's age with them, as they may have had a birthday—or will have one—between the time the story was written and when it goes to print (one former *Slate* intern recalls an awkward assignment where she had to call Martha Minow, a dean and professor at Harvard Law School, for the sole purpose of confirming Minow's age).

Read source material carefully to make sure you have the right person, place, or thing, and be wary of seemingly obvious facts that may have more than one meaning. Dan Sullivan and Dan Sullivan each ran for office in the Alaska Republican primaries in 2014, although they are two different men; Manhattan Beach is both a wealthy seaside community outside Los Angeles and a tiny inland town in Minnesota; and if you're checking a story about beachwear by an Australian writer that'll publish in the U.S., you'll find that Americans have a very different meaning for a piece of clothing called a "thong."

Also beware of obsolete information online or in print. A university website may not reflect a recent change in a professor's title; a company may no longer offer a product at a certain price; and the phone number on a pamphlet for an Argentinian estancia, which a writer grabbed while working on a travel piece, may actually be out of service. When in doubt, call or email a representative from the organization in question to make sure the details are right.

Finally, don't assume that the writer and editor are using specific words correctly, particularly if those words are unfamiliar to you. When in doubt, check definitions to make sure the meaning and context are appropriate.

. . . .

Think Like a Fact-Checker

The next time you read an article or a nonfiction book, pick one of the people mentioned in the story and—without actually contacting them or anyone else—try to confirm the details that were written about them. Were the sources hard to find? Did you notice discrepancies between the story and the information you found? If so, why might the writer have gotten it wrong—or why might the source you found be wrong?

. . . .

NUMBERS AND MEASUREMENTS

If you need to confirm numbers or measurements in a story, keep in mind the context, the source, and common sense. For straightforward measurements, this will be easier (but never slack even with these). Say, for example, you're fact-checking a feature in a food magazine that includes a recipe. Do the measurements make sense? Would anyone ever *really* use a tablespoon of vanilla extract, or is that meant to be a teaspoon? Or say you're fact-checking a story that cites distances that came from a report that was written in a European country. Were the measurements correctly converted from kilometers to miles? Or say a story claims that 8 billion people have purchased a new smartphone. As of early 2022, the entire world population was estimated at a bit more than 7.8 billion. Did the writer mean 8 *million*? Or did they mean a different number of billions, like 1 billion? Or how about a story on a new camera setup, which includes several attachments, that claims the entire kit can be purchased for $500. When you add up the individual prices for all the parts, does the overall price match up? Or how about a case where a writer rounds up or down, rather than using an exact number? It's usually best to use the exact number if it's available, but at the very least, let the writer and editor know the exact versus rounded numbers so they can make an informed decision on which to use. Or how about a case where a writer claimed there was a percent increase. Did they confuse *percent* with *percentage points*? For example: a change from 50 percent to 60 percent is an increase of 10 *percentage points*, but it's an increase of 20 percent.

In other words, always check individual numbers and measurements. And always look at numbers in context.

The more complex the number, the more you need to pay attention. Take statistics, which are regularly twisted and misinterpreted. Look carefully at the sources that the writer used. Are the authors of those sources obviously biased in any way? Do they work for a partisan think tank, for example, or an advocacy group? If so, find a better, more neutral source, and make sure it is a primary one. (Unless the whole point of using that source is to point out its inherent biases, which should be made clear in the story.)

You also need to make sure the writer is using the stats correctly. One common error is to mistake *correlation* for *causation*. Correlation shows how two variables change in relation to each other—maybe they both increase or decrease the same way over time, for instance, or one goes up when the other goes down. But correlation can't tell you if the two are changing at the same time because of cause and effect. That's where causation comes in. To help illustrate the difference, you can line up two sets of data that follow the same trajectory over time but are almost certainly unrelated. Tyler Vigen, a principal at Boston Consulting Group, does just that in his book *Spurious Correlations*, as well as at a blog of the same name. For instance, Vigen graphs the divorce rate in Maine between 2000 and 2009, which more or less follows the rate of the per capita consumption of margarine. But no one would argue—I hope—that the divorce rate in Maine has decreased over time *because* people are eating less of the butter substitute.

That's not to say that legitimate research never relies on correlation. On the contrary, some scientific work, such as epidemiological studies, examines correlations all the time. These studies often look at how exposure to something in our environment—a food, for instance, or a potential carcinogen—might affect a group of people. But such studies will never be able to definitively say that an exposure *caused* a particular

Figure 7. The blog *Spurious Correlations* has found a humorous way to illustrate why correlation does not imply causation. Here, datasets on the divorce rate in Maine and the per capita margarine consumption follow more or less the same ups and downs over time, but they are almost certainly unrelated.

outcome. As a fact-checker, you should always be sure that you understand what a study is suggesting and be sure that a writer isn't taking a finding too far.

We might in this light also consider health reporting, where studies often discuss *relative* risks, which writers often report as *absolute* risks. Relative risk emerges from a comparison between two different test groups, while absolute risk describes the actual likelihood of a specific event happening. Let's say a hypothetical study claims that coffee increase your relative risk of cancer by 25 percent. Inevitably you will see headlines saying, "Coffee Boosts Cancer Risk by 25 Percent," which make it seem as though if you drink a cup of coffee, you're in trouble. But now let's look at this hypothetical study more closely: the authors are comparing a group that drinks coffee to one that does not. The coffee abstainers had a 0.001 percent risk of cancer while the coffee drinkers had a 0.00125 percent risk. That's a 25 percent increase in relative risk, but it's still a tiny risk overall. Now, go enjoy that coffee.

Another example of misunderstood statistics comes from the inevitable headlines that follow announcements from the

International Agency for Research on Cancer, which is part of the World Health Organization. The IARC is tasked with, among other things, looking at the available science on an array of materials and determining how likely it is that those materials cause cancer. The trouble is that the agency organizes these materials not by risk, but by the strength of the evidence. In 2015 their assessment of bacon made the news, with some outlets claiming that it is just as likely to cause cancer as tobacco. In reality, while both tobacco and cured meats are included at the highest level on the IARC list ("Group 1: Carcinogenic to Humans"), this only means that the science that confirms this connection is equally robust. Ultimately, eating bacon is far less risky than smoking when it comes to increasing your chances of getting cancer.

Yet another important statistical concept for a fact-checker to understand is the so-called p-value, which researchers use to determine whether the differences they detect in a study's results are statistically significant or due to random chance. And frankly, there is no simple way to define it. I tried in the first edition of this book and failed.* But here's a new attempt.

---

* In the first edition of *The Chicago Guide to Fact-Checking*, I wrote: "A commonly accepted p-value is 0.05, which translates to the researchers being 95 percent certain that their results represent something real." This isn't entirely accurate, as two sharp readers pointed out (Bethany Brookshire, a science journalist, and Sebastian Lutz, a senior lecturer at Uppsala University who specializes in philosophy of science, philosophical methodologies, and the history of logical empiricism). I made another attempt at writing the passage, and my fact-checker for this edition of the book, Nora Belblidia, found out that I was *still* wrong after talking to both Brookshire and Lutz; she then interviewed the statistician David Spiegelhalter to help clear things up. When you're writing on a complex topic, there is always a tension between getting it 100 percent accurate and making sure that it's understandable to the average reader. Here, multiple times, I erred too far on the side of trying to make it easy to grasp—to the point that it was wrong. All this is to say: as a fact-

Pro Tip: Finding Numbers Online

Google isn't always a great source on its own, but it may help locate key numbers. If you can't confirm a statistic that appears in a story you are checking, try using search terms that include the number and other keywords from the sentence or sentences, and Google may return a primary source. But beware: there may be even better sources that provide more accurate numbers, which likely won't come up in a search such as this. Evaluate whatever source Google spits out just as you would any other.

A commonly accepted p-value is less than 0.05, also written as $P < 0.05$ which, according to David Spiegelhalter, author of *The Art of Statistics*, could be thought of this way: "Out of 100 experiments in which there was not actually any relationship (i.e., the null hypothesis is true in all of them), we would expect five to have $P < 0.05$ and so a false 'discovery' might be claimed." (In statistics, a null hypothesis is that a particular experiment will yield no significant results.) In some areas of study, such as high-energy physics, a 0.05 p-level is laughably high. In other instances, researchers manipulate data until they reach an acceptable p-value—a process that is called p-hacking, which uses statistics improperly in order to squeeze out a desired answer. When in doubt, a fact-checker should call a statistician to help identify whether a paper is using the p-value honestly and correctly—and defining it well, for that matter.

Finally, there may be cases where writers use raw data to

---

checker, you'll need to help your writers and editors land on language that is both correct and easy to read. And any of us can goof it up at any point.

make their own calculations. If possible, have the writer walk you through the math and take a look at the original sources used. Do those sources seem solid? Does the author's logic make sense? Can you find any other sources that help confirm the numbers?

If you're trying to check a stat or calculation and, despite having a solid source, the numbers still seem confusing, that's okay. You aren't required to be an ace statistician or math whiz to be a good fact-checker. Set up a phone call or video chat with an appropriate expert, perhaps through the math department at an accredited university.

. . . .

Think Like a Fact-Checker

The next time you read a magazine article, mark all the numbers. Can you track down reliable primary sources for each one? Which numbers proved the most difficult to check, and why do you think that is?

. . . .

POLLS

News outlets often rely on polls, with good reason: to provide a snapshot of people's opinion on something, from how they feel about the issues of the day to whom they're going to vote for in an upcoming election. Polls are even considered primary sources, since they are a direct collection of data. But that doesn't mean they are always of high quality—that depends entirely on how they were built. It also doesn't mean that journalists should rely on a single poll to confirm something, because even a well-done poll will have limitations. In other words, polls are "not in themselves capital-T Truth—they're one lens on what we know is the truth," says Andrea Jones-Rooy, director of undergraduate studies at NYU's Center for Data Science and a former quantitative researcher at

FiveThirtyEight. Instead, polls offer a view from "one point in time," they add. "But that doesn't mean it's [all] garbage and polls are wrong. The question is, are they systematically biased or off in a particular direction?"

Before a journalist or fact-checker even assesses an individual poll, they should see where it exists in the broader polling ecosystem, says Dhrumil Mehta, an associate professor in data journalism at Columbia University and assistant director of the Tow Center for Digital Journalism (Mehta is also a former FiveThirtyEight colleague of Jones-Rooy). The goal, Mehta says, is to provide as much context as possible for the poll. If the poll is for a presidential election, for instance, you should consider all of the other recent polls on that same topic and see how the responses compare.

Next, Mehta recommends looking at who conducted the poll. Some groups are known entities that have been doing polls for a long time and have a better track record of getting things more or less right—for example, ABC News / *Washington Post*, SurveyUSA, and Monmouth University are well regarded when it comes to election polls. And if the pollster is unknown or hasn't been around for very long, don't forget about shoe-leather reporting, Mehta adds, because fakes and scam artists do exist. Find out: Who created the poll? Are they an actual person or organization with transparent contact information? And are they willing to talk to you about the poll and how it was made? A good pollster will be transparent about who they are. They will also be transparent about how their poll was created, providing a list of the poll's verbatim questions, including the order in which they were asked. A good pollster will also disclose the poll's general demographics (gender, race, political party, and so on) and percentage of people who responded, although, according to Mehta, the absence of a response rate doesn't necessarily mean the poll is untrustworthy. "More transparency is always better than less transparency," he says, "but I wouldn't doubt a survey just because they didn't include that particular piece of information in their methodology."

Also beware of all the different types of organizations that do polls. Some polls are from news outlets and universities. But others come from pollsters hired by political candidates, which could mean they've been working from a similar set of contacts again and again—and those contacts may be biased toward a particular party. Still others are internal campaign polls, which, Jones-Rooy says, makes them "the most nervous," since the people conducting such polls may want to please their bosses, and may ask leading questions or filter only the most positive answers through a press release.

Once you have some context for a poll, you can assess it on an individual level. This means looking at the methodology. Two easy details to look for, according to Jones-Rooy, are the date range when the data were collected and how many people participated. The date range is important because it will be a snapshot of how people felt when the questions were asked; this could show, for instance, if voters were expressing their preference before or after some damaging information came out about a political candidate. The number of people surveyed is important because it shows the sample size. A pollster won't have the time or money to ask all 330 million or so Americans how they feel about, say, gun rights or abortion, so they aim to find a subset that will be more or less representative. According to Jones-Rooy, around 2,000 participants may be enough for a good sample of the U.S. population (going higher to 10,000 or so, they add, doesn't actually increase the accuracy all that much). But beware if the sample size is unusually small, or if the pollsters have failed to include the sample size at all.

The composition of a sample is also relevant. Traditionally, pollsters have used probability to design a good poll, aiming for a random sample with demographics that can be extrapolated to the broader population. One way to assess this part of a pollster's methodology is to consider how they contacted the participants. In probability-based polling, pollsters may pull together participants from existing phone or mailing lists. But they need to take care to make sure that sample is random, and that it isn't skewed—for instance, by underrepresenting an age range, political persuasion, or income bracket (they may also weight the responses to better reflect the broader demographic). Did the pollsters only call people on a land-line? Well, a lot of people don't have one. Did they only call by cell phone? Not everyone will answer an unknown number; if they do pick up, they may quickly disconnect once they realize they're going to have to answer political or sensitive questions. To get at a more representative sample, some polls will try many different forms of communication: calls, texts, emails. A diverse method of contact *may* mean that the respondents are more of a representative sampling. (But beware: mixed meth-ods aren't *always* better than a really well-done phone poll by a highly competent pollster, so be sure to consider how they contacted people in context with all of the other information you are pulling together for a poll.)

Pollsters have also increasingly turned to the internet, usu-ally through opt-in online polls, which has made it easier to collect data from far more people for far less money. Some of these polls may have huge samples—far bigger than a typi-cal probability poll. But online opt-in polls can't rely on ran-dom sampling, because, as the Pew Research Center points out, there isn't a master list of everyone on the internet like there is for all the phone numbers and physical addresses in the United States. That means that pollsters who are working online are often doing what is called nonprobability polling— they aren't able to use the mathematics of probability to make sure they're getting the right information. Instead, they have to go looking for people to poll through advertisements and other means, without knowing if the folks who respond are a truly random sampling of the group of people they're trying to assess, and then apply some fancy statistical methods to try to make it all work. One way to assess such a poll is to really be sure it is coming from a reputable organization, says Mehta. That means not only looking up the organization that the poll is coming from but checking to be sure that they have used this method in the past—and that they have a reasonably good track record of getting predictions right.

Another key piece of a poll's methodology is how its questions are worded. A standard question like *Do you approve/ disapprove of the job Joe Biden is doing as president?* will usually elicit a more clear-cut response than *Who are you going to vote for in the upcoming election?* And in some cases, the wording may push respondents toward a particular answer. These are called leading questions. Example: *How terrible of a job is Joe Biden doing?* Next, look at the order of the questions. If a survey asks a bunch of questions about the economy and then asks at the end, *What's the biggest problem facing America?*, respondents may have been primed to say the biggest problem is the economy, says Jones-Rooy. Sensitive questions may also need careful wording (*Have you ever used illegal drugs?* may not provoke an honest response, but *Do you know anyone who has used illegal drugs?* might.) And if the survey has 50 questions, some respondents may have stopped paying attention or dropped out by the end, which means responses to the last questions may not be as accurate as those to earlier ones.

If you're fact-checking a story with polls and you still aren't quite sure how to assess them on your own, find an expert who can help walk you through them and point out the potential red flags. Also consider not only the polls themselves but how the journalist has used them in their story. Often a writer will just drop a poll result in as though it were an absolute fact. Again, it's a good idea to see what other polls exist on the same topic, to make sure the one the journalist used isn't an outlier. Add to the story key caveats for and limitations of the poll, and if possible, link out to the original source. And make sure the story accurately reflects how the relevant question is worded within the original survey.

QUOTES

Ask three fact-checkers how to confirm a quote and you'll likely get three different answers. Checking quotes also varies depending on the publication, the sensitivity of the quote, the source materials available, and the context. Here are a few ways to do it. Each has benefits. Each has pitfalls.

Audio Recordings

No checker has time to listen to many hours' worth of interview files—assuming the writer recorded an interview in the first place—but sometimes a writer will provide you with both the relevant file as well as the time stamp at which the quote occurs. But even exact words on a recording could be misleading: the quality may be poor or the quote may be taken out of context. If the recording is garbled, double-check the quote's content with the source (see below for tips). For context, take care to listen to the audio both before and after the quote to make sure the way it is used in the story reflects what the person appears to have meant.

Transcripts

It's helpful to check quotes against a transcript if you're pressed for time, because you can run a search for a word or a phrase in the quote. But the quality of a transcript depends on how carefully a writer or a transcription service has followed a recorded interview, again assuming the interview was even transcribed. Maybe they misunderstood a phrase or mistyped a word. One cautionary tale comes from *Wired.* In 2013 the magazine published a story about Dropbox, a company that provides cloud storage so that a person can access their files from any computer. The story quoted the company's cofounder Drew Houston this way: "You think about who needs

Dropbox, and it's just about anybody with nipples." But, due to a transcription error, the wrong quote had made its way into the story. After the story published, the magazine was obliged to make a correction: Houston hadn't said "anybody with nipples" but "anybody with a pulse."

Interview transcripts can come from a variety of sources and they have different levels of quality. In some cases, a journalist may transcribe their own recordings. In others, they may hire a transcription service. Some of these services employ people to do the transcription, while others use artificial intelligence. No matter the source, a fact-checker should take care when using any transcript. Even professional human transcribers may make errors, particularly if the audio is of poor quality or the topic includes a lot of jargon—for instance, if the interviewee is a scientist. And AI-based transcription can also get tripped up if an audio file has a lot of background noise or a speaker uses unusual terms or has a heavy accent. In an ideal case, the journalist will have checked the transcript against the audio file and cleaned up any errors—or made a note in cases where the audio is unintelligible. Sometimes, though, they won't.

Check with the Source

Most publications forbid reading a quote back to sources verbatim—the source may deny it, or want to tweak it so they sound better or smarter or to avoid getting in trouble with, say, their employer. But if you don't have a reliable audio file or transcript, or if the writer handed you a quote scribbled on napkin or claimed to have pulled the quote from memory, you may need to check it with the source.

There are a few ways to do this, and which one you choose will depend on your employer's rules as well as whether the quote is benign or contentious. One option is to ask the source several questions on the same topic to see if you can catch something like the original quote. If their answer is similar to the original quote, it's reasonable to believe that the original quote is legit, although pay attention to not only the words they use but also their tone (are they saying it sarcastically, when the text comes off as earnest, for example?). Another method is to paraphrase the quote and ask if the information within it is true without disclosing that it is a direct quote in the story. Another is to tell the source you are paraphrasing a direct quote to make sure the information within it is accurate, although be sure to explain you can't make changes that don't deal directly with facts (some fact-checkers say this and then read the quote verbatim, especially if there is technical language within it). And even though it's not common, some publications do read the quote verbatim—and tell the source so—with the understanding that the magazine has the final say on whether to make any changes.

What should you do if the quote doesn't check out? Point it out to the editor in your fact-check report. At some publications, altering a quote in any way is forbidden; at others, deleting *um*s and *er*s and smoothing grammatical errors is okay; at others, particularly those that feature writing about technical issues for a general audience, may swap out a bit of jargon for a more digestible word, so long as the source agrees; and at others, quotes may be entirely rewritten to make the text snappy (not recommended!). Another elegant option for quotes that are too riddled with verbal ticks, jargon, or tangential asides: just paraphrase the key parts and attribute it to the source. (This is probably the best approach.) Also be aware that most outlets edit long Q&As for clarity and length, which means these will rarely exactly reflect the original interview. Usually, though, the writer will note that the Q&A has been edited in the piece's introduction.

There is also the matter of checking facts within a quote. If a source says something that is outside their expertise or obvious knowledge, you'll need to check that claim. For example, if an artist references an anecdote about Picasso, whom the artist obviously never met because their lives didn't overlap, find another expert or historical document to make sure that the story is accurate. If it isn't, the quote may not support the piece the way the author intended and it may need to be cut or replaced.

. . . .

Think Like a Fact-Checker
Find a family member or friend who will let you record a short mock interview with them, or watch a video that you can record or otherwise play back. Take notes on what you hear. Later, try to reconstruct a quote with your notes, and then listen to the recording to see if you got it right. Was it difficult to capture the quote correctly? Why might it have turned out that way—was the person a fast talker, or were they speaking about an unfamiliar topic, or was there a lot of background noise?

. . . .

CONCEPTS
Some facts aren't discrete numbers or bits of information; instead, they are abstract, often complex ideas generalized from particular instances. Consider, for example, dark matter—the invisible material presumed to make up the bulk of the mass in our universe—or a political theory used to explain a recent increase in white supremacist groups, or an economic argument for a government providing people with a no-strings-attached basic income.

You will be a floundering novice as to a lot of the subjects you must fact-check; big concepts may require the help of an expert rather than cramming a PhD's worth of background reading into a workday. There are two key approaches for finding the right expert. First, look at the list of interviewees from the story—you are likely already speaking to these people to confirm more specific information. Add a few general questions to their interview list.

Second, look for someone who doesn't appear in the story but is willing to chat about background information. Google will help: search for professors of cosmology to find a dark matter expert, for example, or look for academics who have written on white supremacy or the pros and cons of universal basic income. If you can't find a specific person, search for universities or professional organizations with good reputations in whatever field you need to ask about.

What constitutes "good" will be up to your judgment. Look for accreditations where necessary and be aware that groups with impressive names may still be considered fringe. Always double-check whether an organization is generally respected by experts in whatever field it is supposed to represent. Also be sure to look for real or perceived conflicts of interest, be they financial, personal, or political. If an expert does have a conflict, that doesn't necessarily mean they have to be removed from a story, but their conflict should be clearly disclosed in the text. And you might need to find an additional, independent source—or more than one—to help corroborate the information provided by the source with the conflict.

Once you've found a solid group, email or call the relevant media or press department, explain what you are looking for, and ask for expert recommendations.

. . . .

Think Like a Fact-Checker
The next time you read an article or a book, look for an explanation of how a technical process works, an account of the inner functions of an obscure government agency, a description of a political movement, or any potentially complicated concept. If you were fact-checking the text, what experts or organizations might you turn to in order to confirm the information?

. . . .

ANALOGIES

Writers use metaphor, simile, and other rhetorical tricks to capture complex concepts in a relatable way. But are those analogies accurate? Is it reasonable to call the world a stage or say the universe began with a big bang, or did the writer bite off more than they could hang their hat on?

Sometimes you can confirm an analogy using your own common sense. Take the example from chapter 3 that called certain facts as wriggly as a freshwater eel, impossible to hold in your bare hands. Do freshwater eels even exist? Are they truly wriggly? And are they actually difficult to hold? A fact-checker might confirm that, yes, freshwater eels are a real type of animal and then peruse online videos of people catching eels in their hands, if they can find them. For more straightforward analogies, you might use your own experience as a gut check. Other times, though, an analogy may be used to describe a complex scientific process or an artistic movement or something else that is more esoteric. In these cases, take a look at your source list and work the wording into your list of questions. You may find that the expert strongly disagrees that the analogy is a good one and recommends a replacement.

· ·

Think Like a Fact-Checker

Find an analogy in a news story, headline, nonfiction book, or any other source of information you might consult. How would you fact-check the analogy? Could you do it based on common sense or your own experiences? Or would you need to check with an expert—and if so, what kind of expert? Do you think the analogy was apt considering the story's context? Why or why not? Can you think of a better one?

· ·

IMAGES

Stories are usually accompanied by images, which provide key visual context. You need to confirm that all images in a story show what they claim to show.

Photographs and Videos

Make sure the subject is the right person, place, or thing. Some of this information may come from a publication's art department, a wire service, or directly from a photographer or videographer, but it doesn't hurt to confirm with other sources if you have time—try official websites or press contacts and cross-reference with stock photography or video sites. Anyone with personal knowledge of the photograph or video and its content is always best, but reflect before sending anything directly to one of your sources. In some cases, this may be fine—for example, if you need the world's foremost expert on cane toads to confirm that a photograph indeed depicts a cane toad. But if the image came from an in-house photo shoot, the publication may prefer not to send it out, to protect their work from leaking. And a person who appears in a story may try to talk you out of using a specific photo of them if they think it is unflattering.

Also make sure that the image is oriented correctly. In a more abstract image, perhaps of an unfamiliar animal, has the top been inadvertently switched to the bottom? (That error was really encountered once, by a fact-checker at National Geographic, who happily caught it before it went to print.) Has an image accidentally been flipped (mirrored) so that the left is now at the right—perhaps lettering on a sign will provide a clue?

Captions need fact-checking, too, as does any superimposed text in a video. Are names, locations, and other features identified and spelled correctly? Does the information accurately describe what is in the photo or video shot? A fact-checker at a fashion magazine may need to confirm the material of a piece of clothing—whether that vest is leather or pleather, or that rose-print dress actually shows a different type of flower—as well as the style and designer, while someone working with a photography publication may need to double-check a featured camera's make and model. Also look out for vague descriptions that need more context: a photograph that is simply captioned "City Hall," for example, may need clarification. City Hall in London will look very different from City Hall in New York or Topeka, Kansas.

And beware of fakes. In some cases, an image might be of a real event, but used in the wrong context. For instance, in 2019, as wildfires ravaged the Amazon, several high-profile Twitter accounts posted photos that supposedly showed the devastation. Cristiano Ronaldo, the soccer star, tweeted that "The Amazon Rainforest produces more than 20% of the world's oxygen and its been burning for the past 3 weeks. It's our responsibility to help to save our planet. #prayforamazonia," along with a photo that was actually taken in 2013, in a different part of Brazil. Ronaldo has tens of millions of Twitter followers, and as of late 2021, his post had been shared on Twitter more than 100,000 times and liked nearly 375,000 times. And French president Emmanuel Macron, who has about 7.6 million followers, tweeted an actual photo of the Amazon rain forest on fire, but it was a stock image by a photographer who had died about sixteen years earlier. That particular post gained about 52,000 retweets and about 147,000 likes.

To avoid using a real photo in the wrong context, use a reverse image search, which will show where else the image has appeared online. As of this writing, two popular options for this service are Google's reverse image search feature and TinEye. If Macron had done this for the photo of the Amazon fire, he likely would have found it on a stock photography website and could have looked up the photographer for additional context. (Videos are a little more difficult to search in this manner, but you can take a few screen grabs to search individual frames.)

Some images are even trickier. New technology, particularly advances in a type of artificial intelligence called machine learning, have made it possible to train a computer to create an image or a video from scratch, rather than altering an existing one or putting it into the wrong context. Essentially, researchers can train algorithms to look at photos of a particular thing and recognize new versions of such images—and even create their own. Some of these algorithms can train themselves, too. Worryingly, many of these efforts are already bearing fruit. In 2019, researchers at the tech company Nvidia published work on generative adversarial networks—one approach to machine learning—and were able to make realistic photos of faces of people who don't exist. The computer-generated images are clear, crisp, and so convincing that in 2021, when researchers at Lancaster University and the University of California, Berkeley, asked people to rate the trustworthiness of photos from a selection including both photos of real people and photos generated by Nvidia's tool, they rated the fakes higher. Computer scientists are using similar approaches to train algorithms to create text, speech, and videos.

How do you catch computer-generated photos? Hany Farid, a computer scientist at the University of California, Berkeley, who specializes in digital forensics—and one of the authors on that trustworthiness study—says two important factors to consider are the photo's resolution and its quality. Resolution refers to the number of pixels; the more pixels, the higher the resolution. Quality relates to ways in which the image might be relatively easy or difficult to see: Was it taken at night? Is it grainy? For videos, has the file been compressed to the point that it is choppy? A file can have high resolution but still be of poor quality; it can also have a low resolution but be of high quality. If an image or video has both high resolution and high quality, Farid says, that's "always a good thing, because the easiest way to mask traces of manipulation—and there are always traces—is to reduce the resolution and add artifacts, which help mask little bits you left behind." If an image has low resolution or quality, he adds, "you should be a little nervous."

Another thing to check is the file's metadata, which accompanies many photos and will often show the relevant date, time, and location. How to locate the metadata will differ a little depending on your operating system and whether you are working from a computer or a mobile device. If a photo is of both high quality and high resolution *and* it has metadata showing when and where it was taken, Farid says, "I am feeling pretty good about it," although he notes that caution is still warranted.

After that, the analysis gets pretty technical, and Farid doesn't recommend any amateur photo sleuths trying it out. As a fact-checker, you shouldn't be trying to figure out if a photo is fake based on how a shadow is cast, or whether the sizes or geometries in the image make sense. There are a lot of services online that offer such expertise, but Farid also cautions against using these. "It is crap," he says. "There are all kinds of hacks out there claiming they can analyze photos—and they can't."

Illustrations and Animations

A piece of art is always subjective, but it should be grounded in reality for a nonfiction story. If a drawing, graphic, or animation is supposed to represent an actual person, animal, building, body of water, book, movie, machine, tree, piece of candy, or anything, really, then you should check it against the real-world version of that anything. In a drawing of poison ivy, make sure there are clusters of three leaves, not four; in a portrait of a celebrity, make sure their eyes aren't shown as blue if they are actually brown; and in an animation that shows the mechanism that drives the world's fastest roller coaster, make sure the depiction does not defy the laws of physics. And so on.

Quick Guide: Photos and Videos

Are you unsure whether a photo or video is legit? Here are a few things to check:

- Quality
- Resolution
- Metadata
- Context via a reverse image search

If a photo or video is of low quality or low resolution—or both—there is a higher chance that it has been manipulated. On the flip side, high-quality and high-resolution photos and videos are less likely to have been faked, particularly if they have metadata intact. To be sure a real photo isn't used out of context, try a reverse image search to see where else it lives on the internet (for video, try using a few individual frames).

But nothing replaces old-fashioned reporting, particularly as AI gets better at creating convincing images. Report out what you see in the photo by contacting potential witnesses, establishing general facts about the scene the photo claims to show, and so on.

Infographics

Infographics are only as good as the data on which they were built, so a first step is to make sure the data source is reliable and complete. Check all numbers against the original data and make sure that visual representations make logical sense. The sections of a pie chart should not add up to more than 100 percent. A set of shapes that are supposed to depict relative sizes—say, circles representing several county populations—should physically depict those size differences, so get out the ruler and measure them. A graphical categorization of beer flavor profiles should not attribute a vanilla flavor to Centennial hops.

Maps

Borders in parts of the world are constantly changing, particularly as nations split up or annex one another. Even the number of countries is confusing: as of 2021 there were 193 member states of the United Nations, while the United States recognized 195 countries. Other governments recognized disputed lands, such as Palestine and Taiwan, as countries too. Well-established lines are even sometimes accidentally changed by major news sources: in on-air graphics, CNN once moved London 120 miles to the northeast, NBC allowed Vermont to swallow New Hampshire, and Fox replaced Iraq with Egypt. Always double-check maps against hard-copy atlases or guides and web mapping applications such as Google Maps, to confirm location, spelling, borders, and more. (Caveat: even published atlases and established web mapping applications can have errors, so it is a good idea to consult more than one source.) Other features to check: city names and locations, geographical markers such as major rivers or mountain ranges, and map keys or legends that describe distances or other information. Also pay attention to cardinal directions. Are north, east, south, and west in the appropriate locations? Are you sure? Some older maps may show south at the top of the page and north at the bottom. Make sure you consider the context.

. . . .

Think Like a Fact-Checker

Look up your childhood home or another familiar address on Google Maps. Does the right location pop up? If not, what do you think went wrong?

. . . .

Credits

Finally, make sure that all images are credited to the appropriate entity—the photographer, artist, almanac, and so forth. If you want to double-check that an image belongs to a specific person, see if they have an online portfolio and check whether the image is there, or if the work that you find seems reasonably similar in style to the image you are using (artist information should also be available through a publication's art department).

. . . .

Think Like a Fact-Checker

Think about a topic that you know a lot about—let's use baseball as an example. Go to Google Images and search for "baseball infographics." Do these representations seem accurate to you? If something seems off in one, what do you think should have been changed in order to make it accurate?

. . . .

PHYSICAL DESCRIPTIONS

Not every story will be packed with physical descriptions, but longer narrative pieces will always have the likes of a dusty intersection or the smell of fresh-cut grass or a kid with warm brown eyes. Or perhaps a story will explain the inner workings of a machine and, in doing so, sketch its gleaming surface or whirring hums.

In the best scenario, the writer will supply photos, videos, or detailed notes that they took while reporting the story, or at least provide visual references that they found online. But if not, there are other ways to make sure a scene is accurate. To confirm places, look for photographs and maps online, especially from official sources like a city website. Google Street View may help with specific buildings or intersections, although colors and other details may have changed. You might also confirm descriptions with the people who were interviewed for the story, if they were in the same place, or with a local librarian. For machines or products, look for product web pages and track down a press contact. For people, look for official websites or online bios, or double-check photography that will be published along with the story. You could also ask a source directly. (Once I had to ask a pest control expert whether he indeed had a mustache in 1999.)

. . . .

Think Like a Fact-Checker

The next time you read a description of a place in an article or a book, look up that place and see if it was depicted correctly. How would you have described it? Bonus: find a description of your hometown, or any other place you're very familiar with, in an article online. Does the description contradict how you see this location? If so, why do you think the writer saw it differently?

. . . .

SPORTS

Don't rely on written accounts of a game or a match when you're fact-checking a sports piece. Instead, see if you can find a video of the game online. Watch it to make sure the scores, movements, timing, and so forth match up to the writer's descriptions and interpretations. (You can fast-forward to key moments.)

. . . .

Think Like a Fact-Checker

Read David Foster Wallace's "Federer as Religious Experience," published in the *New York Times* on August 20, 2006. Now see if you can find one of the Roger Federer matches that Wallace describes. When you watch the match, do you see what Wallace saw? Do the basic facts—like scores or movements—check out?

. . . .

HISTORICAL QUOTES AND STORIES

There are snippets of history that twist over time. Maybe a translator confused a word or phrase years ago, or someone inverted a number or letter. Or maybe someone attributed a quote to the wrong person or changed its wording, and the new version carried on indefinitely because it just sounded better that way. The best approach to find out for sure is to dig up the primary source, whether it's a first edition book or a set of letters. It's not always possible under a tight deadline, of course, but if you do have time, a story from Alice Jones, director of research at *National Geographic Magazine*, highlights the great lengths that checking such facts may require.

In 2011 Jones was checking a story about the development of the teenage brain. The story included a Shakespeare quote from *The Winter's Tale*, which, according to the author, read: "There were no age between sixteen and three-and-twenty, or that youth would sleep out the rest; for there is nothing in the between but getting wenches with child, wronging the ancientry, stealing, fighting." But the more Jones looked, the more unsure she was of the exact quote. After looking through sources including *Encyclopaedia Britannica*, dictionaries, and quotation books, Jones found some versions that said "ten and three-and-twenty" instead of "sixteen and three-and-twenty."

Ultimately she contacted the Folger Shakespeare Library in Washington, DC, and a historian there looked up the original folio, which confirmed "ten and three-and-twenty." At some point, perhaps in the eighteenth or nineteenth century, someone changed the line, and it had been written incorrectly ever since. (The quote stayed in the *National Geographic* story, as "ten and three-and-twenty.")

There are ways around these impressive fact-checking acrobatics, particularly if you're in a time crunch. You can recommend removing the quote entirely, or adding that it is *often* cited this way or *usually* attributed to this or that person rather than claiming it outright as fact. This is not ideal. Sometimes, it is necessary.

. . . .

Think Like a Fact-Checker

Try to confirm the following historical quotes. If you are uncertain whether online resources are pointing you in the right direction, identify a library or other organization that has original editions, letters, or other primary sources. (Do not actually call the library or organization; they will be confused if everyone who reads this book does so.)

"Well-behaved women rarely make history."
—Marilyn Monroe
"The only sure things in life are death and taxes."
—Benjamin Franklin
"God does not play dice."
—Albert Einstein

. . . .

PRODUCT CLAIMS

Any company selling a product advertises it in a flattering way, even when the product doesn't work very well. When a journalist writes about a product, sometimes they take the company's words at face value. To make checking these claims stickier, most companies are protective of data that might support or contradict their claims, including proprietary formulas, designs, or studies. So what is a checker to do?

One option is to make sure that any claims in a story are attributed to the company or a spokesperson and not the author—this at least makes it clear where the information came from. Another option is to interview experts to see if the claims that the company makes are even possible (for example, talk to a dermatologist and a biologist who studies skin to gauge the effectiveness of a wrinkle cream, but make sure they don't have financial ties to the company—or one of its competitors). Some magazines test products, too, but keep in mind that this is subjective—a positive result might be due to the placebo effect, that wily psychological trick that makes a product seem to work by sheer force of wishful thinking.

If a product makes a particularly outrageous claim—one that could potentially harm a reader if they were to try it or open the publication to a lawsuit—question whether the story should include it at all. This is especially important for products related to health, like weight-loss pills, diets, or exercise

---

Quick Guide: Elusive Facts

If you can't confirm a fact, or if confirming it will take more time than your deadline allows, evaluate how necessary it is for the story. If it isn't crucial, consider suggesting to the writer or editor that they delete it entirely. If your team balks, add words to make the sentence more accurate. Rather than stating questionable historical anecdotes as fact, for example, perhaps add the words: "According to lore . . ." or "Legend says . . ." or something similar.

As for historical anecdotes, the same holds true: use a primary source when possible. If you can't find one—or if it doesn't exist—think of ways to present the stories that don't claim that they are factual. If using the anecdote no longer makes sense in light of these hedges, consider proposing it be cut.

plans. Or, if it must be included, make sure the story has context that appropriately questions the product's validity.

. . . .

Think Like a Fact-Checker
Watch an infomercial on television or online and write down all the claims that you'd want to double-check before including them in a story. Next to each claim, make a list of the types of experts or resources you would use to confirm or refute it.

. . . .

LANGUAGES OTHER THAN ENGLISH

Some research departments purposefully hire fact-checkers who speak languages other than English—the *New Yorker*, for example, has had checkers fluent not only in Spanish and French but also in Arabic, German, Hebrew, Mandarin, Portuguese, Russian, and Urdu. Not every publication has the resources for such a wide linguistic spread, though. So how do you fact-check information, phrases, and so on that appear in a language other than your own?

First, find out whether any of the writer's sources speak the language, or whether they employed a translator during certain interviews. If the information is straightforward, you may be able to check it during a quick interview with either person.

But if there are no appropriate sources or translators—or if the information is sensitive and twisting it might benefit those same people in some way—find a third party who can help dig into the words' true meanings. Email a university language department or a specific professor with expertise, or check with a translation service.

Keep in mind that some languages may have unique regional characteristics. In 2012 the Associated Press created a

Spanish-language style book, *Manual de Estilo*, to help journalists in the Americas use universally understood words, since there are so many differences from one locale to the next.* While universal terms might be best for certain stories, like an international news article, regional dialects and phrases might be more appropriate for others, like a narrative travel piece about a small town. For example, someone who says they're going to take the *guagua* to the market means something very different depending on whether they are in the Dominican Republic or in Chile.

OUTLETS OUTSIDE THE UNITED STATES

Fact-checking isn't uniformly common worldwide or even within any country. As such, you likely won't have much opportunity to work as an editorial fact-checker outside the United States (although there are many political fact-checking groups that have sprung up worldwide). However, it's important to consider these differences when you're reading publications from elsewhere in the world, particularly if you are working with a writer who is quoting or otherwise sourcing from them. If this happens, take a moment to research the publication and the location where it is published and consider whether it seems trustworthy.

Newspapers and magazines operating in countries with censorship laws or state-run media are another issue. Salar Abdoh, an Iranian writer, recalls working on a story in which a man and a woman met in an American bar. Abdoh knew he couldn't get that past his country's censors, so he changed it to a café in his piece. "As a writer, these are simple things, but even these can make you question your role," he says. And

* NPR's *On the Media* did a related episode on July 4, 2014, and it is available online at http://www.onthemedia.org/story/spanish-ap-style-guide/.

while it may be a simple thing, it's important to keep in mind that details both small and large may be altered—if a bar must be a café, what other ways may the truth be changed?

"COMMON KNOWLEDGE"

When a fact-checker asks for a source, one of the most irritating responses a writer can give is "Well, that's just common knowledge." By now, from reading this book, you know that even the simplest claims need to be double-checked. As the old journalism adage goes: if your mother says she loves you, get a second source. (Try to find the primary source for that chestnut.) No matter how obvious a fact or statement may seem, use your checker skills to check it out. For example, consider this piece of common knowledge: Washington, DC, is the capital of the United States. Think about how it is that you know this is true. Likely, you've read or heard this hundreds of times—so many that it'd feel silly to spend time looking it up in a primary source during a hypothetical fact-check. But now consider working on a story that mentions the U.S. capital in 1791. Would you gloss over this piece of common knowledge—that the capital is DC—or would you remember to check that in this year it was actually Philadelphia?

HEADLINES AND COVER LINES

Editors and writers want an article's headline to be eye-catching, and the same goes for a magazine's cover lines (the blurbs that appear on the cover that describe some of the stories inside). There isn't room for nuance or hedging when you're trying to sell a magazine or get a reader to click a link on the internet. Inevitably, fact-checkers balk at these pithy descriptions. Try your best to balance the need for pure accuracy with the publication's need to promote a story. And if the headline is truly a problem that could hurt the publication in the long run, have snappy alternatives ready.

. . . .

Think Like a Fact-Checker

Go to a magazine rack and take a look at the cover lines. Which grab your attention? Why? Now pick up one of the magazines and take a look at the headlines inside. Read one of the articles advertised by a cover line. How well did the cover line and headline describe it? Did you notice wording that seemed to sensationalize the story? What changes would you have made?

. . . .

FACTS FROM ANONYMOUS OR SENSITIVE SOURCES

Fact-checking basics remain the same no matter the topic, but investigative or controversial pieces may require a delicate approach. In an investigative story, sources may have been reluctant to give information to the reporter; they may be doubly gun-shy about confirming it with a checker. They may even need special protection—government whistleblowers, for instance, might face legal action for revealing confidential information. Be prepared to do some hand-holding as you go through the fact-check, and think about how you might coax the source into answering your questions, *before* you contact them. In some cases, the source will have arranged to be anonymous—make sure you understand from the writer who these sources are. The writer should also provide you with the name and contact information, which you need to keep anonymous. (You should also confirm that the writer has kept the people anonymous in the story when promised.)

It may be similarly tricky to check sensitive documents that can't be shared through usual means. One example comes from the weekly magazine *Der Spiegel* in Germany. Bertolt Hunger—a checker there who specializes in terrorism, police, and intelligence services—was one of several people responsible for confirming stories about the NSA leaks through documents provided to the magazine's writers and editors by Edward Snowden. The publication didn't allow any of the supporting documents to be copied to a computer that was connected to the internet, and in some cases they required the materials to be hand-delivered from other cities. "We try to be especially careful with interpretations; we stick very close to the documents when we quote them," Hunger says. "As a colleague of mine says: *Immer mit dem Arsch an der Wand lang.*" (Always along the wall with the ass close to it.)

SENSITIVE SUBJECTS: TRAUMA, ABUSE, AND MORE

Other types of stories that require a delicate approach include those with details about trauma, abuse, marginalized communities, and personal identity. Although the fact-checking should remain rigorous, a fact-checker and the broader editorial team should take care in approaching sources for these stories, both for the original reporting and for the fact-check. Although each story is unique and must be approached on a case-by-case basis, one key step in considering a sensitive topic is to "do as much background research off the get-go as you can," says Allison Baker, head of research at *The Walrus*, a Canadian magazine, as well as a 2021–22 journalist in residence at the Future of Journalism Initiative (FJI) at Carleton University. "Don't go in with a blank notebook," she adds. "Come in with as much grounding information as you can." For instance, if the person you are interviewing goes by they/them pronouns but they are identified differently by your publication, the relationship with that source—and the broader community of people who identify as nonbinary—may be harmed.

Or, in a story regarding a specific Indigenous nation in Canada, that community may have a different name depending on whom you ask, says Viviane Fairbank, former head of research at *The Walrus* and Baker's fellow 2021–22 FJI journalist in residence. The federal government may use one name, while the community itself uses another. Even members of the same community may give you a different answer, depending on their age, where they live, or personal preference. "If you don't have that information from your own contextual research when you're asking someone to confirm the name, first of all you might just be alienating them so that they don't trust you," she says. (She also recommended asking for a source's preference on spelling Indigenous names and words, as that can vary too.) Even if you don't alienate the source, she adds, if you haven't done your homework, you may not be able to fully assess their answer and ask the right follow-up questions to contextualize it accurately. (Fairbank and Baker are also co-authors of a guide on fact-checking, with a focus on the ethical challenges of and best practices for stories about marginalized communities and sensitive topics.)

Fairbank also recommends having a clear conversation about fact-checking with sources at the earliest stage of reporting. In other words, the journalist should explain the fact-checking process to the source in their very first interview, so that the source isn't surprised when they need to repeat information for a separate person later on. If the source wants specific accommodations for the fact-check, that should also be discussed early on—for instance, if they would prefer to do the fact-check in person, or have a fact-checker of a specific gender or background, or if they would like to have a support person in the room while they recount a traumatic experience. Although the editorial staff might not be able to satisfy every request, it still helps to be clear on everything from the start. When the fact-checker is ready to speak to the source, Baker adds, they should confirm the agreed-on accommodations and reassess them as needed.

Not every editorial team will have a system like this in place, however. Sometimes, a freelance journalist might not know to alert a source to the fact-checking process, or an editor might not typically ask their team to approach stories in this way. As a fact-checker, whenever you are assigned a story with sensitive material, it is worth asking both the editor and the journalist directly whether the source is expecting you and whether there is anything you need to know about how to approach them. If you find that the team didn't prepare the source for a fact-check, you may want to collectively decide how best to approach them, says Fairbank. For instance, since the writer already has a longer relationship with the source, it may make the most sense for the writer to introduce the fact-checker and the process in general, even if the story is already reported and written.

Fact-checkers should also take care in how they pose questions to sources when the subject matter is sensitive—for instance, when the source is a victim of sexual assault. Rather than jumping straight into rigid yes-or-no questions, which can come across as interrogative, the fact-checker might walk them through it more gently, says Fairbank. For instance, before you start the questions, you might say something like: *Now I'm going to ask you about your assault. Are you ready to talk about that?*

When your editorial team is unsure about how to proceed with a particular story—particularly if no one on the team comes from the community that the story is about—you should consider hiring a sensitivity reader. Sensitivity readers can help flag offensive content, poor word choices, biases, stereotypes, and more—all of which can introduce factual errors. Sensitivity readers may also offer new wording to replace the questionable or inaccurate material.

. . . .

Think Like a Fact-Checker

Think back to a time when you had to ask someone you know a difficult question that you knew they didn't want to answer.

How did it go? If it went poorly, how might you have adjusted the tone of your voice and the words that you used to make it easier? Now get a piece of paper and pencil and write down some ideas on how you'd apply this approach to asking someone you *don't* know a question that you know they don't want to answer.

. . . .

CONFLICTING FACTS

You may also find a range of sources that hold conflicting views of a situation or interpretation of facts. For example, what happens if multiple eyewitnesses recall a scene in radically different ways? Or how about cases where two political scientists—experts in the same field—disagree on the potential impact of a new federal policy? What should you do if there is no immediately clear agreement? One option is to make this lack of agreement clear in the story: give the reader enough information to show the different conclusions and nuance. "Some things will just always be controversial, and I think we can address them in stories. We don't have to come down on one singular truth all the time," says science and health editor Katie Palmer, who also formerly worked as a fact-checker at *Wired*. "If something is positioned as being a fact in the story and you get seven different people disagreeing on it, you just readjust the words."

For sensitive stories, consider the power dynamics at play when two sources have conflicting stories (for instance, the personal account of a person who was harmed by the police as compared to the official report of the same interaction). These power dynamics should be at the top of your mind when it comes to contextualizing the facts. For instance: What is that particular police department's record on how it has interacted with the community? How about the police officers involved?

And how does this particular situation fit into the broader conversation about policing?

. . . .

Think Like a Fact-Checker

The next time you are reading or watching a controversial news story, pay attention to how the writer or reporter treats the information. What experts and points of view do they use? Do you think they added enough voices to give the controversy depth and context? Why or why not?

. . . .

GRAY AREAS

Despite journalism's collective attempt at objectivity, there is no way for any reporter, writer, or producer to be entirely clearheaded on every topic. They're all human beings with their own perspectives, experiences, and opinions. So how do you check those gray areas—the ones that aren't entirely fact-based, but instead extrapolate from the facts and add a splash of subjectivity? For example, what should you do if an article makes bold claims about the effectiveness of a controversial new medical procedure, which the writer has undergone and endorses wholeheartedly? Or what if the gray area is subtler, such as a description of a person or scene that doesn't ring quite true to what you have seen, read, or heard from the sources?

One way around gray areas is to add in as much nuance as you're able, making it clear what facts, exactly, the claim is based on, as well as filling in the reasoning behind it. In the example of the medical procedure, this may mean including not only the author's experience and perspective, but also any scientific literature or medical expert's view that puts the effectiveness of that treatment in a broader context. In the example about the off description of a person or scene, perhaps include some of the other language that came from different sources, or point out that not everyone sees the person or place in the same light.

Another option is to add hedge words, changing, for example, "will" to "may" or slipping in a "perhaps," "supposedly," or "partially." Writers and editors hate this, and for good reason: it takes the teeth out of their work. The key is to keep your perspective and push for hedges only in sensitive cases, says Jennifer Conrad, the former research director at *Vogue*: "Words

---

Quick Guide: Hedge Words

Sometimes a sentence will come across as too strong, but the writer or editor won't want to change it. One way to address this is by using hedge words, which take the edge off. The higher the stakes that the claims in a sentence make, the more important it is to consider adding a hedge. These words are also helpful when you're on a tight deadline and have no better option. As Shannon Palus, a former fact-checker at *Popular Science* and *Discover*, puts it: "Hedge words are the error bars of writing."

Here are examples:
- About
- Appear
- Likely
- Mainly
- More or less
- Partially, or in part
- Perhaps
- Presumably
- Quite
- Supposedly

---

like that can be important when you're writing about medical studies where the findings suggest an outcome but the results aren't completely conclusive. If you're working on a profile of a new restaurant that serves 90 percent of its dishes on blue plates, I think it's okay to say meals come out on blue plates without qualifying that a few dishes are served in white bowls."

In an ideal situation, the team will collectively come to wording that is clear, meaty, and also correct. But this doesn't always happen. At the very least, raise your point and—you guessed it—keep good records of your conversations with the writer and editor.

. . . .

Think Like a Fact-Checker

Pick a current event that's been in the news this week and look for relevant stories in historically left-leaning and right-leaning publications. How did each use the facts to build their story? How were the articles different, and how were they the same?

. . . .

LITIGIOUS MATERIAL

As discussed in chapter 1, part of the reason for a fact-check is to catch statements that could embroil the publication in litigation. As a fact-checker, it isn't your job to be an expert in the law surrounding defamation, copyright, and invasion of privacy. But it is important to familiarize yourself with the basics and keep an eye out for any language that might fall into these categories. From there, the story should go to the publication's lawyer.

According to Rob Bertsche at Klaris Law—who represents a range of publications, including national weekly magazines, monthly regional publications, news websites, podcasts, video, and daily and weekly newspapers and sites—each outlet has different customs and practices for how much the fact-checker is involved in the legal review. In some cases, the fact-checker will work directly with the lawyer and go through the sourcing for iffy claims. In other cases, the lawyer will work instead with the editor or the writer—in which case the fact-checker may have to make a bigger effort to get their voice heard. The best practice, Bertsche says, "particularly on complex or controversial pieces, is to have a telephonic or in-person review that includes writer, fact-checker, and editor." Find out the process for your publication and ask about the expectations for your role in checking potentially litigious information.

After the lawyer looks at a story, they will tell the publication what risks it's taking on by publishing the piece. From here, the editorial staff—and in particular the editor in chief— will need to decide whether to make changes or let the story stand as it is. "The business is uncovering stories and having a responsible journalistic standard, which includes publishing often quite contentious details," says Yvonne Rolzhausen, research chief at *The Atlantic*. "As long as we feel that we've backed them up enough, then we're all in an open conversation about what the risks are."

PLAGIARISM AND FABRICATION

Catching plagiarism before it publishes can save your outlet from deep professional and public embarrassment. In 2021, for instance, David Mikkelson, cofounder of the well-known fact-checking website Snopes, was found to have plagiarized dozens of articles under a fake name or general byline. Snopes launched in the mid-1990s and is perhaps the oldest site to systematically take down online hoaxes. As *BuzzFeed News*, which broke the plagiarism story, put it, Mikkelson had "long presented himself as the arbiter of truth online, a bulwark in the fight against rumors and fake news." The website was arguably a political target even before Mikkelson's misdeeds were revealed; the plagiarism and pseudonym gave critics more ammunition to push back not only on the credible work that Snopes had published, but also on fact-checking more broadly.

Plagiarism can be hard to catch on your own, but as you read a piece, along with its source materials, keep an eye out for language that seems out of place. If a section of a story sounds oddly familiar even the first time you've read it, stop and ask yourself if you remember it from your background reading. Also stay attuned to bits of writing that sound different from the voice in the rest of the piece—a clue that they may have been lifted.

An even easier route, in these internet days, is to copy and paste the story into an online plagiarism checker. There are many paid versions, such as at Grammarly, and free ones, such as at Duplichecker. Generally, such websites flag sections that look suspect and note the sources from which they may be plagiarized. (Beware false positives: confirm that each flagged section truly is plagiarism before alerting your editor.)

Fabrication, too, can be hard to spot depending on how well writers who are dedicated to such lies cover their tracks. In the mid- to late 1990s, when Stephen Glass made up material, to varying degrees, for pretty much all the articles he wrote for the *New Republic*, he was able to trick the fact-checkers because he knew how they operated: he once headed the magazine's fact-checking department. And so, especially since the web wasn't yet a robust research tool, he was able to make up sources and events, as well as the backup materials that supported them. Glass completely fabricated people, conversations, voice-mail messages, business cards, and more. The fact-checkers for those stories didn't have much of a chance because he was purposely trying to dupe them.*

---

* Stephen Glass was eventually blacklisted from journalism. His reputation followed him even after he switched careers, went to law school, and passed the bar in both New York and California. The New York bar

More recently, in 2018, it was revealed that the writer and editor Claas Relotius pulled a similar move at *Der Spiegel*, in Germany. Relotius had been working for the news magazine for seven years and had won multiple journalism awards. But it turned out that he embellished, altered quotes, and outright fabricated information, including from people he had never interviewed. The case was all the more astonishing because *Der Spiegel* had a world-renowned fact-checking department, which at one point included 70 fact-checkers, with many holding doctorate degrees and other specialized training. Still, the team didn't always double-check all of Relotius's claims, and according to Bertolt Hunger, a longtime checker there, the journalist's stories didn't always go through the usual fact-checking process. Most stories at *Der Spiegel* are fact-checked by specialists—a story on a right-wing party in Germany, for example, would be checked by a specialist in extremism or political parties. But Relotius's stories usually went to a fact-checker who wasn't a specialist in the vast range of topics the journalist covered. Hunger also points out that higher-ups at the magazine wanted the types of stories that Relotius put out. So, apparently, did other journalists and the general public—the stories were popular among both peers and readers. Relotius apparently felt pressure from this desire. According to a report on the scandal from *Der Spiegel*, during his confession, he said, "It wasn't about the next big thing. It was the fear of failure." And: "The pressure not to fail grew as I became more successful." (It's worth noting that both Glass and Relotius were considered superstars at their respective publications, which they were able to hide behind. A good fact-checker should not be afraid to point out errors—diplomatically—in even the most famous writers' work.)

---

told him his moral character application would be rejected, and so he withdrew it; California effectively banned him from practicing.

Then there is the case of Mike Daisey, a monologist and writer. One of his popular theatrical monologues described a trip he took to China, in which he recalled horrible conditions in factories that produce iPhones and other electronics. In 2012 Daisey performed the piece on the radio show *This American Life*. Later, after the piece aired, it became clear that Daisey made up some of the experiences described in the story—he exaggerated the number of factories he visited, the ages of the workers, and may have made up some of his encounters entirely. Daisey was found out in part when *This American Life* later interviewed his translator, who noted differences between her account and his. The radio show retracted the entire episode and dedicated another one to how the truth came out. In the prologue, Ira Glass (no relation to Stephen Glass), the show's host, says: "The most powerful and memorable parts of the story all seem to have been fabricated."

Later in the episode—which is filled with a lot of awkward silences—Glass confronts Daisey directly. When he lists specific inaccuracies from the original piece, Daisey responds: "I stand by it as a theatrical work. I stand by how it makes people see and care about the situation that's happening there. I stand by it in the theater and I regret, deeply, that it was put into this context on your show."

"Are you going to change the way that you label this in the theater?" Glass asks. "So that the audience in the theater knows that this isn't, strictly speaking, a work of truth, but in fact what they're seeing is really a work of fiction that has some true elements in it."

"Well, I don't know that I would say in a theatrical context that it isn't true. I believe that when I perform it in a theatrical context—in the theater—that when people hear the story in those terms that we have different languages for what the truth means," Daisey says.

"I understand that you believe that, but I think you're kidding yourself in the way that normal people who go see a person talk—people take it as a literal truth," Glass says. "I thought the story was literally true seeing it in the theater."

The exchange underscores a difference in perspective between fact and truth, and one that should be made clearly to readers and audience members for all works of nonfiction. And Daisey is not the only artist with this perspective on Truth with a capital *T*, as opposed to the truth that we largely assume is based on facts. In a 2007 *New York Times* interview, the director Werner Herzog is asked about alleged liberties he took with the facts in some of his documentaries. He replies that the search for deeper truth illuminates, whereas "if you're purely after facts, please buy yourself the phone directory of Manhattan. It has four million times correct facts. But it doesn't illuminate."

It may be nearly impossible to catch someone who is truly out to trick a fact-checker, just as it may be difficult to argue a point with a writer who is seeking some sort of truth that isn't based on facts, but on feelings. Still, one method for spotting fabrication before it makes it into print or on air is to ask yourself: Does this story sound too good to be true? If the answer is yes, be extra cautious and skeptical in your work.

Fact-checking doesn't mean much if you aren't checking a story against solid sources. If you're fact-checking someone else's work, the writer will ideally, though relatively rarely, provide sources for most or all of the story. When the writer does provide sources, you will need to evaluate those sources. This is a matter of experience and consideration. When the source material is lacking in quality or quantity, you will have two choices: (1) pester the writer to provide better materials (this may be especially necessary if the sources in question are interview transcripts and other materials you can't access) or (2) find relevant sources on your own.

Whether you're in the position of evaluating a writer's source material or finding your own, keep in mind the distinction between primary and secondary sources, and use primary sources whenever possible. Think of these as raw material—the original wellspring of information. Examples include eyewitness reports, government documents, diaries, letters and emails, photographs, interviews, speeches, audio and video recordings, and historical records.

Secondary sources, such as biographies and encyclopedias, build on primary sources and interpret or summarize them in some way. When a writer relies on secondary sources, dig up relevant primary materials to make sure the information wasn't lost in translation. For example, if a biography includes quotations from letters, contact the entity—perhaps a museum—that has those documents. If you aren't able to do this, evaluate the biography and ask yourself whether or not you should trust it. Or, another way to treat this sort of material is to be sure to include the source in the text of the story, in order to provide transparency for the reader. Rather than stating something from the biography as fact, add, for example: "According to Walter Isaacson's biography of Steve Jobs . . ."

Be aware, though, that not all primary sources are necessarily of high quality or trustworthy, while some secondary sources have a high level of accuracy. When it comes to primary sources, an expert may have financial conflicts of interest that influence their perspective; an eyewitness to a crime might not fully remember the details; and an opinion poll may have shoddy methodology. High-quality secondary sources may include a well-done scientific analysis of multiple original studies, called a meta-analysis; a well-sourced and contextualized biography; and a historian relaying an anecdote about original papers they have analyzed from an archive. Also be aware that some sources can be either primary or secondary, depending on how they are used. A newspaper article, for example, may be primary if a writer used it to show that a particular event was covered by the press, while that same article could be secondary if the writer is using it to confirm a statistic.

Although the following list isn't exhaustive, it includes the categories of sources you'll encounter most often as a fact-checker. Some categories may include both primary and secondary sources. For example, a person who experienced or witnessed an event may be a primary source, but a reporter who wrote about that event will be a secondary source. On the internet, you will find both primary sources (video footage of interviews, government documents, and so on) and secondary sources (commentary, reviews, and so on).

PEOPLE

You may talk to a range of people in the course of a fact-check: eyewitnesses, experts, spokespeople, anonymous sources, and more. For each, ask yourself: How do I know this person is telling the truth? Do they have anything to gain from stretching the facts or telling an outright lie, or is it possible their memory might be spotty? And what is their relationship to the story or information—are they in a position to truly know what they say they know?

This doesn't mean you have to grill each source on the phone to wring the truth from them. In fact, you should do the opposite, approaching them with kindness and tact (more on this soon). But it does mean that you should look up the person, figure out whether their expertise is legitimate, and ask whether you should consider other voices to make sure the story they are telling you is true or is at least presented with sufficient context.

Take eyewitnesses, for example, who may not remember an event as clearly as they think they do. Are there other people who were there? Can you talk to them in order to corroborate the story? Or are there photographs or videos that help clarify the scene?

For academics and other experts, consider their credentials. Is their school accredited? Is their work controversial? It's okay to include contentious views in a story, but it's important to put them in context. For example, you can find doctors who are against vaccination and scientists who are climate change skeptics, but the scientific consensus is clear on both of these topics: vaccines are generally safe and effective, and climate change is real and underway. If a writer includes a dissenting voice, don't let that voice speak for the whole of a field. Don't give it equal footing, either. While most journalism requires balance between conflicting views, science journalism is a little different—instead, it should weight the scientific evidence. The classic example is a hypothetical news story about the shape of our planet. It wouldn't be fair to the reader to quote a planetary scientist and then give an equal word count to the president of the Flat Earth Society. The same goes for fringe experts on current topics that are controversial not because of the science or the research, but because of politics.

Quick Guide: Primary vs. Secondary Sources

Primary sources are the closest you can get to the origin of a fact. Examples include

- Eyewitness reports
- Correspondence
- Autobiographies
- Diaries
- Interview or speech transcripts
- Audio and video recordings
- Government documents (hearings, laws, etc.)
- Photographs
- Surveys or polls
- Original scientific experiments
- Newspapers or online media

Secondary sources may be a step or more removed from a primary source. Examples include

- Magazines
- Histories
- Biographies

When you talk to spokespeople, be aware that although they can be a wealth of knowledge, it's also their job to make their client look great. If a spokesperson makes a claim about how their product works, or what their celebrity is up to, or the important world-changing work their organization is doing, look for other sources that can confirm the information. And also consider that a spokesperson or public relations representative may not have the right information. One example comes from Danielle Emig, who has fact-checked at *InStyle* among other outlets. While working on a story about clothes, Emig recalls asking a PR contact what the material a particular shirt

- Encyclopedias
- Criticism
- Reviews
- Scientific reviews and meta-analyses
- Newspapers or online media

But beware: some primary sources may not be of high quality, and you'll need additional sourcing to corroborate whatever they say, while some secondary sources may be quite accurate. And some sources may be used as either a primary or a secondary source, depending on the context. Note, for example, that newspapers and online media appear on both lists. Whether a news outlet is a primary or a secondary source depends on the type of story (news vs. editorial) and the quality of the paper. It also depends on how you use the source. Take the example of Elan Gale from chapter 1—the man who fabricated a fight with a fictional woman on a flight over Thanksgiving. Most of the sourcing for those stories came from online media, because the point of that example was that those outlets reported his hoax as the truth.

was made from, and the PR contact responded that the fabric was gingham. In reality, the *pattern* was gingham—a checkered design, often in blue and white although it can be other colors. The *fabric*, or what the material was made from, was in this case polyester-cotton.

Anonymous Sources

When a writer has used an anonymous source, they should provide the fact-checker with phone numbers, emails, or other information so you can get in touch with the person. The writer should have also given the source a heads-up that you will be in touch. If you aren't sure whether the writer did this, ask—if they say no, ask if they could make an introduction.

It may be risky to trust anonymous sources without double-checking the information they've provided with yet more sources. Consider *why* they have chosen to be anonymous, as well as whether they have anything to gain by leaving their name out of the story. Could harm come to them if they disclose their name—will it make them a target for violence or jeopardize their job? Or are they using anonymity so they can bad-mouth another person without taking responsibility for those comments? The writer and editor should judge an anonymous source before you ever get this far, but if you are unsure about the quality of an anonymous source—or how to confirm that they are who they say they are—tactfully talk through your concerns with your editor or the writer, depending on whom you feel more comfortable approaching.

Single Sources

When part of a story relies on a single person, keep in mind that you will need to confirm the information with outside sources. Take this example from Ryan Krogh, a former research editor at *Outside*. In 2007 Krogh had to fact-check an as-told-to first-person survival story for the magazine in which two French explorers got lost in the Amazon in French Guiana for fifty-one days. In order to survive, they said they had to eat, among other things, hairy tarantulas, which they claimed had to be cooked to the point that the spiders' venom burned off. In one harrowing description, the narrator said he did not cook a spider enough and the venom made him horribly sick. But when Krogh checked that part of the story with a spider expert from the American Museum of Natural History, he learned that it was more likely the barbed nettle-like hairs on the spider that caused the man so much pain. Cooking the spiders, which the locals in the region do regularly, burns the hairs off, which is why it isn't always a problem. Because it was an as-told-to story, the editors left the original text intact but published it along with a note explaining the more likely cause of the explorer's illness.

Relying on a single source can be devastating. One infamous cautionary example comes from *Rolling Stone*. In November 2014, the magazine published a feature titled "A Rape on Campus," which focused on a young woman named Jackie (a shortened version of her first name) who said she had been gang-raped at a University of Virginia fraternity party. The account, written by Sabrina Rubin Erdely, was vivid and wrenching, and the story went viral. Not long after, readers and other journalists questioned the piece's accuracy, and by December *Rolling Stone* issued an editor's note online that retracted at least part of the story. Ultimately, the magazine asked the *Columbia Journalism Review* to conduct an independent investigation, which the latter would eventually call "a work of journalism about a failure of journalism."

The main problem with Erdely's work, according to the *CJR* report, was that she relied almost solely on Jackie for much of her reporting, even re-creating dialogue from three friends based on the young woman's account without going to those people and confirming what they had said. Erdely also didn't confirm that the alleged ringleader of the rape—a student called Drew in the story, although that was a pseudonym—existed, or that the party where Jackie had said she'd been raped actually happened on the day and at the location indicated in the story. None of these claims held up under scrutiny. As *CJR* noted: "The magazine set aside or rationalized as unnecessary essential practices of reporting that, if pursued, would likely have led the magazine's editors to reconsider publishing Jackie's narrative so prominently, if at all."

The quality of a fact-checking department is only as good as an organization lets it be—fact-checking needs both support and independent authority to thrive. According to the *CJR* report, *Rolling Stone*'s head of fact-checking at the time, Coco

McPherson, said that the decisions not to reach out to the three friends during the fact-check of Erdely's story "were made by editors above my pay grade." Here, that mistake came at a high cost. An associate dean at the University of Virginia sued *Rolling Stone*; the magazine's publisher, Wenner Media; and Erdely; a jury awarded the dean $2 million from Erdely and $1 million from the magazine and publisher, although the case eventually settled for an undisclosed amount. The fraternity chapter sued *Rolling Stone* for $25 million, which ended in a reported settlement of $1.65 million. And individual members of the fraternity also sued for defamation; although a judge dismissed the claims in 2016, at least some of the plaintiffs reportedly won an appeal in 2017 and settled for an undisclosed amount later that year.

Of course, with limited time and resources, it isn't always possible to exhaustively vet every source. At some point, both the writer and the checker must decide that they've talked to enough people—and the right people—to get an accurate story. Each time you do this, however, think about the ways in which a source may be shaky or outright wrong. If a story seems too good to be true, or if you are looking at it from only one person's perspective, it's possible that the story has holes. This isn't always the case, but it's worth raising these issues with your editor.

Attribution Definitions

In addition to evaluating the quality of a person as a source, you also need to consider what promises—if any—the writer made regarding attribution. Such agreements should be made before the interview, but they also may be made during it, and they involve how the material from the interview may be used and whether the source can be directly quoted or included in any way. Ideally, the writer should communicate any special promises to the fact-checker at the beginning of the fact-check process, but if not, there should be some record of those agreements in the interviews or correspondence with the source. You may need to nudge the writer to provide this information.

The following general attribution definitions were adapted from New York University's *NYU Journalism Handbook for Students: Ethics, Law and Good Practice.*

On the record: Anything the source said can be published or aired and attributed to the source. This is the assumed default in every interview, so if the rules aren't laid out in advance, everything in the conversation is publishable and attributable.

On background: The information can be published, but the source can't be named. Sources often use this for sensitive information, and it may be wise to confirm it elsewhere.

Not for attribution: The information can be published but it can't be attributed specifically to the source. The journalist can, however, include the source's job or position, the description of which must be agreed on between the source and the journalist.

Off the record: The information can't be used or attributed to the source, but if the journalist is able to confirm the information with other sources, it can be published (though still not attributed to the original source). Sometimes an interview that starts on the record will switch to off the record when the source wants to reveal something but is shrewd enough to know they don't want it in print. In these cases, both the journalist and the source have to agree that the material will remain off the record; if the journalist doesn't agree and the source keeps talking anyway, it is technically fair game. If the parties both agree to go off the record, the journalist must request to go back on the record as soon as the sensitive portion of the interview has ended, or else everything else the source says will also be off the record—even if it wasn't intended to be.

The journalist should also make it clear in the transcript or notes what parts are on and off the record.

As the NYU handbook points out, journalists and sources alike don't always understand the distinctions between these definitions—particularly the differences between on background, not for attribution, and off the record. Consider, too, whether the source is media savvy, such as a political hack or a publicist, or naive with little or no experience interacting with a journalist. The latter may need more explanation to make sure they understand the terms. Whoever the source is, make sure their understanding with the writer is clear, and alert your editor if a source tries to back out of a statement because of a misunderstanding over attribution.

Navigating Relationships with Sources

This brings us to a key point: navigating the relationship with a source can be just as tricky as working with editors and writers. Often, dealing with sources is like "setting off a series of controlled explosions," says Peter Canby, the former fact-checking head at the *New Yorker*. You may be delivering either good news or bad news; if it's the latter, it's better to deal with the fallout early, before the story goes to print.

You may have to deal with a wide range of characters, from politicians who don't want to confirm unsavory facts to victims of a crime who are reluctant to relive a painful memory. You'll probably need to be firmer with the politician and more compassionate with the crime victim but, regardless, always do your best to explain that participating in the fact-check is in their best interest. This is their last chance to contribute to the story. Sources who have been interviewed before may be more aware of the fact-checking process, but others will not understand what it is you are trying to do. You will need to clearly and kindly explain who you are and why you're asking them questions they've already answered. And if you've decided to record your conversations, bring this up as tactfully and transparently as you can. One approach is to explain that you want to make sure you have a good record of the conversation, perhaps blaming slow fingers that may not be able to type or write fast enough to catch everything.

You may also need to explain that your questions might seem out of context (and they often will be, by necessity), but that you'll try to fill in as much context as you can if they don't understand what you're asking. And any time you speak with a source, make sure to start with the easiest questions and work your way to the most sensitive or controversial material. This will help you build a rapport, however brief. If they get angry at the tougher questions and try to end the conversation, at the very least they'll have already answered the rest. (If you have direct communication with the writer, ask early on if there are any sources that may be difficult during the fact-check, to help you mentally prepare for the call or video chat.)

Sources may ask to read the story rather than submit to a fact-check. This is almost always against a publication's rules, because it gives the source the impression that they have editorial control in how the final piece is presented. If a source asks for the full draft, politely tell them you'll lose your job if you do that and carry on with your fact-check. (You might explain the fact-checking process, too, and say that while you don't think *they'd* try to ask for changes in the piece that aren't related directly to the facts, other interviewees might, which is why you must adhere to a blanket policy not to send out unpublished article manuscripts.) Sources may also try to get you to change certain phrases or words, even when there are no factual errors. Don't make any promises that you can't keep, but do tell them that you'll relay their concerns to your editor, who has the final say, and follow through on that promise. It might be that the editor doesn't mind the change because it doesn't significantly affect the piece, which could leave everyone happy.

Sources may also balk at the number of questions you have to ask, as well as at basic queries that seem entirely answerable through a Google search. Explain early on that you know some of the questions may seem as though you could answer them elsewhere, but that you have to ask because you're required to by the publication—be as deferential and as apologetic as you need to be in order to get the source to answer these questions. (A note on celebrity press people: one checker from a national magazine says he'll often catch PR folks confirming their client's information via Wikipedia, so be wary when checking facts this way. If you suspect this is happening during your fact-check, corroborate the information through other sources.)

Although writers usually have up-to-date contact information for their sources, there are cases when stories publish months or even years after they've been in touch. In these cases, you may have to track sources down. In today's hyperconnected society, this is often pretty easy: if you cannot reach them by phone, try email, text messages, Facebook, Twitter, Instagram, or any other social media platform. Use resources like Google or Whitepages or available phone books. Some outlets may also have accounts with specialized services that can help you find contact information, such as LexisNexis, which provides, among other things, public records searches. It's always worth asking your editor if such resources are available to you.

Sometimes the source won't want to be found, which will make your job even harder. Riley Blanton, a former checker at *GQ*, who is now a research editor at the *New York Times Magazine*, recalls fact-checking a *GQ* feature about a man named Christopher Thomas Knight who lived alone in the woods for twenty-seven years, surviving, in part, by robbing nearby homes for food and other supplies. Then he was caught in the act and arrested. The author of the *GQ* story, Michael Finkel, struck up a mail correspondence with Knight and eventually visited him in jail, although he wasn't allowed to record their conversations. Finkel's story, based in part on those interactions, didn't publish until after Knight was released and had again disappeared, and it was Blanton's job to track the so-called hermit down for the fact-check.

The local police wouldn't give up Knight's location, so Blanton turned to public records to find where Knight went to school as well as contact information for a woman he suspected was Knight's mother. After a week or so of searching and with a looming deadline, he called the woman up and explained who he was. Blanton says that she paused and then yelled at someone in the background, and soon Knight was on the phone. He was not open to doing a full fact-check despite Blanton's best efforts, but he did confirm that Finkel had visited him in jail. Between that, the correspondence, interviews with other sources, and police records that confirmed all of the items Knight had stolen over the years, Blanton was able to confirm the story.*

INTERVIEW RECORDINGS AND TRANSCRIPTS

When checking quotes, paraphrases, and other key information that comes from a person, both interview recordings and transcripts provided by the writer are helpful—especially when that person isn't available for a follow-up interview. But keep in mind that even these primary sources may not be entirely foolproof. As discussed in chapter 4, transcripts may have errors, such as words or sections where the person who transcribed the interviews thought they heard one thing when the source said another. If a snippet from a transcript seems strange or inappropriate considering the source or the sub-

---

* Yes, Finkel is the same writer who got in trouble for creating a composite character in the 2001 *New York Times Magazine* piece "Is Youssouf Malé a Slave?" Fair or not, Finkel and a handful of other writers continue their careers after factual screw-ups, although they're typically subject to intense scrutiny from their peers.

ject, go back to the recording to check for discrepancies. If that isn't possible, get the interviewee on the phone or video chat to step through the information.

Recordings, too, aren't perfect. When you check a quote or any other information against a recording, listen for at least a few minutes both before and after to make sure the writer didn't pull anything out of context, whether inadvertently or otherwise. When in doubt, contact the source.

SEARCH ENGINES AND WIKIS

As a resource for information, the web can be either very good or very bad. It all depends on how well you run searches and evaluate information.

Neither Google nor Wikipedia—or any other search engine or crowd-sourced online resource—should be considered a final source for any fact (unless that fact is specifically about these respective companies and came from their spokespeople and other knowledgeable sources). But resources like these can help you scour the internet to find reliable sources.

"My feeling is that Google is a very important engine and a gateway—if you are going to be a good fact-checker, you use Google as a gateway to what might be an authoritative source," says the veteran checker Cynthia Cotts. "But if you use Google to get to Wikipedia, you are not going to be a successful fact-checker."

Google can be an excellent tool for finding all sorts of strong primary and secondary sources. Trying to find an obscure academic paper or double-check to see if a quote was plagiarized from another publication? You can run searches for exact phrases within quotation marks. Trying to wade through a large number of hits that are unrelated to your target? You can use advanced searches to home in on the results most suited to your needs. Say, for example, you are looking up information related to chocolate chips, but you definitely don't want to read about chocolate chip cookies. You can run an "advanced"

Google search for the words "chocolate" and "chips" and exclude all web pages that include the word "cookies." (You could get the same result by typing into the search bar: "chocolate chips -cookies.") Want to limit your search to a specific website? Just type in "site:" in front of the website name, followed by the search terms (to find information on this book, you could try "site:press.uchicago.edu fact checking"). Want to run two searches at once? If you want all results from *either* search, try "search one" OR "search two." You can also find out where a photograph originated on the internet using a reverse search on Google Images; find exact times across the world; quickly look up word definitions; and get measurement and currency conversions. (For more Google search tips, as well as how to use the features mentioned here, go look at Google's support website. In fact, you can find it by Googling "Google search tips.")

As for crowd-sourced websites, the most popular is arguably

Pro Tip: Evaluating Sources

An excellent guide on how to confirm the quality of a source—whether online or print or person—comes from a piece by the journalist Michelle Nijhuis on the blog *The Last Word on Nothing*: "The Pocket Guide to Bullshit Prevention." Although she goes into far greater—and more amusing—detail, the basic steps are to ask:

1. Who is telling me this?
2. How do they know this?
3. Given #1 and #2, is it possible that they are wrong?
4. If the answer to #3 is "yes," find another, unrelated source.
5. Repeat until answer to #3 is "pretty f—ing unlikely."

Wikipedia, a living encyclopedia that is constantly updated by volunteers. Wikipedia doesn't always have a great reputation among fact-checkers, since it's a dynamic site—anyone could edit any page anonymously and either purposely or accidentally introduce errors. But research shows that it can actually be quite good, depending on the topic. Wikipedia should never be a fact-checker's last stop, but it's quite useful for background reading, which you should confirm with other sources, as well as a way to find primary sources, which are often footnoted at the bottom of each entry.

As for other resources on the internet, one strategy for evaluating the reliability of online information is called SIFT, developed by Michael Caulfield, a research scientist at the Center for an Informed Public at the University of Washington, and Sam Wineburg, a professor emeritus at Stanford's Graduate School of Education. SIFT is an acronym distilling the process into four steps:

1. **S**top.
2. **I**nvestigate the source.
3. **F**ind better coverage.
4. **T**race claims, quotes, and media to the original context.

Another approach comes from the late 1990s, in the early days of the internet, when university librarians were figuring out how to guide undergraduates on using web-based sources for research. Based on a 1998 paper by Jim Kapoun published in *College & Research Libraries News*, most libraries suggest that when you evaluate the quality of a website, ask yourself: Can you tell who made the website and why? Is the author a credible source, and do they provide contact information so you can get in touch with additional questions? Does the other information on the page seem legitimate, and can you verify it using trusted sources? Has the information been updated in the past few months? Does the page link to other websites that are credible? Are there any misspellings, broken links, or other mistakes that give you pause about the site's overall quality? Does the main purpose of the site appear to be to provide information, or is it pushing a specific point of view or trying to sell products?

If you aren't sure about a particular website based on this evaluation, move on and find one that has a clearer origin and more credibility. For example, if you are seeking basic information about the president of the United States, look at the Whitehouse.gov website or search for resources through the Library of Congress, rather than relying on www .ThePresidentLies.com (not a real website, at least at the time this book was written).

MAPS AND ATLASES

Always make sure any map or atlas you are using as a reference is up-to-date (unless you are checking a piece that references historical events or geographies). Google Maps and Google Earth are based, in part, on satellite imagery, so are generally accurate—although there are exceptions, so it's wise to find additional sourcing to corroborate what you find. You might compare these to other maps, too. One place to find a wide range of maps is the USA.gov website (just search for "maps"). Other good geographic sources include the U.S. Board on Geographic Names, *Merriam-Webster's Geographical Dictionary*, and the Getty Thesaurus of Geographic Names (getty.edu/research/tools/vocabularies/tgn/).

In some cases, you may be using the maps to double-check geographical statements in a story. For example, if a writer says Kyoto, Japan, is around 500 miles southwest of Tokyo, you'll need a map to check both the distance and the direction. (And for the record, that statement contains a factual error. Can you spot it?) In other cases, you may be fact-checking the map itself. Here, keep in mind not only the obvious details, such as borders, keys, and relative distances, but also colors and other more subtle features, to make sure the image isn't signaling something it shouldn't. Take, for example, a story from Todd Hermann, Director of Editorial Research at National Geographic Partners. His team once hired a third-party company to provide maps for a documentary about the Taliban in Afghanistan, in order to show the locations of certain areas mentioned in the show. The maps showed the borders of nearby countries, too, including Pakistan and India. During a fact-check, Hermann realized that not only did the map have outdated borders, giving more of the disputed Kashmir region to India than it actually has, but that Pakistan was depicted in striped shades of deep saffron, white, and green—the national colors of India.

PRESS RELEASES

Never trust a press release as a final source, even though the information comes directly from an organization. Their quality may vary from one place to another, and while some may be accurate and even-toned, others are aggressively optimistic or riddled with errors.

Sometimes the press release may even have information that its author thinks is accurate but isn't. Take this story from Mara Grunbaum, a writer and former fact-checker at *Discover* magazine. Grunbaum once had to fact-check a story about newly discovered exoplanets, which are planets that orbit a star other than our sun. One exoplanet in the story had received a lot of media attention because, according to a NASA press release, it was unusually similar to Earth (scientists are especially interested in planets like ours because these could hypothetically sustain life). When Grunbaum checked specific relevant measurements with the scientists who had discovered the planet, they went back to their calculations and realized they'd made a mistake. The planet wasn't Earthlike at all, but instead was much larger and hotter, similar to the hundreds of other newfound exoplanets.

In other cases, press releases may be purposely misleading.

Drug companies, for example, may leave the Food and Drug Administration's concerns over safety or efficacy out of their product press releases, even though the FDA clearly states those concerns in official letters to the companies. In 2015, researchers from the FDA published a study in the *BMJ* in which they compared 61 such letters sent between 2008 and 2013 to public press releases published by the companies. The letters were to inform the companies that their relevant drugs weren't approved for a specific use, and these letters were not available to the public. Less than half of the related press releases mentioned the deficiencies, and 21 percent didn't match any of the information provided by the FDA letters. And a 2014 study—also published in the *BMJ*—found that 40 percent of press releases in a survey of 462 related to biomedical research and health "contained exaggerated advice."

BOOKS

Even though books seem authoritative, they are rarely fact-checked. Because of this, it is important to evaluate each on a case-by-case basis before trusting it as a source. The first step is to look up the author. Are they an authoritative figure on the topic—an expert, academic, or other professional with good credentials? Or are they associated with an organization that would gain from a one-sided perspective, such as a partisan think tank, an advocacy group, or an industry association? Understanding the author's motives for writing the book will offer a clue about its thoroughness (that's not to say the book will be wrong, exactly, but that it may omit key context or facts that contradict the author's thesis).

For example, consider the task of finding an accurate modern history of the infamous insecticide DDT, which was banned for use in the United States in 1972 after it was linked to environmental damage. In searching for such a book, you'd likely come across these three contenders: *The Excellent Powder: DDT's Political and Scientific History*, by Donald Roberts and Richard Tren; *DDT Wars: Rescuing Our National Bird, Preventing Cancer, and Creating the Environmental Defense Fund*, by Charles F. Wurster; and *DDT and the American Century: Global Health, Environmental Politics, and the Pesticide That Changed the World*, by David Kinkela. If you look up each author, you find that Roberts and Tren were on the board of Africa Fighting Malaria, which is pro-DDT; Wurster is a cofounder of the Environmental Defense Fund, which was formed to help take down DDT; and Kinkela is a professor of history at the State University of New York at Fredonia. Which of these authors has a stake in the story? Which may have a strong perspective or opinion on DDT? And which would you choose to find the most unbiased perspective?

Take a look at the publisher, too. Is the book self-published or from a mainstream publisher or university press? None of these will necessarily mean a book is good or bad, but keep in mind that a self-published book may have had even less oversight than one from a publishing house. As for traditional publishers, check out their reputation. Are they well respected? What other books have they published? In the example above about the DDT histories, the Roberts and Tren book is self-published, while the other two came from university presses. Does this change your decision on which book you would trust?

Another clue as to the quality of a book is the author's supporting research. Look for sources listed in footnotes, endnotes, or a reference section. Are they authoritative sources, or a bunch of Wikipedia links? How many sources did the author use? The higher the quality of the sources, and the greater the number, the higher your confidence may be in the book.

Finally, finding some books that could serve as sources, especially older or more specialized ones, can be difficult, and not every checker will have access to a good library. Try using Google Books, Amazon previews, and other online sources, which are often text searchable. It is rare for an entire book to be available on these sites, but you may be able to get the information you want. Librarians are also great resources, whether they're at universities, your local library, or libraries in nearby big cities if yours is relatively small or sparsely stocked. From these experts, you may be able to get more information about and from inaccessible books.

NEWSPAPERS

As already discussed in chapter 3, newspapers are typically on the newspaper fact-checking model, which means they don't usually employ independent fact-checkers. That doesn't mean that newspapers don't verify the information in stories before their publication, but that they don't necessarily have a dedicated fact-checker to do the work. Still, it's always worth remembering that stories in newspapers—and in other publications on the newspaper model—aren't employing the same number of editorial safety nets as you may find at other publications.

As a fact-checker, you usually won't use a newspaper as a primary source. But you will likely read a lot of newspaper articles—mostly online—as you work, whether you're looking for related reporting or trying to triangulate some basic information by looking it up across multiple outlets. So keep in mind: some newspapers are better than others. And all publications, whether their editors would like to admit it or not, have a point of view. (Speaking of editorial perspective, you should know the different types of writing a newspaper or other outlet publishes, from news to opinion to analysis, and be able to distinguish between them. An opinion or analysis piece will be permitted more subjectivity.)

You should familiarize yourself with publications that are well respected and highly read—although remember that correlation doesn't necessarily mean causation. In the U.S., a similar set of publications often tops both lists. According to Muck Rack, a media database that caters to people in public relations, as of this writing the top five U.S. newspapers by total visits online are: the *New York Times*, the *Washington Post*, the *New York Post*, *USA Today*, and the *Wall Street Journal.* By circulation, according to the market research company Statista, the top five as of January 2019 were *USA Today*, the *Wall Street Journal*, the *New York Times*, the *New York Post*, and the *Los Angeles Times*. Rankings, of course, are subjective, but the *Columbia Journalism Review* made a list of the top 100 newspapers in 1999, based on surveys from more than 100 editors: their top five had the *New York Times* ranked first, followed by the *Washington Post*, the *Wall Street Journal*, the *Los Angeles Times*, and the *Dallas Morning News*. Of course, 1999 was a long time ago, and many of the papers on the list have suffered their own scandals and budget cuts in recent years. And just because a newspaper has a good reputation doesn't mean it is infallible. It's always worth reading widely and corroborating information.

You can find similar lists for publications in other countries or regions. And whenever you encounter an outlet you aren't familiar with, vet them just as you would any other source. In this case, you might ask: Who is the publisher? Do they have a reputation for being particularly partisan? How is the publication funded? Has the publication been transparent about how it separates its newsgathering from however it makes money? Does the outlet appear to show a clear line between news and opinion and advertorials?

As for finding newspaper articles, most will be available on the paper's website or through Google News searches. If you are hired as a fact-checker for a specific outlet, you may find they subscribe to LexisNexis, a database of newspaper articles. Other free newspaper databases may be available through your local public library. When you read through a newspaper article, pay attention to any corrections or editor's notes. Usually, these appear at the bottom of the story, although especially egregious errors might be corrected at the top. And databases such as LexisNexis may not always show corrections with the original story, instead including them as a separate entry.

No matter where or when an article published, don't forget to find backup sources to confirm the information in it. One relevant cautionary tale comes from Stephen Ornes, a science writer and writer in residence at Vanderbilt University. In 2007 Ornes wrote a short piece for *Discover* magazine about a few unusual cases when a Nobel Prize had been stolen. Two of the examples Ornes found were true stories. The third, he located in a newspaper article. It referenced a woman named Kay Miller, who said her 1985 Nobel Peace Prize had been stolen and later recovered from the trunk of a man's car, along with a gun and dozens of driver's licenses. Ornes published the piece with a brief mention of Miller's ordeal, only to get an angry email from the group that actually won the 1985 Peace Prize. It turned out that Miller's prize was a commemorative replica that had been awarded to a student delegation—a medal that she maintained was an actual Nobel.

Also beware of fake news. Although the term's definition has shifted over time, it more or less refers to content that is false and intentionally presented to look like it came from a regular news publication. The goal of fake news may be to make money through advertising, by publishing inflammatory content that users are likely to click. Or it may be political, spreading conspiracies or lies about a politician or candidate. Always look closely at a publication's URL, the bylines and bios of its writers, and the sourcing it includes—or fails to include—within the stories.

OTHER PUBLICATIONS

Of course, there are all sorts of publications beyond newspapers: print magazines, digital magazines, blogs, digital publications with multiple verticals, publications with both print and digital output, and more. It's hard to say which will employ

Quick Guide: Using Media as a Secondary Source
Sometimes it isn't possible to track down solid primary sources, particularly if you are on a tight deadline. If you have to use secondary sources such as a newspaper or online outlet, aim to use three or more articles from different publications to corroborate the information. But beware: not all publications do an independent fact-check and they aren't all of equal quality. Also, if one outlet got a story wrong, the mistake may have been picked up by dozens of others. Pay attention to where a news story originally published (if it got picked up by another site, it should be linked to or referenced somewhere), and make sure to use stories that include original reporting (i.e., the writer cites reasonable primary or secondary sources, rather than attributing the entire piece to another reporter at another outlet).

fact-checkers and which will not. As with newspapers, though, it's better not to use any other type of publication as a primary source. (There are exceptions. See "Primary vs. Secondary Sources" on p. 128.) A fact-checker might use other types of publications as background reading, to see how other reporters have covered a story or to flag potential errors of omission. If you are reading publications that you aren't familiar with, be sure to vet them.

ACADEMIC LITERATURE

Journal articles can be great primary or secondary sources, and many are accessible for free online. Primary journal articles include research conducted by the authors themselves and described as such in the publication. Secondary journal articles include reviews and meta-analyses, which pull to-gether works of other authors to look at the state of a field or to conduct a deep analysis across multiple works, respectively.

Whether the article is a primary or a secondary source, one way to find it is simply to Google the citation: author name, article title, and journal information including the volume and page numbers. Sometimes, such searches reveal a free copy—usually as a PDF file—either on a database or on the author's own website. There are also many academic databases that help locate papers. Good resources include Google Scholar and JSTOR (Journal Storage). For medical papers, look at PubMed, a search engine provided by the U.S. National Insti-tutes of Health. If you can't find a free copy of the entire article (some journal websites only provide the abstract), email the author or authors to see if they can send a copy to you. Explain that you need it for research or for fact-checking a story. In most cases, they will be happy to oblige. Universities usually subscribe to academic journals, so if you have a past or cur-rent affiliation with a school you may be able to access papers directly. A lot of media outlets also have subscriptions—for instance, an outlet that mainly publishes science journalism may subscribe to some of the top relevant scientific journals. Whether you are a staff or freelance fact-checker, check with your editor to see if you can access these accounts.

But beware: not all journal articles are necessarily accurate or up-to-date. This is especially the case in science, a field that is dynamic and constantly self-correcting. Looking at academic journals is helpful, but make sure you find a trust-worthy expert in a field to help navigate through drifts of aca-demic literature. This is especially important in fields that are hijacked by politics, such as climate change. There may very well be single papers that appear to disprove certain aspects of climate change, but it's important to understand how these papers fit into the larger body of research. Another trick for surveying a subject's landscape is to look for recent review

Pro Tip: How to Read a Scientific Paper

Most science papers have six major sections: abstract, introduction, methods, results, discussion, and references. The abstract gives an overview of the research, including highlights of the study's intent and its findings. The introduction provides background information to help give the research context. The methods section describes how the authors conducted the work and should give enough detail so that anyone with expertise in the same field can understand and replicate the steps. The results section states what the authors found and may include figures, tables, and other data. The discussion section typically puts the results in a broader context, spelling out what the authors think the results mean. And the references, of course, list any other papers that the authors cite.

Experts usually read papers differently than a layperson would, perhaps skipping around to different sections and reading the work multiple times. All the while, an expert will be assessing the research, looking for hints that all of the data was published along with the study, the methods are sound, the statistics and other analyses are done well, and the hypothesis is reasonable. And since science is built not on individual papers but on cumulative research, an expert will also be able to tell how a study fits into a larger body of work.

As a fact-checker, you will likely read these papers differently for two reasons: the material may be over your head, and you'll almost certainly be pressed for time. Where a fact-checker finds relevant information depends on which parts of the research are cited in the story you are checking. Most of the information for a fact-check will be in either the abstract or the discussion section, which means a checker could go directly to those to look up the paper's findings. In other cases, a writer may describe how an experiment was conducted, which means the checker should look in the methods section. In any case, make sure to read the entire section to verify that it was used in context in the story you are checking. If you need help understanding the paper, or you aren't sure the story you are checking describes it accurately, get in touch with the paper's author and ask.

Also keep in mind that a writer may have pulled some background facts from the paper's introduction. Usually this section will be a secondary source, because the information comes from previous research. If a writer uses anything from the introduction, see if the corresponding original source is cited in the references and check that paper (sometimes this process becomes a rabbit hole, where papers cite one another but never lead back to a truly original source).

Finally, as with any source, look up the author's and publisher's credentials. If you are unsure whether the paper is a good one, or if you need help vetting it, find an expert who can help walk you through the work. This expert shouldn't be one of the authors of the study—although you should also talk to an author—but an independent researcher who knows the field in question and has no stakes in how the paper is presented in the media.

Other tips:

- Read accompanying press releases. You'll need to beware of the spin, but they may help you understand the gist of the work or define key jargon.
- Look for accompanying editorials in the same journal issue, which may help put the work into a large context.
- Confirm that the findings support the conclusions (and if you aren't sure, ask an independent expert).
- Look for the paper's limitations, which the authors usually disclose near the end.
- Look for statements of conflicts of interest, which usually appear at the end.

articles—again, a secondary source—which typically pull together and analyze all of the relevant research in a form that is
relatively easy to read even for the nonexpert.

Also be aware of various trends in academic publishing.
One is open-access journals, which provide free articles, usually by passing on the publishing costs to authors. The general intention is to bring research to the public and to other
researchers as quickly and openly as possible. While some
open-access publishers have good reputations and peer review, there are also seedy groups that will publish anything
so long as authors cough up hefty publishing fees. This means
that anyone can publish a paper if they have the money to do
so, and the quality of journals operating in this manner suf-
fers because of it. These open-access publications are called
predatory journals. One of the more famous lists of them was
made by Jeffrey Beall, formerly the scholarly communications
librarian at the Auraria Library at the University of Colorado
Denver, who created a blacklist on *Scholarly Open Access*
titled "Beall's List: Potential, Possible, or Probable Predatory
Scholarly Open-Access Publishers." Beall took the original
list down in 2017 because, he says, he "felt pressure from my
university and intense pressure from the predatory publishers
themselves." As of this writing, there are still versions of the
list available online (Beall says he has no connection to any
existing lists, although some were based on his original work).
No matter what list of predatory journals you look at, these
should be a starting point, rather than an end point: always
do your own vetting.

Another trend in academic publishing is the preprint. Although preprints have been around in some fields since the
1990s, their use has exploded more recently—particularly
during the COVID-19 pandemic, when scientists were publishing studies relevant to the coronavirus and its spread on
preprint servers at a fast clip, and journalists were increasingly referencing such work in articles for the general public.

In traditional publishing, it can take a long time for research to make it out to other academics and the general public. Some fields have turned to preprints to speed the process along. A preprint is essentially a scientific paper that publishes before it has gone through a rigorous peer review—and before, or during, its submission to a traditional journal. While there is some debate as to whether journalists should report on preprints at all, one thing is clear: if a journalist mentions such work, they should vet it with independent experts, and their article should make it clear to the reader that the research has not yet gone through peer review.

SIX ||| **Record Keeping**

Keeping track of your fact-checking sources is vital. This is true when you're in the midst of a fact-check, of course, but it's equally true after the story is filed, published, and in recycling bins nationwide or otherwise forgotten—even years after, in fact. Every good fact-checker has a clear system for organizing their source material. There's no right or wrong way to do it: just make sure you're consistent and that whatever system you use helps you locate interview notes, emails, reports, and any other source materials quickly.

There are several reasons why you or your editors may need access to your research files. So far, we've mainly explained this in the context of the editorial stet (if you've already forgotten, that's the copyedit notation meaning "let it stand" that essentially ignores suggested changes). If you track each stet from your editor or the writer, it will help you when those stets inadvertently preserved an error—which you'll know soon enough, as readers contact the outlet to point out all the story's faults. Inevitably, your boss will forward said correspondence to you and ask: "What went wrong?" If you weren't the person who made the mistake, you'll want proof that you did your job and what went wrong was someone else.

For a fact-checker, there are several other reasons to keep records, too. Publications often revisit stories or pursue ones on similar topics, and you may want to access your old files to reuse source material (this is also true for writers who need to fact-check their own work, who may pillage old research to build new stories). Digital articles also live far longer than print used to, which means a reader may spot a potential error months or years from now.

Then there are the legal matters. For stories that may open a publication to lawsuits, backup materials will be key. Rob Bertsche from Klaris Law says publications should keep source records at least as long as it takes for the statutes of limitations—the amount of time in which a person can legally initiate a lawsuit—to run out for defamation, invasion of privacy, and any other potential grounds for litigation. The statutes of limitations vary between states and countries, so look up the rules wherever you work to figure out the timing that best suits you. For example, if the state statute of limitations for defamation is two years, the publication should normally keep source materials for at least two years; the materials should stick around longer if the piece has been revised—for instance, if a correction or other update was issued—or is a matter of dispute.

PAPER BACKUP

Keeping hard copies of documents and other source materials isn't especially common in today's digital age, but some publications do still store fact-checking backup in an old-school filing cabinet. If this is the case where you work—or even if you're a self-employed researcher working from home and simply prefer paper—you'll probably want manila file folders, expanding file pockets, and either filing boxes or cabinets. (If you're freelancing for a publication, they may provide special instructions on how to keep your files. You may also want to keep a copy at home, if you're working remotely.) How you organize everything will vary depending on your—or your employer's—preferences, but it will usually go something like this. Each story will get its own set of manila folders, labeled with the magazine issue (date, year, and so on) and story title. Or if you're working with online stories, the folder will have the date, website section, and so on. One folder—or more, if needed—will contain hard copies of the story itself, whether they're printed Word documents or proofs. And another folder or set of folders will contain the source material organized, perhaps, by source type, author, or any other way that makes it easy to locate a specific document inside. For big stories with loads of backup, you may need several folders separated by source type (one file for interview transcripts, one for reports, and so on).

However you organize your files, they'll likely go in a larger expanding file pocket with other stories from the same issue of

---

Quick Guide: Labeling Records

Whether you're keeping hard-copy records, electronic records, or both, you'll want to make sure to label them clearly so that if you return to the material weeks—or even months or years—from the time you worked on the story, you'll be able to easily find each source. Here are some tips:

- Make a folder for each outlet you work for and label it with the outlet's name.
- Create subfolders within that folder, labeled by story (e.g., "Beyoncé Knowles Profile").
- Create additional subfolders and label them by type of source material: interviews, reports, images, etc.
- Label interview transcripts or recordings with the interviewee's last name (e.g., "Knowles interview. mp3").
- Label reports with the author or organization name and the date (e.g., "Billboard hits 2008.pdf").
- Pick a format and stick with it so it's easy to locate specific files.

Pro Tip: Hard-to-Store Sources

Websites change over time and may even disappear entirely. If you use online information as a source, either print it as a PDF or take a screenshot (or print it as a paper copy, although this could get cumbersome if you use a lot of web sources). For books and other published materials that are too big and expensive to file away, make a list of titles and other key publishing information so you can locate them again. For interview recordings and other audio or video content—which likely will exist somewhere digitally—make a list of the file names and where they are stored. And if there are any other materials that can't go in a filing folder or cabinet, make lists of those, too, along with whatever information you need in order to find them again. (For books, particularly rare ones that were difficult to procure, you may want to scan the relevant pages and copyright information to save as an electronic file.)

the magazine. These will then go into file boxes or cabinets organized in chronological order, so it's easy to go back and find the specific magazine or online publication date, and then the specific story folder or folders.

How long an outlet keeps your fact-check files will depend on both the statutes of limitations and storage space. Some publications eventually move files to an off-site storage facility, keeping them anywhere from a few years to indefinitely.

ELECTRONIC BACKUP

There are a variety of ways to organize digital files. One free option, so long as you have a computer, basically re-creates a filing cabinet using labeled digital folders: each folder can

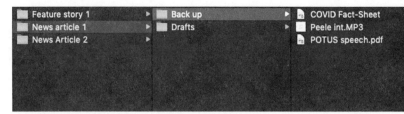

Feature story 1 ▶	Back up ▶	COVID Fact-Sheet
News article 1 ▶	Drafts ▶	Peele int.MP3
News Article 2 ▶		POTUS speech.pdf

Figure 8. Be sure to clearly name each file so that it is easy for other people—and you, after a long time has passed and you aren't as familiar with the documents—to identify.

have multiple subfolders, and those folders may also contain any electronic file format (audio files for interviews, PDFs of reports, and so on). (You could also check out various online services that help organize documents, such as Overview Docs, which uploads your research material and helps make it searchable.) Inevitably, these tips will get stale as new technologies become available, but the basic logic behind the filing system will likely be helpful no matter what digital tools you have at your disposal.

If you are fact-checking for multiple outlets, make a folder for each, clearly label it, and follow the filing steps outlined above by story and by outlet. For each story, create a folder and rename it according to the story's headline (or an obvious nickname, if the headline is too long). Then, within the folder, make several subfolders. How many you need and what you name them will depend on your preferences. You may, for example, want to keep things simple: a folder for story drafts and another folder for source material. Or, if you have a lot of sources that may be difficult to sift through, you may want to use multiple folders separated into each type of source (transcripts, audio files, images, reports, and so on).

As for the electronic documents that you keep in each folder, make sure the file names are clearly marked so it is easy for anyone to go in and find each iteration of the story draft, as well as, say, the transcript for the Jordan Peele interview or the COVID-19 fact sheet or the president's most recent speech on health care reform.

To save the information from websites or other online sources in case they change or disappear, make an electronic copy—for example, by taking a screenshot or saving as a PDF. For books, open a plain text document in your word-processing software of choice and make a list of the titles and relevant copyright information. This goes, too, for writer's notebooks, print archives from libraries, or any other materials that aren't available digitally.

Where you keep these folders depends on where you work. If you're an in-house checker at a publication and other people

---

Pro Tip: Saving Online Sources

Things change on the internet all the time. Links go dead, websites go through a redesign, social media posts disappear. Every time you find a source online, you should screenshot, download, or save it as a PDF file (most operating systems allow you to print any document as a PDF using, more or less, the same menu options you'd use to print to paper).

If you forgot to save a key website or post and—*gasp*—it's gone, don't despair quite yet. You may be able to find it through the Wayback Machine, a digital internet archive, or other similar services; cached web pages (older versions of pages stored by search engines for use when current pages aren't available); or, in the case of damning social media posts, you may be able to find places where other folks have taken screenshots (just be sure to authenticate the posts). Once you find whatever you're looking for: save a copy.

need to access your documents, you may simply keep your records on your own computer. Some outlets also have a shared drive that is linked to everyone's computers, in which case you should also save your files there. Follow the format for all of the other folders on the shared drive—for example, if each issue of a magazine has its own folder, with story-related subfolders within it, do the same with your work. If you're working remotely and don't have access to your computer desktop or shared computer drives, you may need to send your files to your boss through Dropbox, Hightail, or any other file-sharing service.

And if you're saving your files at home, use your hard drive, an external drive, a cloud storage service, or any other storage you prefer—or a combination of these, to have extra copies. Just be sure that if you are saving sensitive documents on the cloud, you are aware of the company's security and privacy policies.

As with the hard-copy files, how long you keep your electronic materials will depend on both statutes of limitations and the preference of you and your employer. It's much easier to store digital files, because they take up far less room, so it may be that you have old shared drives or other storage that have materials that date back many years. Old fact-checking files may be a good resource when you're looking for good materials for your next fact-check job, particularly if you work on stories that are on the same general topic.

And then the process begins anew.

Itching to put your newfound fact-checking skills to work? Here's your chance. Over the next several pages, you'll find two exercises relevant to the information you've learned in this book. Answers are available in appendix 1. (No peeking!)

EXERCISE 1

Underline the facts in the following passage. How many can you find?

|||

The smell feels illicit even though it's not: a pleasant blend of pine, cedar, and skunk. It hangs in the air of a refurbished brick warehouse in downtown Spokane, permeating each drafty room. One of the only residents on this early January evening is ODO Oil, a company that processes cannabis oil, but there are big dreams of a sprawling cannabis business district with recreational shops and kitchens baking pot-infused treats. Upstairs, 60 rundown hotel rooms may eventually be converted to pot-friendly condos. For now, the main floor is mostly empty, save for a few televisions in the storefront windows broadcasting a CNN rerun about cannabis onto the snowy, empty streets outside.

I'm visiting ODO with Alan Schreiber, a scientist who plans to do business here. The company's lab director, Steve Lee, is telling us about the history of the building, but Schreiber promptly interrupts. "I want to see my product. I just want to talk about what's going on," he says.

"Absolutely," Lee says. He guides us downstairs to the main processing room. It's loud and hot and filled with $1-million-worth of extraction machines, which wrest the oil from dried, ground cannabis plants. The extraction concentrates the compounds that give pot its oomph—dozens of chemicals called cannabinoids, which include tetrahydrocannabinol, or THC, the main psychoactive ingredient. A guy in Tyvek coveralls and protective gloves pulls a lever to spritz a first-run of raw oil into a clear plastic cup. If we're being charitable, the oil looks like melting caramel gelato; if not, it'd easily be mistaken for the contents of a baby's diaper.

We make our way to a secondary processing room, quieter and cooler, where the oil is filtered and spun until it has the deep viscous clarity of buckwheat honey. Lee holds up a Mason jar of the stuff, estimated at $18,000 wholesale. He explains that in order to land on store shelves as inhalable cartridges, or as an ingredient in cookies, candy or other edible goods, the oil must go through state-mandated safety and quality tests from a third-party lab to assure that it's free of contaminants such as bacteria, mold, and remaining solvents. The labs also determine the potency.

Schreiber, a former academic entomologist and pesticide toxicologist who is now essentially a hired gun in agricultural pest control, then turns to me. "I'm going to make a statement, and he's going to agree with it or not agree with it, or maybe counter it," he says, nodding at Lee. "He doesn't have to test that for pesticide residues."

Lee agrees. "Currently in Washington State there is no mandate that we have to test for pesticides," he says.

Excerpt from "The Scientist Pot Farmer,"
by Brooke Borel, *Undark*, April 7, 2016

EXERCISE 2

Mark each of the following sources as (1) primary or secondary and (2) high-quality or low-quality.

Note that some sources may be primary in some uses and secondary in others. Identify and explain these situations. Likewise, articulate how you would evaluate the quality of each source. What credentials are meaningful? What situations might vary a given source's quality?

1. Photographs
2. Maps
3. A public opinion poll
4. Court transcripts
5. An interview with an oncologist about cancer
6. An interview with an oncologist about the history of cancer
7. A televised presidential debate
8. A scientific study
9. A scientific review or meta-analysis
10. A statistic in the abstract of a scientific study
11. A person attending a political rally
12. History books
13. A farmer whose crops were destroyed by a flood
14. A newspaper article
15. A politician speaking on climate change
16. Audio or video footage
17. An official biography
18. An unofficial biography
19. An autobiography
20. The bouncer at a bar who threw out a named patron for doing illegal drugs

Conclusion

When I revisit the conclusion from the first edition of this book, I wince at my naivete. Back when I wrote it, the biggest fact-checking challenges facing the industry, at least as I saw it, were in-house errors and internet hoaxes, in which media outlets credulously reported false stories—like one from 2014 in which a Russian man said his phone ringtone, which played Justin Bieber, saved him from a bear attack, a story that got picked up by *BuzzFeed News*, MTV, the *New York Post*, and more. Sure, there were plenty of conspiracy theorists back then, from anti-vaxxers to flat-earthers to Alex Jones. There were also lots of bot farms and click farms to deal with, but these collections of fake social media accounts mostly seemed to be used to gain more online clout—and, for some people, to make more money. As the *New Republic* put it in 2015, "just as fast as Silicon Valley conjures something valuable from digital ephemera, click farms seek ways to create counterfeits." Still, back then, it seemed like newsrooms could somehow handle this weird digital ecosystem, so long as we collectively infused our reporting with a little more rigor and added a few more fail-safes in our processes.

I also saw glimmers of hope. Political fact-checking groups were multiplying, popping up in countries all over the world and working to hold powerful politicians accountable for their words. The hoax-busting site Snopes had a sizable following. Journalists were uncovering questionable news agencies and networks of trolls. Popular online columns helped point out viral hoaxes, and social media companies were rolling out plans to flag misinformation and rank articles by accuracy.

I was wrong to feel optimistic. Since 2016, it's become clear that the problems we are facing are much bigger than fact-checking alone can handle. The promises and protocols I found comforting back then aren't doing as much to preserve fact-checking and journalism as I had hoped. Political fact-checking doesn't appear to be as effective for audiences who view the work as inherently biased. Social media platforms like Facebook may actually benefit from viral misinformation— it's a boon to their business model, because they make more money the more people engage, no matter the veracity of the content. The platforms' limited attempts to flag false content have produced underwhelming results—and, in many ways, totally backfired. My favorite columns that focused on taking down hoaxes stopped publishing. The cofounder of Snopes was revealed as a plagiarist, working under a pseudonym on his own site. Bot farms are still prolific, and they've evolved, often aiming to push conspiracies and sway elections.

Conspiracy theorists have just gotten louder and, in many cases, gone mainstream; data show that most of this activity has come from the Far Right, promoting conspiracies from Pizzagate to QAnon to lies about the COVID-19 pandemic. Some of these conspiracies have even aimed to rend the very fabric of democracy. In early 2022, to name one example, an investigation from ProPublica and the *Washington Post* identified more than 650,000 Facebook posts containing misinformation and violent threats related to the results of the 2020 presidential election, posted between Election Day 2020 and the January 6, 2021, insurrection at the U.S. Capitol. Many of the posts called for civil war and executions. The journalists also found that Facebook did little to curb the flow of false claims, based on interviews with former employees.

Unfortunately, it's only going to get worse. During a 2021 interview, the computer scientist Hany Farid, from the University of California, Berkeley, told me that in the future, one of the biggest worries for fact-checkers should be synthetic media, which is a media landscape created or altered by artificial intelligence. We are already seeing the beginnings of this world. Computer scientists are using artificial intelligence—mainly machine learning—to make computer-generated images and videos (commonly known as deepfakes), as well as text and audio. Here's how it works, more or less: researchers develop algorithms to learn from many, many examples. In order for an algorithm to be able to create an image of a horse, for instance, the researchers will feed it hundreds or thousands of images of horses—different colors, sizes, and breeds. Eventually, the algorithm understands how to create its own picture of a horse. The same goes for audio clips: an algorithm will hear many clips of someone's voice, and then use those examples to learn to speak like them. And so on.

Right now, synthetic media has limitations. Although algorithms can make photos of a person that are hyperrealistic, the images typically only show people from the shoulders up. The technology isn't yet capable of making a full scene from scratch—for instance, conjuring a riot or war that never happened. But mind-blowing examples of synthetic media *are* already possible, with some time and effort. In 2021, for instance, a series of TikToks showing the actor Tom Cruise in goofy scenarios—retelling a joke he supposedly heard from Mikhail Gorbachev, performing a magic trick, eating candy, and more—were all deepfakes. Their creator, visual and AI effects artist Chris Umé, used an actor and shot scenes in real-life settings, then applied an AI model trained on videos of the real Tom Cruise to fill in the facial details. Someday, such scenes will be possible with far less effort. Synthetic media is "on a meteoric rise," Farid told me. "There is going to be a lot of movement on this, and a lot of cool but troubling technology that can be weaponized. And it is going to be a fast-moving space. Every three to four months, we see advances."

(Of course, bad actors don't even need high-tech algorithms to weaponize information and manipulate media—many low-tech disinformation campaigns have been successful. People believe what they want to believe.)

Then there is the metaverse, a digital world that is a combination of technologies, from augmented reality to virtual reality. It's a little hard to get your mind around the concept, because it is still so new. As *Wired* put it in 2021: "To a certain extent, talking about what 'the metaverse' means is a bit like having a discussion about what 'the internet' means in the 1970s. The building blocks of a new form of communication were in the process of being built, but no one could really know what the reality would look like." So, the metaverse might mean playing immersive video games, as is already possible with products like the Oculus VR headsets, or interacting in three-dimensional online worlds to socialize, conduct business, seek entertainment, consume media, and more. Already, Meta, formerly Facebook, has created a three-dimensional world where people can gather face-to-face or, more accurately, avatar-to-avatar.

Tech companies are investing heavily in this virtual world. Right now, virtual reality headsets are a little clunky and inaccessible for many people. But it's inevitable that the tech will improve and get cheaper. The social media platforms that are designing the metaverse will offer services that are more and more complex. How will we know the real identities of the people to whom we are talking? How will we share media within this world, and how will advertisers share media with us? Will our interactions with others feel more *real* and emotionally compelling, heightening our reactions of passionate solidarity or outrage? The metaverse will surely provide new forms of entertainment, but there will be ample opportunity for the downsides of our existing social media to deepen and expand: spreading false information, preying on users' emotions, manipulating content, connecting like-minded conspiracy enthusiasts, and fracturing society. In these embryonic days of the metaverse, users have already reported harassment and abuse.

How will we navigate these shadow worlds? How will journalists, nonfiction writers, historians, editors, and fact-checkers help everyone make sense of these spaces?

The answers aren't yet clear, but that doesn't mean we should give up hope. The work of journalism and nonfiction writing—it matters. Democracy can't exist without a free and honest press. Humans can't survive as a species if we don't understand our past and perceive the consequences of dangers ranging from climate change to the spread of diseases to the bad behavior of world leaders. Some people will always seek out facts and accurate news; they are here in the real world, they'll exist even in a sea of synthetic media, and they'll be in the metaverse. The job of fact-checkers, journalists, and editors is to help make a record of the world, both for the people who are seeking truth now and for future generations. But we need to be collectively aware of how the online ecosystem in which we all exist is changing. We need to watch these new technologies so we know how they work and how they're evolving. Only then will we be able to figure out how they can be manipulated.

Some groups are proposing to use technology to help preserve facts and truth. Collaborations between computer scientists and journalists, for instance, aim to use machine learning and other AI techniques to build automated fact-checkers, which, if they ever actually work, would trawl the internet and flag falsehoods. Companies and newsrooms are joining together to help promote authenticated digital content, from photos to documents, using software that can show the content's provenance. Here, the goal is to shift the responsibility of the fact-check: rather than forcing fact-checkers and journalists to figure out if a photo is real, this system wants photographers to use a digital signature that will follow that photo around the internet; then, *anyone* who wants to authenticate the image can quickly run a check of that provenance data.

Still others are trying to figure out how to apply blockchain technology to journalism. You may mostly associate blockchain with the cryptocurrency Bitcoin and other financial applications. But the basic concept behind the technology has many possible applications, because it creates an immutable and transparent digital ledger of transactions that is distributed among its users—in other words, it can make a record that is exceedingly difficult to tamper with. For a cryptocurrency, this means that a user can purchase a coin (or a fraction of a coin), and then anyone can follow how it is used. Blockchain technology can also be decentralized, so that no single group has full control. Some proponents have argued that blockchain could provide a new funding model for journalism. Readers would own a stake in a publication and collectively help guide it, thereby doing away with the influence of advertisers or billionaire owners. Blockchain technology could also help to create a clear and unchangeable ledger of key information related to an article, like the byline and time of publication, according to the Tow Center for Digital Journalism at Columbia University, and "secure content and publication data securely and immutably."

While I'm glad that there are people who are thinking about how to apply technology to help curb mis- and disinformation, I've been around long enough to know that the purveyors of lies are motivated to find their way around any technological barrier meant to stymie them. I've tested AI fact-checkers and, frankly, they haven't impressed me. So far, it's just too tricky to find a data set to train the AI models—they require an enormous base of information in order to learn, plus an understanding of nuance and tone that computers just can't handle yet. As for digital provenance, smart computer scientists and

AI experts have told me that creating verifications for digital content will always be an arms race—people who want to make a fake will mimic the latest technology, just as currency counterfeiters find a way to make convincing watermarks, holograms, and light-shifting inks. As for blockchain technology, the proposals for its use in journalism so far haven't taken off. I worry that even when someone comes up with just the right model, the average reader won't engage with the technology or support it by buying in. And people who are motivated to disregard reality aren't going to be any more convinced by an immutable content ledger than they are by our current systems of verification. So, we can't count on technology to save us. The work of human fact-checkers—and anyone else who is interested in presenting a correct record of events—will always be relevant.

During my research for this edition of the book, I reinterviewed some of the journalists I talked to for the first edition. One of those journalists was Adrienne LaFrance, who is currently the executive editor of *The Atlantic*. Back in 2014, when I started working on the first edition, LaFrance was the author of a series at *Gawker* called Antiviral: Here Is What's Bullshit on the Internet This Week. The concept was simple: LaFrance dissected viral hoaxes from Twitter and elsewhere online, showing why they weren't real (and why people needed to stop sharing them). When I caught up with LaFrance in late 2021, we talked about how different the internet felt compared to 2014. If she rebooted the column, she joked, the concept would have to flip: "Here Is What's *Not* Bullshit on the Internet This Week." I asked LaFrance if the original column seemed quaint, with all that has happened since then. She agreed, but with an important caveat. "I'd say it was grounded in a philosophy that I think we need ever more of. Which is, the default should be skepticism," she told me. Rather than relying on hearsay, everyone should be asking good questions and looking for legitimate sources. "We as a society need to be thinking critically," she added. "Not that everyone has to be a journalist, but that's certainly what journalists should do for people—is to have that posture."

She's right. So let's get to work.

Acknowledgments

It may seem extra nerdy to anyone outside the fact-checking business, but it was really fun to research and write this guide, especially for this former fact-checker. But I couldn't have written the book alone. An enormous thank-you goes to all of the checkers, researchers, journalists, and writers who gave me their time, either by responding to my surveys, submitting to long interviews, or both; to my kind readers on the first edition, John Banta, Rob Bertsche, Alice Jones, Erika Villani, and Luke Zaleski; to the University of Chicago Press reviewers, for their wisdom; to my fact-checkers Meral Agish, on the original edition, and Nora Belblidia, on the second, for setting me straight more times than I'd like to admit (though I take responsibility for any mistakes that snuck into the final text); to Julia Calderone, for her good humor during our proofreading sessions; to Deborah Blum and the rest of the staff at the Knight Science Journalism Program at MIT, for all of their support in my various fact-checking projects; to Patti Wolter, for all the conversations about the craft of fact-checking (and all those keynote speeches); to Jen Schwartz, for the smart comments on early drafts of the introduction and conclusion, as well as for the friendship; to my editor Mary Laur, for her sharp insight and vision, and to Christie Henry, for connecting us; to Mollie McFee for tracking down hard-to-find images and more; to Erin DeWitt and Stephen Twilley, for their meticulous copyediting for the first and second editions, respectively; to Lauren Salas and Carrie Adams, on the first and second editions, respectively, for their marketing skills;

to Kevin Quach and Jill Shimabukuro; and to my agent, Paul Lucas, who always supports my ideas no matter how wide they wander.

And love and thanks to Maggie, Arte, and Mike.

EXERCISE 1 ANSWER KEY

I identified 129 facts in the passage. The exact number may vary depending on how you break up certain phrases. See footnotes for details.

|||

The smell[1] feels illicit[2] even though it's not[3]: a pleasant blend of pine, cedar, and skunk.[4] It hangs in the air[5] of a refurbished brick warehouse[6] in downtown Spokane,[7] permeating each[8] drafty room.[9] One of the only residents[10] on this early January

1 "smell": Confirm with sources present that there was a smell.

2 "feels illicit": Confirm that cannabis, and by extension the smell that indicates its presence, is illegal in most jurisdictions in the U.S., where this story takes place.

3 "even though it's not": Confirm that cannabis is legal in Washington State.

4 "a pleasant blend of pine, cedar, and skunk": While this is subjective, a fact-checker could still ask sources present whether the description is apt.

5 "It hangs in the air": Confirm with sources present that the building smelled consistently like cannabis.

6 "refurbished brick warehouse": Confirm description of building.

7 "in downtown Spokane": Confirm the building's location.

8 "permeating each": Confirm with sources present that the smell occurred throughout the building.

9 "drafty room": Confirm with sources present that the rooms felt drafty.

10 "One of the only residents": Confirm the number of business residents in the building, and that ODO Oil is one of them.

evening[11] is ODO Oil,[12] a company that processes cannabis oil,[13] but there are big dreams of a sprawling cannabis business district[14] with recreational shops[15] and kitchens baking pot-infused treats.[16] Upstairs,[17] 60[18] rundown[19] hotel rooms[20] may eventually be converted to pot-friendly condos.[21] For now, the main floor[22] is mostly empty,[23] save for a few[24] televisions[25] in

11 "on this early January evening": Confirm date and time with sources present.

12 "ODO Oil": Confirm name and spelling.

13 "a company that processes cannabis oil": Confirm company's products.

14 "but there are big dreams of a sprawling cannabis business district": Confirm plans of business district with developers/owners.

15 "recreational shops": Confirm as part of proposed business district.

16 "kitchens baking pot-infused treats": Confirm as part of the proposed business district.

17 "Upstairs": Confirm that the hotel rooms are located upstairs.

18 "60": Confirm number of hotel rooms.

19 "rundown": While this is subjective, confirm that it is fair to describe the rooms' appearance this way.

20 "hotel rooms": Confirm that the rooms are, indeed, hotel rooms.

21 "may eventually be converted to pot-friendly condos": Confirm as part of the business district plan.

22 "main floor": Confirm that sources were on the building's main floor in the described scene.

23 "mostly empty": Confirm with sources present that this is an apt description.

24 "few": Confirm the number of televisions.

25 "televisions": Confirm the presence of televisions.

the storefront windows[26] broadcasting a CNN rerun about cannabis[27] onto the snowy,[28] empty streets[29] outside.[30]

I'm visiting ODO[31] with Alan Schreiber,[32] a scientist[33] who plans to do business here.[34] The company's lab director,[35] Steve Lee,[36] is telling us[37] about the history of the building,[38] but Schreiber promptly interrupts.[39] "I want to see my product. I just want to talk about what's going on," he says.[40]

26 "in the storefront windows": Confirm the location of televisions.

27 "broadcasting a CNN rerun about cannabis": Confirm the topic and date of the programming aired during the tour.

28 "snowy": Confirm that there was snow on the ground.

29 "empty streets": Confirm that no one was visible on the streets from inside.

30 "broadcasting . . . outside": Confirm that television screens were visible from the street.

31 "I'm visiting ODO with Alan Schreiber": Confirm Schreiber's presence at the Spokane cannabis center and that the author accompanied him.

32 "Alan Schreiber": Confirm name and spelling.

33 "a scientist": Confirm job description.

34 "who plans to do business here": Confirm that Schreiber is planning to do business at the Spokane cannabis center.

35 "The company's lab director": Confirm title.

36 "Steve Lee": Confirm name and spelling.

37 "is telling us": Confirm that Lee told the group this story.

38 "about the history of the building": Confirm content of Lee's story.

39 "but Schreiber promptly interrupts": Confirm that Schreiber interrupted.

40 "'I want to see my product. I just want to talk about what's going on,' he says": Confirm quote and attribution.

"Absolutely," Lee says.[41] He guides us[42] downstairs[43] to the main processing room.[44] It's loud[45] and hot[46] and filled[47] with $1-million-worth[48] of extraction machines,[49] which wrest[50] the oil[51] from[52] dried,[53] ground[54] cannabis plants.[55] The extraction[56] concentrates[57] the compounds[58] that give pot its oomph[59]—dozens[60] of chemicals[61] called cannabinoids,[62] which include[63]

41 "'Absolutely,' Lee says": Confirm quote and attribution.

42 "He guides us": Confirm that Lee led the group to a new spot in the building.

43 "downstairs": Confirm that ODO's processing room is downstairs in the building.

44 "to the main processing room": Confirm the room description.

45 "It's loud": Confirm noise level.

46 "hot": Confirm temperature.

47 "filled": Confirm that the equipment indeed fills the room.

48 "$1-million-worth": Confirm cost of equipment.

49 "extraction machines": Confirm machine type and function.

50 "wrest": Confirm description of what machine does.

51 "the oil": Confirm material that the machine extracts.

52 "from": Confirm direction of extraction.

53 "dried": Confirm description of material.

54 "ground": Confirm description of material.

55 "cannabis plants": Confirm the material the machines are extracting from.

56 "extraction": Confirm action.

57 "concentrates": Confirm action.

58 "compounds": Confirm that the extracted materials can be called "compounds."

59 "give pot its oomph": Confirm that these particular compounds are the active ingredients in cannabis and that "oomph" is an appropriate way to describe them.

60 "dozens": Confirm number of compounds.

61 "chemicals": Confirm synonym for "compounds" in this context.

62 "called cannabinoids": Confirm name and spelling.

63 "include": Confirm that the following specific compounds/chemicals are examples of the previously stated "dozens."

tetrahydrocannabinol,[64] or THC,[65] the main[66] psychoactive[67] ingredient.[68] A guy[69] in Tyvek[70] coveralls[71] and protective[72] gloves[73] pulls[74] a lever[75] to spritz[76] a first-run[77] of raw oil[78] into a clear[79] plastic[80] cup.[81] If we're being charitable, the oil looks like melting caramel gelato;[82] if not, it'd easily be mistaken for the contents of a baby's diaper.[83]

64 "tetrahydrocannabinol": Confirm name and spelling.

65 "THC": Confirm abbreviation and spelling.

66 "main": Confirm that there are no other psychoactive compounds that could be considered more prominent.

67 "psychoactive": Confirm that THC is psychoactive.

68 "ingredient": Confirm as synonym for compound/chemical.

69 "guy": Confirm gender.

70 "Tyvek": Confirm attire material.

71 "coveralls": Confirm attire style.

72 "protective": Confirm that gloves were indeed intended for protection.

73 "gloves": Confirm that the person wore gloves.

74 "pulls": Confirm direction of action.

75 "lever": Confirm description of item that the person pulled.

76 "spritz": Confirm that the material came out in a spritz/spray and not in some other fashion (for example, a trickle or a gush).

77 "first-run": Confirm that this was the first processing stage.

78 "raw oil": Confirm the oil should be called "raw" at this processing stage.

79 "clear": Confirm color.

80 "plastic": Confirm material.

81 "cup": Confirm container type.

82 "the oil looks like melting caramel gelato": Confirm description of raw oil.

83 "easily be mistaken for the contents of a baby's diaper": Confirm description.

We make our way[84] to a secondary processing room,[85] quieter[86] and cooler,[87] where the oil[88] is filtered[89] and spun[90] until[91] it has the deep[92] viscous[93] clarity[94] of buckwheat honey.[95] Lee holds[96] up[97] a Mason jar[98] of the stuff,[99] estimated at $18,000 wholesale.[100] He explains[101] that in order to land on store shelves[102] as inhalable cartridges,[103] or as an ingredient

84 "We make our way": Confirm the same group moved through the building.

85 "to a secondary processing room": Confirm that this was the next stop on the tour.

86 "quieter": Confirm noise level in relation to previous room.

87 "cooler": Confirm temperature in relation to previous room.

88 "oil": Confirm material processed in second room.

89 "filtered": Confirm that this action takes place in the secondary processing room.

90 "spun": Confirm that this action takes place in the room, after the filtration.

91 "until": Confirm the duration of the filtering and spinning.

92 "deep": Confirm the depth/darkness of the oil's color.

93 "viscous": Confirm the oil's consistency.

94 "clarity": Confirm how transparent/opaque the oil appears.

95 "buckwheat honey": Confirm that the filtered/spun oil resembles buckwheat honey in color, consistency, and clarity.

96 "Lee holds": Confirm that Lee was the one who held the oil.

97 "up": Confirm the direction that he held the oil.

98 "Mason jar": Confirm the container type.

99 "the stuff": Confirm that the Mason jar indeed contained the filtered/spun oil.

100 "estimated at $18,000 wholesale": Confirm value of oil in Mason jar.

101 "He explains": Confirm that it was Lee who gave the following context.

102 "in order to land on store shelves": Confirm that Lee was talking about the oil as a commercial product.

103 "inhalable cartridges": Confirm example of a commercial product that could include the cannabis oil from ODO.

in cookies,[104] candy[105] or other edible goods,[106] the oil must go through[107] state-mandated[108] safety[109] and quality tests[110] from a third-party lab[111] to assure that it's free of contaminants[112] such as bacteria,[113] mold,[114] and remaining solvents.[115] The labs[116] also determine the potency.[117]

Schreiber,[118] a former[119] academic[120] entomologist[121] and

104 "ingredient in cookies": Confirm example of a commercial product that could include the cannabis oil from ODO.

105 "candy": Confirm example of a commercial product that could include the cannabis oil from ODO.

106 "or other edible goods": Confirm example of a commercial product that could include the cannabis oil from ODO.

107 "the oil must go through": Confirm that it is the oil, and not the whole product, that must go through the testing.

108 "state-mandated": Confirm that the testing is required by state law specifically.

109 "safety": Confirm the category of state-mandated testing.

110 "quality tests": Confirm the category of state-mandated testing.

111 "from a third-party lab": Confirm who/what does the state-mandated testing.

112 "assure that it's free of contaminants": Confirm the purpose of the testing.

113 "bacteria": Confirm example of targeted contaminant in the testing.

114 "mold": Confirm example of targeted contaminant in the testing.

115 "remaining solvents": Confirm example of targeted contaminant in the testing.

116 "The labs": Confirm that the same third-party labs do the additional testing.

117 "also determine the potency": Confirm description of additional testing.

118 "Schreiber": Confirm that Schreiber is the person speaking.

119 "former": Confirm Schreiber's academic appointment status.

120 "academic": Confirm whether Schreiber was indeed ever an academic.

121 "entomologist": Confirm job description.

pesticide toxicologist[122] who is now essentially a hired gun in agricultural pest control,[123] then turns to me.[124] "I'm going to make a statement, and he's going to agree with it or not agree with it, or maybe counter it," he says, nodding[125] at Lee.[126] "He doesn't have to test that for pesticide residues."[127]

Lee agrees.[128] "Currently in Washington State there is no mandate that we have to test for pesticides," he says.[129]

122 "pesticide toxicologist": Confirm job description.

123 "now essentially a hired gun in agricultural pest control": Confirm job description.

124 "then turns to me": Confirm whom Schreiber was speaking to.

125 "nodding": Confirm gesture Schreiber made.

126 "at Lee": Confirm whom Schreiber was indicating.

127 "'I'm going to make a statement, and he's going to agree with it or not agree with it, or maybe counter it,' he says . . . He doesn't have to test that for pesticide residues'": Confirm quotes and attribution.

128 "Lee agrees": Confirm that Lee agreed with Schreiber's statement.

129 "'Currently in Washington State there is no mandate that we have to test for pesticides,' he says": Confirm quote and attribution.

EXERCISE 2 ANSWER KEY

While journalists should aim for primary sources whenever possible, there are some cases where a secondary source is useful. And there are also cases where a primary source isn't particularly trustworthy. Here are some ways you might categorize the following sources.

1. Photographs: Primary, but make sure they are real (reverse image search; TinEye; contact photographer). High or low quality. Double-check the framing, the caption information, and whether the images are available from other angles or photographers.

2. Maps: Could be both primary and secondary and both high- and low-quality. When was the map made? How was it made? How is it cited? Who made it, using what tools? For example: say you want to describe Lower Manhattan in New York circa 1725. A map of the area made in 1725 would be a primary source. But a map made in 2019 reconstructing 1725-era Lower Manhattan would be secondary.

3. A public opinion poll: Primary. Quality depends on the methodology.

4. Court transcripts: Primary. Typically high-quality, but consider the country and court in which the case took place.

5. An interview with an oncologist about cancer: Primary if they stick to their experience and expertise. Potentially high-quality, but vet for conflicts of interest, crackpot theories, affiliations, etc.

6. An interview with an oncologist about the history of cancer: Secondary. A better expert would be a historian who specializes in this field or primary sources that you might find in archives or libraries. Low-quality.

7. A presidential debate broadcast: Primary. High-quality for checking candidate quotes; a mix of high- and low-quality

for specific claims, depending on the candidate and their sourcing.

8. A scientific study: Primary, as long as reference is to original research in the study. Quality can vary, so cross-check with third-party experts and look for signs of potential quality (peer review, journal reputation, etc.).

9. A scientific review or meta-analysis: Secondary. Quality depends on methodology.

10. A statistic in the abstract of a scientific study: Primary if the stat comes from the original research in the study. Secondary if the abstract cites other research. Could be high- or low-quality depending on the methodology and original source.

11. A person attending a political rally: Primary for color and context but secondary for any claims about policy, statistics, etc. Quality depends on how the source is used, but in general this will not be a high-quality example for any statements of substance. Even if this source describes policy or constitutional issues accurately, for example, it is better to confirm the claims with an unbiased expert or a data set.

12. History books: Secondary. Can be high- or low-quality, depending on the author and methodology.

13. A farmer whose crops were destroyed by a flood: Primary for the fact that the crops were destroyed, secondary for any details about why the flooding occurred or other technical matters. Quality will depend on how the source is used. For example, if the farmer claims the flooding is connected to climate change, it's best to find a qualified scientist to assess that claim.

14. A newspaper article: Could be primary or secondary depending on how it is used. For instance, if a story cites a newspaper article as evidence that an event appeared in a particular publication, it is primary. But specific information in the article is generally secondary. The

quality depends on the newspaper, the reporter, the reporting, and more.

15. A politician on climate change: Secondary unless they have a degree or valid research experience in climate science or a relevant field. Even then, it's better to find another, less potentially biased source. The quality depends on how the source is used, but in general a politician shouldn't be the final say on a scientific topic.

16. Audio or video footage: Primary, but make sure it is real. The quality could be high or low. Ask: How was it edited? Is the clip taken out of context? Who released it?

17. An official biography: Secondary, as it isn't a firsthand account by the subject. The quality depends on both the author and the subject. Vet them. If the subject has a dirty track record, for example, an official biography may gloss over misdeeds and misstate or twist facts.

18. An unofficial biography: Secondary, as it isn't a firsthand account by the subject. The quality depends on both the author and the subject. Vet them. In some cases, an unofficial biography may be more truthful than an official one.

19. Autobiography: Primary, as it written by the subject. But the quality depends on whether we trust their account.

20. A bouncer at a bar who threw out a named patron for doing illegal drugs: Primary for the fact that the bouncer threw out the patron. Either primary or secondary for the illegal drugs. Did the bouncer see or confiscate drugs? Were the drugs confirmed to be illegal? The quality depends on how the bouncer is used in the story. Always corroborate, particularly for sources who accuse someone of a crime.

BOOKS AND BOOK CHAPTERS

Brouse, Cynthia. *After the Fact*. Toronto: Cynthia Brouse and Ryerson University School of Journalism, 2007. (A brief fact-checking guide.)

Canby, Peter. "Fact-Checking at *The New Yorker*." In *The Art of Making Magazines: On Being an Editor and Other Views from the Industry*, ed. Victor S. Navasky and Evan Cornog. New York: Columbia University Press, 2012. (One of the biggest names in fact-checking discusses his craft.)

Calvert, Clay, Dan V. Kozlowski, and Derigan Silver. *Mass Media Law*. New York: McGraw-Hill Education, 2023. (Look for used copies or previous editions, as this legal text is expensive.)

D'Agata, John, and Jim Fingal. *The Lifespan of a Fact*. New York: W. W. Norton, 2012. (D'Agata, an essayist, and Fingal, a fact-checker, reenact their back-and-forth over fact-checking D'Agata's piece "About a Mountain." More fact-checking performance art than fact-checking reality, the book raises questions about the meaning of fact versus truth. In 2018 and 2019, an adaptation appeared on Broadway starring Daniel Radcliffe, Cherry Jones, and Bobby Cannavale.)

Kovach, Bill, and Tom Rosenstiel. *The Elements of Journalism: What Newspeople Should Know and the Public Should Expect*. New York: Three Rivers Press, 2007. (A primer on journalism.)

McInerney, Jay. *Bright Lights, Big City*. New York: Vintage, 1984. (A novel about a fact-checker at a high-brow New York magazine. It was later made into a film starring Michael J. Fox.)

Silverman, Craig, ed. *Verification Handbook: A Definitive Guide to Verifying Digital Content for Emergency Coverage*. Maastricht: European Journalism Centre, 2014. (Especially helpful for fact-checkers or writers who spend most of their time breaking news online.)

Smith, Sarah Harrison. *The Fact Checker's Bible: A Guide to Getting It Right*. New York: Anchor Books, 2004. (The author pulls from her experiences as a fact-checker at the *New Yorker* and head of fact-checking at the *New York Times Magazine*.)

Zweig, David. *Invisibles: The Power of Anonymous Work in an Age of Relent-*

less Self-Promotion. New York: Portfolio / Penguin, 2014. (A nonfiction book about unseen—but important—jobs, including the job of the fact-checker. The author is a former fact-checker.)

ARTICLES AND ESSAYS

Bissinger, Buzz. "Shattered Glass." *Vanity Fair*, September 1998. https://www.vanityfair.com/magazine/1998/09/bissinger199809. (The original article describing the journalistic misdeeds of Stephen Glass.)

Dzieza, Josh. "John D'Agata's Fact-Checking Battle." *Daily Beast*, February 21, 2012. http://www.thedailybeast.com/articles/2012/02/21/john-d-agata-s-fact-checking-battle.html. (More commentary on *The Lifespan of a Fact*.)

Eveleth, Rose. "Hurricane Sandy: Five Ways to Spot a Fake Photograph." *BBC Future*, October 31, 2012. http://www.bbc.com/future/story/20121031-how-to-spot-a-fake-sandy-photo. (A handy guide to the inevitable dramatically Photoshopped images that appear during breaking news and catastrophic events.)

Fisher, Marc. "Who Cares If It's True?" *Columbia Journalism Review*, March 3, 2014. (An essay on fact-checking, as well as on old versus new media.)

Gessner, Dave. "Everything You Ever Wanted to Know about Truth in Nonfiction but Were Afraid to Ask: A Bad Advice Cartoon Essay." *Bill and Dave's Cocktail Hour*, March 28, 2015. http://billanddavescocktailhour.com/everything-you-ever-wanted-to-know-about-truth-in-nonfiction-but-were-afraid-to-ask-a-bad-advice-cartoon-essay/. (An illustrated essay exploring the meaning of creative nonfiction and a writer's obligation to the reader in presenting work as fact, truth, and the result of honesty.)

Johnson, Bobbie. "Why Facts Matter." *Medium*, December 10, 2013. https://medium.com/@bobbie/why-facts-matter-bf66dfb5c5e8#.riutj7h8v. (An essay about internet hoaxes and why *Matter*, a Medium publication, fact-checked their pieces.)

Kachka, Boris. "Will Book Publishers Ever Start Fact-Checking? They're Already Starting." *Vulture*, June 23, 2015. http://www.vulture.com/2015/06/will-book-publishers-ever-start-fact-checking.html. (A brief survey of the state of fact-checking in book publishing.)

McPhee, John. "Checkpoints." *New Yorker*, February 9, 2009. https://www.newyorker.com/magazine/2009/02/09/checkpoints. (McPhee's ode to his fact-checker, Sara Lippincott.)

Nijhuis, Michelle. "The Pocket Guide to Bullshit Prevention." *The Last Word on Nothing*, April 29, 2014. http://lastwordonnothing.com/2014/04/29/the-pocket-guide-to-bullshit-prevention. (Provides excellent suggestions on deciding whether to trust a source.)

O'Neil, Luke. "The Year We Broke the Internet." *Esquire*, December 23, 2013. http://www.esquire.com/news-politics/news/a23711/we-broke-the -internet/. (The author examines the proliferation of hoaxes online, as well as his role in boosting awareness of these hoaxes.)

Rolzhausen, Yvonne. "How to Fact Check *The Atlantic*." *Atlantic*, January 25, 2018. https://www.theatlantic.com/notes/2018/01/how-to-fact-check-the -atlantic/551477/. (The head of the fact-checking department at a well- known magazine walks the reader through checking a short excerpt from "What ISIS Really Wants," a story that published in 2015.)

Rosin, Hanna. "Hello, My Name is Stephen Glass, and I'm Sorry." *New Republic*, November 10, 2014. https://newrepublic.com/article/120145 /stephen-glass-new-republic-scandal-still-haunts-his-law-career. (One of Stephen Glass's former colleagues and friends revisits his fabrication scandal.)

Schulman, Michael. "Daniel Radcliff and the Art of the Fact-Check." *New Yorker*, October 15, 2018. https://www.newyorker.com/magazine/2018/10 /15/daniel-radcliffe-and-the-art-of-the-fact-check. (In preparation for his role in *The Lifespan of a Fact*, a Broadway show adapted from the 2012 book of the same name, Daniel Radcliffe learned how to fact-check at the *New Yorker*.)

Schultheis, Emily. "*Der Spiegel* Made Up Stories. How Can it Regain Readers' Trust?" *Atlantic*, October 1, 2019. https://www.theatlantic.com /international/archive/2019/01/der-spiegal-fabrication-scandal-global /579889/. (A look at the 2019 fact-checking scandal at the German magazine *Der Spiegel*, which was previously well known for its large fact- checking team.).

Shafer, Jack. "The Return of Michael Finkel." *Slate*, July 27, 2007. http://www .slate.com/articles/news_and_politics/press_box/2007/07/the_return _of_michael_finkel.html. (The comeback tale of Finkel, a writer who was caught presenting a composite character as a real person in a 2001 *New York Times Magazine* feature.)

Silverman, Craig. "The 'Lifespan of a Fact' Blends Fiction with Nonfiction to Explore the Nature of Truth." *Poynter*, March 5, 2012. http://www .poynter.org/2012/the-lifespan-of-a-fact-blends-fiction-with-nonfiction -to-explore-nature-of-truth/164447/. (An examination of the D'Agata and Fingal book.)

Somaiya, Ravi, and Leslie Kaufman. "If a Story Is Viral, Truth May Be Taking a Beating." *New York Times*, December 9, 2013. https://www.nytimes .com/2013/12/10/business/media/if-a-story-is-viral-truth-may-be -taking-a-beating.html. (An examination of viral news stories, as well as the fact that some outlets who publish hoaxes also produce serious journalism.)

Swetala, Christopher. "Fact-Check Yourself before You Wreck Yourself." *Transom*, April 25, 2017. https://transom.org/2017/fact-check-fact-wreck/. (A fact-checker at *This American Life* discussed the art and importance of fact-checking.)

Warzel, Charlie. "2014 Is the Year of the Viral Debunk." *BuzzFeed News*, January 23, 2014. http://www.buzzfeed.com/charliewarzel/2014-is-the-year-of -the-viral-debunk#.xdLpKp2BP9. (A discussion of the way that journalists combat viral hoaxes.)

Wen, Tiffanie. "The Hidden Signs That Can Reveal a Fake Photo." *BBC Future*. June 29, 2017. https://www.bbc.com/future/article/20170629-the -hidden-signs-that-can-reveal-if-a-photo-is-fake. (Tips on identifying fake photos on the internet.)

AUDIO

Gladstone, Brooke. "Checking in on Fact Checking." *On the Media*, September 20, 2012. https://www.wnycstudios.org/podcasts/otm/segments /239015-checking_fact_checking. (Brooke Gladstone tackles the state of fact-checking across media.)

Glass, Ira. "Retraction." *This American Life*, March 16, 2012. https://www .thisamericanlife.org/460/retraction. (Ira Glass and others from the radio program analyze a retracted story by monologist Mike Daisey.)

Neary, Lynn. "Checking Facts in Nonfiction." *Weekend Edition*, June 8, 2019. https://www.npr.org/2019/06/08/730898366/checking-facts-in -nonfiction. (Lynn Neary explores fact-checking—or the lack thereof—in nonfiction books.)

Sullivan, Margaret. "In Praise of Radically Transparent Journalism." Interview by Bob Garfield. *On the Media*, November 30, 2017. https:// www.wnycstudios.org/podcasts/otm/segments/in-praise-radically -transparent-journalism. (An interview with Margaret Sullivan from the *Washington Post*, in which she calls for more transparency in journalism.)

References

For each chapter, selected sources are listed in alphabetical order.

INTRODUCTION

Alizada, Nazifa, Rowan Cole, Lisa Gastaldi, Sandra Grahn, Sebastian Hellmeier, Palina Kolvani, Jean Lachapelle et al. "Autocratization Turns Viral." Democracy Report 2021. Varieties of Democracy Institute, 2021.

Bankoff, Caroline, and Margaret Hartmann. "What We Know about Charleston Gunman Dylann Storm Roof." *New York Magazine*, June 19, 2015. http://nymag.com/daily/intelligencer/2015/06/what-we-know-about -the-charleston-gunman.html.

Banta, John. Email message to author, August 13, 2021.

Banta, John. Interview with author, March 19, 2015.

Barber, Tony. "Rise of Autocracies Spells End to the West's Global Supremacy." *Financial Times*, November 6, 2019. https://www.ft.com/content /cc420908-e910-11e9-aefb-a946d2463e4b.

Barry, Dan, David Barstow, Jonathan D. Glater, Adam Liptak, and Jacques Steinberg. "Correcting the Record: Times Reporter Who Resigned Leaves Long Trail of Deception." *New York Times*, May 11, 2003. https://www .nytimes.com/2003/05/11/us/correcting-the-record-times-reporter-who -resigned-leaves-long-trail-of-deception.html.

Benkler, Yochai, Casey Tilton, Bruce Etling, Hal Roberts. Justin Clark, Rob Faris. Jonas Kaiser, and Carolyn Schmitt. "Mail-In Voter Fraud: Anatomy of a Disinformation Campaign." Berkman Klein Center, October 1, 2020.

Borel, Brooke. Fact-Check Survey (unpublished), 2014.

Borel, Brooke, Knvul Sheikh, Fatima Husain, Ashley Junger, Erin Biba, and Deborah Blum, and Bettina Urcuioli. "The State of Fact-Checking in Journalism." Knight Science Journalism Program at MIT, June 2018.

Brenan, Megan. "Americans' Trust in Media Dips to Second Lowest on Record." Gallup, October 7, 2021. https://news.gallup.com/poll/355526 /americans-trust-media-dips-second-lowest-record.aspx.

Burrough, Bryan. "The Inside Story of the Civil War for the Soul of NBC

News." *Vanity Fair*, April 7, 2015. https://www.vanityfair.com/news/2015/04/nbc-news-brian-williams-scandal-comcast.

Calkins, Laurel. "Alex Jones Must Pay $965 Million for His Sandy Hook Lies." *Bloomberg Law*, October 13, 2022. https://news.bloomberglaw.com/bankruptcy-law/alex-jones-must-pay-almost-1-billion-for-sandy-hook-lies.

Collins, Dave. "Alex Jones Ordered to Pay $965 Million for Sandy Hook Lies." *Associated Press*, October 12, 2022. https://apnews.com/article/shootings-school-connecticut-conspiracy-alex-jones-3f579380515fdd6eb59f5bfoe3e1c08f.

Cooke, Janet. "Jimmy's World." *Washington Post*, September 28, 1980.

Coronel, Sheila, Steve Coll, and Derek Kravitz. "*Rolling Stone* and UVA: The Columbia University Graduate School of Journalism Report." *Rolling Stone*, April 5, 2015.

Cox, Kate, Theodora Ogden, Victoria Jordan, and Pauline Paillé. "COVID-19, Disinformation and Hateful Extremism." RAND Corporation, July 14, 2021. https://www.rand.org/pubs/external_publications/EP68674.html.

Das, Ronnie, and Wasim Ahmed. "Rethinking Fake News: Disinformation and Ideology during the Time of COVD-19 Global Pandemic." *IIM Kozhikode Society & Management Review* 11, no. 1 (2022): 146–59.

Douglas County Sheriff's Department. "Remember when we said to follow official sources only." Facebook, September 10, 2020. https://www.facebook.com/permalink.php?story_fbid=pfbido2mTaavtNGZtTbhFHxnViLpHez84kUV1sSBedRrtKi9MEErJJU60NPyToq5RS9biyil&id=100871513330688.

Downie, Leonard, Jr. "The Trump Administration and the Media." Committee to Protect Journalists, April 16, 2020. https://cpj.org/reports/2020/04/trump-media-attacks-credibility-leaks/.

Eromosele, Diana Ozemebhoya. "Cousin: Dylann Roof 'Went Over the Edge' When His Girl Crush Started to Date a Black Guy." *The Root*, June 22, 2015.

Fabry, Merrill. "Here's How the First Fact-Checkers Were Able to Do Their Jobs before the Internet." *Time*, August 24, 2017. https://time.com/4858683/fact-checking-history/.

Fact Checker (column). *Washington Post*. https://www.washingtonpost.com/news/fact-checker/.

Fichtner, Ullrich, "Der Spiegel Reveals Internal Fraud." *Spiegel International*, December 12, 2018. https://www.spiegel.de/international/zeitgeist/claas-relotius-reporter-forgery-scandal-a-1244755.html.

Graziano, Franki. "A Jury Decides Alex Jones Owes Nearly $1 billion for Sandy Hook Lies." NPR, October 13, 2022. https://www.npr.org/2022

/10/13/1128624069/a-jury-decides-alex-jones-owes-nearly-1-billion-for
-sandy-hook-lies.

Hansen, Evan. "Violations of Editorial Standards Found in Wired Writer's Blog." *Wired*, August 31, 2012. https://www.wired.com/2012/08/violations -of-editorial-standards-found-in-wired-writers-blog/.

Higgins, Tucker. "The Bizarre Political Rise and Fall of Infowars' Alex Jones." CNBC, September 14, 2018. https://www.cnbc.com/2018/09/14/alex -jones-rise-and-fall-of-infowars-conspiracy-pusher.html.

Human Rights Watch. "Hungary: Editor's Sacking a Blow to Press Freedom." July 24, 2020. https://www.hrw.org/news/2020/07/24/hungary-editors -sacking-blow-press-freedom.

Illing, Sean. "'I Made Mistakes': Jill Abramson Responds to Plagiarism Charges around Her New Book." *Vox*, February 8, 2019. https://www.vox .com/2019/2/8/18206892/jill-abramson-plagiarism-book-merchants-of -truth.

Lewandowsky, Stephan. "Climate Change Disinformation and How to Combat It." *Annual Review of Public Health* 42 (2021):1–21.

Lewis, Tanya. "How the Pandemic Remade Science Journalism." *Scientific American*, March 2022. https://www.scientificamerican.com/article/how -the-pandemic-remade-science-journalism/.

Lührmann, Anna, Seraphine F. Maerz, Sandra Grahn, Nazifa Alizada, Lisa Gastaldi, Sebastian Hellmeier, Garry Hindle, and Staffan I. Lindberg. "Autocratization Surges—Resistance Grows." Democracy Report 2020. Varieties of Democracy Institute, 2020.

Malooley, Jake. "Jill Abramson Plagiarized My Writing. So I Interviewed Her about It." *Rolling Stone*, February 13, 2019. https://www.rollingstone .com/culture/culture-features/jill-abramson-jake-malooley-plagiarism -interview-794257/.

Maraniss, David. "Post Reporter's Pulitzer Prize Is Withdrawn." *Washington Post*, April 16, 1981.

Martellucci, Cecilia Acuti, Maria Elena Flacco, Rosaria Cappadona, Francesca Bravi, Lorenzo Mantovani, and Lamberto Manzoli. "SARS-CoV-2 Pandemic: An Overview." *Advances in Biological Regulation* 77 (2020): 100736. https://pubmed.ncbi.nlm.nih.gov/32773099/.

Martineau, Paris. "How an InfoWars Video Became a White House Tweet." *Wired*, November 8, 2018. https://www.wired.com/story/infowars-video -white-house-cnn-jim-acosta-tweet/.

McGrath, Matt. "Climate Change: Huge Toll of Extreme Weather Disasters in 2021." *BBC News*, December 27, 2021. https://www.bbc.com/news /science-environment-59761839.

Meese, James, Jordan Frith, and Rowan Wilken. "COVID-19, 5G Conspiracies and Infrastructural Futures." *Media International Australia* 177, no. 1 (2020): 30–46.

Mongelli, Lorena, and Rebecca Harshbarger. "Charleston Shooter Tried to Kill Himself, but 'He Ran Out of Bullets.'" *New York Post*, June 21, 2015. http://nypost.com/2015/06/21/charleston-shooter-tried-to-kill-himself -but-he-ran-out-of-bullets/.

Mooney, Taylor. "Misinformation about Amazon Fires Could Mean More Blazes in 2020." *CBS News*, March 1, 2020. https://www.cbsnews.com /news/amazon-fires-brazil-president-bolsonaro-misinformation-cbsn -originals-documentary/.

Moos, Julie. "Timeline of Jonah Lehrer Plagiarism, Fabrication Revelations." *Poynter*, August 31, 2012. https://www.poynter.org/reporting-editing/2012 /timeline-of-jonah-lehrer-plagiarism-fabrication-revelations/.

Moynihan, Michael. "Jonah Lehrer's Deceptions." *Tablet*, July 30, 2012. http://www.tabletmag.com/jewish-news-and-politics/107779/jonah -lehrers-deceptions.

New Republic. "To Our Readers." June 29, 1998.

Pogrebin, Robin. "Boston Columnist Is Ousted for Fabricated Articles." *New York Times*, June 19, 1998.

Politifact. Accessed July 1, 2022. https://www.politifact.com/.

Pulitzer Prizes. "1998 Pulitzer Prizes." Accessed June 30, 2022. https://www .pulitzer.org/prize-winners-by-year/1998.

Raines, Howell. "My Times." *Atlantic*, May 2004.

Reed, Betsy. "A Note to Readers." *Intercept*, February 2, 2016. https:// theintercept.com/2016/02/02/a-note-to-readers/.

Reinhold, Robert. "Washington Post Gives Up Pulitzer, Calling Article on Addict, 8, Fiction." *New York Times*, April 16, 1981.

Remnick, David. "The Cost of Trump's Assault on the Press and the Truth." *New Yorker*, November 29, 2020. https://www.newyorker.com/magazine /2020/12/07/the-cost-of-trumps-assault-on-the-press-and-the-truth.

Reporters Without Borders. "Jair Bolsonaro." July 1, 2021. https://rsf.org/en /predator/jair-bolsonaro.

Rosin, Hanna. "Hello, My Name Is Stephen Glass, and I'm Sorry." *New Republic*, November 10, 2014.

Rosin, Hanna. Interview with author, November 17, 2015.

Rosin, Hanna, and Lina Misitzis. "The End of Empathy." *Invisibilia*, April 12, 2019. https://www.npr.org/2019/04/11/712276022/the-end-of-empathy.

Salinger, Tobias. "Dylann Roof 'Kind of Went over the Edge' When Love Interest Who Spurned Him Chose African-American Guy: Report." *New*

York Daily News, June 22, 2015. http://www.nydailynews.com/news
/crime/dylann-roof-raged-black-guy-girl-report-article-1.2266378.

Schaub, Michael. "Jill Abramson's Book Contains Inaccuracies, Vice Correspondents Claim." *Los Angeles Times*, January 15, 2019. https://www
.latimes.com/books/la-et-jc-jill-abramson-book-20190115-story.html.

Smith, Sarah Harrison. *The Fact Checker's Bible: A Guide to Getting It Right.*
New York: Anchor Books, 2004.

Steel, Emily. "Brian Williams Says Fabrications Came from 'Bad Urge inside
of Me.'" *New York Times*, June 19, 2015. https://www.nytimes.com/2015
/06/20/business/media/brian-williams-apologizes-matt-lauer-nbc
-interview.html.

Toronto Sun. "Was Jealousy behind Massacre?" June 23, 2015.

Treen, Kathie, Hywel T. P. Williams, and Saffron J. O'Neill. "Online Misinformation about Climate Change." *WIREs Climate Change* 11, no. 5 (2020):
e665.

Tritten, Travis. "NBC's Brian Williams Recants Iraq Story after Soldiers Protest." *Stars and Stripes*, February 4, 2015.

Tsavkko Garcia, Raphael. "Bolsonaro's Social Media War with the Press
Keeps Bleeding into the Real World." *Slate*, July 6, 2020. https://slate
.com/technology/2020/07/brazil-president-bolsonaro-attacks-press
-journalists.html.

Van den Bulck, Hilde, and Aaron Hyzen. "Of Lizards and Ideological Entrepreneurs: Alex Jones and Infowars in the Relationship between Populist
Nationalism and the Post-Global Media Ecology." *International Communication Gazette* 82, no. 1 (2020): 42–59. https://journals.sagepub.com
/doi/pdf/10.1177/1748048519880726.

Watts, Jonathan. "Jair Bolsonaro Claims NGOs behind Amazon Wildfire
Surge—but Provides No Evidence." *Guardian*, August 21, 2019. https://
www.theguardian.com/world/2019/aug/21/jair-bolsonaro-accuses-ngos
-setting-fire-amazon-rainforest.

Wemple, Erik. "How the Media Dealt with the Intercept's Retracted Story on
Dylann Roof's 'Cousin.'" *Washington Post*, February 3, 2016. https://www
.washingtonpost.com/blogs/erik-wemple/wp/2016/02/03/how-the-media
-dealt-with-the-intercepts-retracted-story-on-dylann-roofs-cousin/.

Zaleski, Luke. Interview with author, December 9, 2021.

CHAPTER ONE

Alba, Davey. "Twitter Permanently Suspends Marjorie Taylor Greene's Account." *New York Times*, January 2, 2022. https://www.nytimes.com/2022
/01/02/technology/marjorie-taylor-greene-twitter.html.

Anderson, Meg. "Trump's Latest Campaign Weapon: The Mirror." NPR, September 10, 2016. https://www.npr.org/2016/09/10/493407606/trumps-latest-campaign-weapon-the-mirror.

Anonymous (@YourAnonNews). "Police on scanner identify the names of #BostonMarathon suspects in gunfight, Suspect 1: Mike Mulugeta. Suspect 2: Sunil Tripathi." Twitter, April 19, 2013, 2:00 a.m. https://twitter.com/youranonnews/status/325141840561074176.

Associated Press. "AP News Values & Principles." Accessed June 22, 2015. http://www.ap.org/company/News-Values.

Bauder, David. "Media Outlets Apologize after Falsely Reporting Giffords' Death." Associated Press, January 10, 2011.

BBC News. "YouTube to Remove All Anti-Vaccine Misinformation." September 29, 2021. https://www.bbc.com/news/technology-58743252.

Beaupre, Lawrence. "Using Unnamed Sources." *AJR*, December 1994.

Bertsche, Rob. Interview with author, March 25, 2015.

Bertsche, Rob. Email message to author, August 13, 2021.

Bertsche, Rob. Email message to author, March 31, 2022.

Bidgood, Jess. "Sunil Tripathi, Student at Brown, Is Found Dead." *New York Times*, April 25, 2013.

Binder, Matt. "No, Walmart Will Not Be Accepting Litecoin. Here's How People were Duped." *Mashable.* September 13, 2021. https://mashable.com/article/litecoin-walmart-fake-news.

Bilton, Nick. "The Health Concerns in Wearable Tech." *New York Times*, March 18, 2015.

Borel, Brooke. "Fact-Checking Won't Save Us from Fake News." FiveThirtyEight, January 4, 2017. https://fivethirtyeight.com/features/fact-checking-wont-save-us-from-fake-news/.

Borel, Brooke, Knvul Sheikh, Fatima Husain, Ashley Junger, Erin Biba, and Deborah Blum, and Bettina Urcuioli. "The State of Fact-Checking in Journalism." Knight Science Journalism Program at MIT, June 2018.

Boseley, Sarah. "Simon Singh Libel Case Dropped." *Guardian*, April 15, 2010.

Boston Globe. "Terror at the Marathon." Metro Special. Accessed June 23, 2015. http://www.bostonglobe.com/metro/specials/boston-marathon-explosions.

Brandom, Russell. "The New York Times' Smartwatch Cancer Article Is Bad, and They Should Feel Bad." *The Verge*, March 18, 2015. http://www.theverge.com/2015/3/18/8252087/cell-phones-cancer-risk-tumor-bilton-new-york-times.

British Chiropractic Association and Dr. Singh, England and Wales Court of

Appeal (Civil Division) Decisions [2011] WLR 133, [2010] EWCA Civ. 350, [2011] 1 WLR 133.

Byers, Dylan (@DylanByers). "RT @KallMeKG: BPD scanner has identified the names : Suspect 1: Mike Mulugeta Suspect 2: Sunil Tripathi. #Boston #MIT. Twitter, April 19, 2013, 1:57 a.m. https://twitter.com/DylanByers /status/325140977725616128.

Canby, Peter. "Fact-Checking at *The New Yorker.*" In *The Art of Making Magazines: On Being an Editor and Other Views from the Industry*, ed. Victor S. Navasky and Evan Cornog. New York: Columbia University Press, 2012.

Canon, Gabrielle. "What the Numbers Tell Us about a Catastrophic Year of Wildfires." *Guardian*, December 25, 2021. https://www.theguardian.com /us-news/2021/dec/25/what-the-numbers-tells-us-about-a-catastrophic -year-of-wildfires.

Carlson, Jen. "'Bachelor' Producer Publicly Shames Fellow Airline Passenger on Twitter." *Laist*, November 29, 2013. http://laist.com/2013/11/29/elan _gale_angry_notes.php.

CNN. "CNN Correction: Supreme Court Ruling." June 28, 2012. http:// cnnpressroom.blogs.cnn.com/2012/06/28/cnn-correction/.

Coghian, Andy. "Simon Singh Wins Libel Battle Against Chiropractors." *New Scientist*, April 15, 2010.

Con Edison (@ConEdison). "#ConEd - No Con Edison employees are trapped in a building. The story spreading is a rumor." Twitter, October 29, 2012, 10:13 p.m. https://twitter.com/ConEdison/statuses /263116397238960128.

Congressional Research Service. "Wildfire Statistics." October 4, 2021. https://sgp.fas.org/crs/misc/IF10244.pdf.

C-SPAN. "Facebook and Twitter CEOs Testify on Regulating Social Media Content." November 17, 2020. https://www.c-span.org/video/?478048-1 /facebook-twitter-ceos-testify-regulating-social-media-content.

C-SPAN. "Senate Hearing on Social Media Algorithms." April 27, 2021. https://www.c-span.org/video/?511248-1/senate-hearing-social-media -algorithms.

Der Spiegel. "The Relotius Case: Final Report of the Investigation Commission." May 24, 2019. https://cdn.prod.www.spiegel.de/media/67c2c416 -0001-0014-0000-000000044564/media-44564.pdf.

Erdman, Jonathan. "U.S. Has Had Most Wildfires Through June in 10 Years, and We're Headed into the Peak Months." Weather Channel, June 23, 2021. https://weather.com/safety/wildfires/news/2021-06-22-most-us -fires-in-2021-through-june-in-10-years.

Fairyington, Stephanie. "In the Era of Fake News, Where Have All the

Fact-Checkers Gone?" *Columbia Journalism Review*. February 23, 2018. https://www.cjr.org/business_of_news/fact-checking.php.

Fichtner, Ullrich, "Der Spiegel Reveals Internal Fraud." *Spiegel International*, December 12, 2018. https://www.spiegel.de/international/zeitgeist/claas -relotius-reporter-forgery-scandal-a-1244755.html.

Finkel, Michael. "Is Youssouf Malé a Slave?" *New York Times Magazine*, November 18, 2001.

Gertz v. Robert Welch, Inc., No. 72–617. 418 U.S. 323 (1974).

Getty. "Sir John Frederick William Herschel." Accessed June 30, 2022. https://www.getty.edu/art/collection/person/103KHK.

Goldstein, Tom. "We're Getting Wildly Differing Assessments." *SCOTUSblog*, July 7, 2012. http://www.scotusblog.com/2012/07/were-getting-wildly -differing-assessments/.

Great Projects Film Company. "Yellow Journalism." PBS. Accessed December 30, 2015. http://www.pbs.org/crucible/frames/_journalism.html.

Griffen, Scott. "Out of Balance: Defamation Law in the European Union and Its Effects on Press Freedom." International Press Institute, July 2014.

Gruzd, Anatoliy, and Philip Mai. "Going Viral: How a Single Tweet Spawned a COVID-19 Conspiracy Theory on Twitter." *Big Data & Society*, July 20, 2020.

Herschel, John. "Great Astronomical Discoveries Lately Made by Sir John Herschel, L.L.D. F.R.S.," *Supplement to the Edinburgh Journal of Science*, August 25, 1835. http://hoaxes.org/text/display/the_great_moon_hoax_of _1835_text.

Hogan, Beatrice. Email with author, August 23, 2021.

Hogan, Beatrice. Interview with author, February 20, 2015.

Holpuch, Amanda. "Hurricane Sandy Brings Storm of Fake News and Photos to New York." *Guardian*, October 30, 2012.

House Committee on Energy & Commerce. "Hearing on 'Disinformation Nation: Social Media's Role in Promoting Extremism and Misinforma- tion.'" March 25, 2021. https://energycommerce.house.gov/committee -activity/hearings/hearing-on-disinformation-nation-social-medias-role -in-promoting.

Facebook. "How Facebook's Third-Party Fact-Checking Program Works." June 1, 2021. https://www.facebook.com/journalismproject/programs /third-party-fact-checking/how-it-works.

Huffington Post Canada. "Epic Note Passing between Passengers Gets UGLY On U.S. Thanksgiving (TWEETS)." November 28, 2013. http://www .huffingtonpost.ca/2013/11/28/elan-gael-passenger-fight_n_4357360 .html.

Immerwahr, Daniel. "All Over the Map: Jared Diamond Struggles to Understand a Connected World." *New Republic*, June 11, 2019. https://newrepublic.com/article/154142/jared-diamond-upheaval-book-review.

Issac, Mike. "Facebook Mounts Effort to Limit Tide of Fake News." *New York Times*, December 15, 2016. https://www.nytimes.com/2016/12/15/technology/facebook-fake-news.html.

Isaac, Mike. "How Facebook's Fact-Checking Partnership Will Work." *New York Times*, December 15, 2016. https://www.nytimes.com/2016/12/15/technology/facebook-fact-checking-fake-news.html.

Jamieson, Amber, and Olivia Solon. "Facebook to Begin Flagging Fake News in Response to Mounting Criticism." *Guardian*, December 15, 2016. https://www.theguardian.com/technology/2016/dec/15/facebook-flag-fake-news-fact-check.

Kaczynski, Andrew, and Rosie Gray. "Reports: Chechen Brothers—Not Missing Brown Student—Are Suspects." *BuzzFeed News*, April 19, 2013. http://www.buzzfeed.com/andrewkaczynski/nbc-reports-overseas-figures-not-missing-brown-student-are-s#.ypx2ZoGLY.

Kaplan, Sarah, and Brady Dennis. "2021 Brought a Wave of Extreme Weather Disasters. Scientists Say Worse Lies Ahead." *Washington Post*, December 17, 2021. https://www.washingtonpost.com/climate-environment/2021/12/17/climate-change-extreme-weather-future/.

Kennerly, Max (@MaxKennerly). "Her book is published by Houghton Mifflin Harcourt. Like @AnandWrites said while dissembling the many errors in Jared Diamond's Upheaval (published by Little, Brown), there is a systemic failure here: the big publishers don't think it's important to fact check books they publish." Twitter, May 24, 2019, 7:16 a.m. https://twitter.com/MaxKennerly/status/1131896864150818821.

LaFrance, Adrienne. Interview with author, November 7, 2014.

LaFrance, Adrienne. Interview with author, December 1, 2021.

Legal Information Institute. "Defamation." Cornell University Law School. Accessed June 22, 2015. https://www.law.cornell.edu/wex/defamation.

Levin, Sam. "'They Don't Care': Facebook Factchecking in Disarray as Journalists Push to Cut Ties." *Guardian*, December 13, 2018. https://www.theguardian.com/technology/2018/dec/13/they-dont-care-facebook-fact-checking-in-disarray-as-journalists-push-to-cut-ties.

Madrigal, Alexis. "#BostonBombing: The Anatomy of a Misinformation Disaster." *Atlantic*, April 19, 2013.

Mantica, Gina. "Is YouTube's Crackdown on Vaccine Misinformation Going to Be Effective?" *The Brink*, October 5, 2021. https://www.bu.edu/articles/2021/youtube-vaccine-misinformation-policy-effective/.

Martel, Frances. "News Organizations Retract Reports of Rep. Giffords' Death; She Is Alive." *Mediaite*, January 8, 2011. http://www.mediaite .com/tv/report-rep-gabrielle-giffords-passed-away-after-point-blank -shooting-in-tuscon/.

Masson v. New Yorker Magazine, Inc. No. 89–1799, 501 U.S. 496 (1991).

Masson v. New Yorker Magazine. Nos. 87–2665, 87–2700. 960 F.2d. (9th Cir. 1992).

McDermid, Brendan. "Con Edison Workers Trapped in New York Power Plant by Sandy: Reuters Witness." Reuters, October 29, 2012. http://www.reuters .com/article/us-storm-sandy-coned-idUSBRE89T03D20121030.

Mohney, Gillian. "Airplane 'Note War' Goes Viral on Twitter." *ABC News*, December 1, 2013.

Moscona, Ron. "Defamation Claims in UK Require Proof of 'Serious Harm.'" JD Supra, July 3, 2019. https://www.jdsupra.com/legalnews/defamation -claims-in-uk-require-proof-26759/.

Moran, Lee. "'Bachelor' Producer Elan Gale Gets into Air Rage Battle aboard Delayed Flight on Thanksgiving," *Daily News*, December 3, 2013.

Mosseri, Adam. "Addressing Hoaxes and Fake News." Facebook, December 15, 2016. https://about.fb.com/news/2016/12/news-feed-fyi -addressing-hoaxes-and-fake-news/.

National Archives (U.K.). "Defamation Act." Accessed June 30, 2022. https:// www.legislation.gov.uk/ukpga/2013/26/section/4/enacted.

National Federation of Independent Business v. Sebelius. No. 11–393. 567 U.S. (2011).

National Weather Service. "Hurricane/Post-Tropical Cyclone Sandy, October 22–29, 2012." Department of Commerce. Accessed June 23, 2015. http://www.nws.noaa.gov/os/assessments/pdfs/Sandy13.pdf.

Neary, Lynn. "Checking Facts in Nonfiction." *Weekend Edition*, June 8, 2019. https://www.npr.org/2019/06/08/730898366/checking-facts-in -nonfiction.

Neumann, Ross (@rossneumann). "This has to be a dream RT @KallMeKG: BPD scanner has identified the names : Suspect 1: Mike Mulugeta Suspect 2: Sunil Tripathi. #Boston #MIT." Twitter, April 19, 2013, 1:59 a.m. https://twitter.com/rossneumann/status/325141515108233216.

Newton, Casey. "A Partisan War Over Fact-Checking Is Putting Pressure on Facebook." *The Verge*, September 12, 2018. https://www.theverge.com /2018/9/12/17848478/thinkprogress-weekly-standard-facebook-fact -check-false.

Newton, Casey. "Facebook Partners with Fact-Checking Organizations to Begin Flagging Fake News." *The Verge*, December 15, 2016. https://www

.theverge.com/2016/12/15/13960062/facebook-fact-check-partnerships
-fake-news.

New York Times. "Ethical Journalism: A Handbook of Values and Practices
for the News and Editorial Departments." September 2004.

New York Times. "Heed Their Rising Voices" (advertisement). March 29,
1960.

New York Times Co. v. L. B. Sullivan. No. 39. 376 U.S. 254 (1964).

O'Connell, Michael. "'Bachelor' Producer Achieves Twitter Celebrity after
Thanksgiving Flight Altercation." *Hollywood Reporter*, November 11, 2013.

Oltermann, Philip. "The Inside Story of Germany's Biggest Scandal since the
Hitler Diaries." *Guardian*, December 9, 2019. https://www.theguardian
.com/books/2019/dec/09/germany-exposure-journalist-claas-relotius.

O'Neil, Lauren. "Bachelor Producer Elan Gale Live-Tweets Epic Feud with
Rude Passenger." CBC, November 29, 2013. http://www.cbc.ca/newsblogs
/yourcommunity/2013/11/bachelor-producer-elan-gale-live-tweets-epic
-feud-with-rude-airline-passenger.html.

O'Sullivan, Donie. "Facebook Fact-Checkers to Trump Supporters: We Are
Not Trying to Censor You." CNN, October 29, 2020. https://www.cnn
.com/2020/10/29/tech/fact-checkers-facebook-trump/index.html.

Ossola, Alexandra. "No, Wearable Electronics Are Not Like Cigarettes." *Popular Science*, March 18, 2015.

Palank, Jacqueline. "High Court Won't Take Up Scottie Pippen Defamation
Suit." *Wall Street Journal*, June 16, 2014.

Park, Miles, and Shannon Bond. "5 Takeaways from Big Tech's Misinformation Hearing." NPR, March 25, 2021. https://www.npr.org/2021/03/25
/981203566/5-takeaways-from-big-techs-misinformation-hearing.

Pekarsky, Michelle. "Airline Passenger Exchanges Notes, Gets Slapped by
Woman He Considered Rude to Flight Crew." Fox4KC, November 29,
2013. http://fox4kc.com/2013/11/29/airline-passenger-exchanges-notes
-gets-slapped-by-woman-he-considered-rude-to-flight-crew/.

Pippen v. NBC Universal Media, LLC. No. 13–1355. 134 S.Ct. 2829 (2014).

Posetti, Julie, and Alice Matthews. "A Short Guide to the History of 'Fake
News' and Disinformation: A Learning Module for Journalists and
Journalism Educators." International Center for Journalists, July 23,
2018. https://www.icfj.org/news/short-guide-history-fake-news-and
-disinformation-new-icfj-learning-module.

Reuters. "Nicki Minaj's Covid-19 Vaccine 'Swollen Testicles' Claim Is False,
says Trinidad Health Minister." CNN. September 16, 2021. https://www
.cnn.com/2021/09/16/americas/nicki-minaj-vaccine-story-false-scli-intl
/index.html.

Rodrigo, Chris Mills. "Critics Fear Facebook Fact-Checkers Losing Mis-information Fight." *The Hill*, January 20, 2020. https://thehill.com/policy/technology/478896-critics-fear-facebook-fact-checkers-losing-misinformation-fight.

Salmon, Felix, and Margaret Harding McGill. "YouTube Allows COVID Mis-information to Stay Up." *Axios*, October 7, 2021. https://www.axios.com/2021/10/07/youtube-allows-covid-misinformation-germany.

Shapiro, Emily. "Robert Durst Dies in Custody." *ABC News*, January 10, 2022. https://abcnews.go.com/US/robert-durst-dies-custody/story?id=82182614.

Shepard, Alicia C. "NPR's Giffords Mistake: Re-Learning the Lesson of Checking Sources." NPR Public Editor, January 11, 2011. https://www.npr.org/sections/publiceditor/2011/01/11/132812196/nprs-giffords-mistake-re-learning-the-lesson-of-checking-sources.

Shepard, Alicia C. "On Deep Background." *AJR*, December 1994.

Shontell, Alyson. "An Incredible Note-Passing War Broke Out on a Thanks-giving Day Flight and Things Escalated Quickly." *Business Insider*, November 29, 2013.

Showler and Davidson v. Harper's Magazine. No. 06–7001. U.S. App LEXIS 7025 (10th Cir. 2007).

Sense about Science. "Libel Reform Campaign." Accessed August 5, 2022. https://senseaboutscience.org/activities/libel-reform/.

Silverman, Craig. "A Year Later, False Reports of Rep. Giffords' Death Still Reverberate for the Press." *Poynter*, January 8, 2012. http://www.poynter.org/news/mediawire/158541/a-year-later-false-reports-of-rep-giffords-death-still-reverberate-for-the-press/.

Sonderman, Jeff. "CNN, Fox News Err in Covering Supreme Court Health Care Ruling." *Poynter*, June 28, 2012. http://www.poynter.org/news/mediawire/179144/how-journalists-are-covering-todays-scotus-health-care-ruling/.

Stern, Joanna. "Why Elan Gale Made Up an Epic 'Note War' on a Thanksgiv-ing Flight." *ABC News*, December 4, 2013.

Stockton, Nick. "The Times' Attack on Wearables Is an Attack on Science." *Wired*, March 18, 2015.

Straits Times. "Twitter Rejects Call to Remove Chinese Official's Fake Australian Troops Tweet." December 2, 2020. https://www.straitstimes.com/asia/australianz/new-zealand-raises-concerns-with-china-over-australian-soldier-image.

Thompson, Juan. "Retracted: Dylann Roof's Cousin Claims Love Interest Chose Black Man over Him." *Intercept*, June 18, 2005. https://theintercept

.com/2015/06/18/cousin-of-charleston-suspect-says-black-man-stole
-roofs-love-interest/.

Tierney, John. "How Facebook Uses 'Fact-Checking' to Suppress Scientific
Truth." *New York Post*, May 18, 2021. https://nypost.com/2021/05/18/how
-facebook-uses-fact-checking-to-suppress-scientific-truth/.

Twitter. "COVID-19 Misleading Information Policy." Accessed August 25, 2021. https://help.twitter.com/en/rules-and-policies/medical
-misinformation-policy.

Twitter. "COVID-19: Our Approach to Misleading Vaccine Information." Accessed August 25, 2021. https://blog.twitter.com/en_us/topics/company
/2020/covid19-vaccine.

Twitter. "Updates to Our Work on COVID-19 Vaccine Misinformation." Accessed August 25, 2021. https://blog.twitter.com/en_us/topics/company
/2021/updates-to-our-work-on-covid-19-vaccine-misinformation.

Twitter Public Policy (@Policy). " We're stepping up internal & external
efforts to protect the public conversation & help people find authoritative
health information on #Coronavirus / Covid-19." Twitter, May 4, 2020,
9:34 a.m. https://twitter.com/Policy/status/1235212091923013632?s=20.

U.K. Parliament. "Defamation Act." House of Commons, Session 2012–13.
Accessed August 26, 2021. https://bills.parliament.uk/bills/983.

U.S. Department of State. "Daniel Brooks Baer." Accessed March 22, 2015.
http://www.state.gov/r/pa/ei/biog/214014.htm.

U.S. Department of State. "Ground Rules for Interviewing State Department Officials." Accessed June 22, 2015. http://www.state.gov/r/pa/prs
/17191.htm.

Van Meter, Jonathan. "Waiting in the Wings." *Vogue*, September 2012.

Vetter, David. "YouTube Is Serving Up Climate Misinformation. This Top
Scientists Says Google Should Ban It." *Forbes*, December 7, 2021. https://
www.forbes.com/sites/davidrvetter/2021/12/07/youtube-is-serving-up
-climate-misinformation-this-top-scientist-says-google-should-ban-it
/?sh=6aac09dce365.

Vida, István Kornél. "The 'Great Moon Hoax' of 1835." *Hungarian Journal of
English and American Studies* 18, no 1/2 (Spring/Fall 2012): 431–41.

Vogue. "Editor's Note." October 2012.

Watts, Alan, and Louisa Robertson. "Defamation Act 2013: A Publisher's
Charter." Thomson Reuters Practical Law. Accessed June 30, 2022.
https://uk.practicallaw.thomsonreuters.com/6-530-5205.

YouTube. "COVID-19 Medical Misinformation Policy." Accessed January 6,
2022. https://support.google.com/youtube/answer/9891785?hl=en.

Zaleski, Luke. Interview with author, December 9, 2021.

Zarrell, Rachel. "This Epic Note-Passing War on a Delayed Flight Won Thanksgiving [Updated]." *BuzzFeed News*, November 28, 2013. http://www.buzzfeed.com/rachelzarrell/this-epic-note-passing-war-on-a-delayed-flight-wins-thanksgi#.lnW27BvZR.

Zerofsky, Elisabeth. "The Deep Pathology at the Heart of a Scandal at Der Spiegel." *New Yorker*, January 30, 2019. https://www.newyorker.com/news/dispatch/the-deep-pathology-at-the-heart-of-the-scandal-at-der-spiegel.

Zielinski, Sarah. "The Great Moon Hoax Was Simply a Sign of Its Time," *Smithsonian Magazine*, July 2. 2015. https://www.smithsonianmag.com/smithsonian-institution/great-moon-hoax-was-simply-sign-its-time-180955761/.

Zimmer, Carl. Email message to author, February 9, 2015.

Zimmer, Carl. Email message to author, August 26, 2021.

Zimmer, Carl. Interview with author, August 31, 2021.

CHAPTER TWO

Beers, Dan, dir. *Fact Checkers Unit (FCU)*. New York: Moxie Pictures, 2007.

Cotts, Cynthia. Email message to author, August 13, 2021.

Cotts, Cynthia. Interview with author, March 22, 2015.

Cummings, Corinne. Email message to author, August 26, 2021.

Cummings, Corinne. Interview with author, March 13, 2015.

Mailer, Norman. "Oswald in the U.S.S.R." *New Yorker*, April 10, 1995.

Mailer, Norman. *Oswald's Tale: An American Mystery*. New York: Random House, 1995.

Rolzhausen, Yvonne. Interview with author, March 3, 2015.

Rolzhausen, Yvonne. Interview with author, January 13, 2022.

Schiller, Lawrence. www.lawrenceschiller.com.

CHAPTER THREE

Abdoh, Salar. Interview with author, November 13, 2014.

Agish, Meral. Interview with author, February 10, 2015.

Aikins, Ross. Interview with author, February 2, 2015.

Alkon, Cheryl. Interview with author, January 22, 2015.

Alter, Alexandra. "It's a Fact: Mistakes Are Embarrassing the Publishing Industry." *New York Times*, September 22, 2019. https://www.nytimes.com/2019/09/22/business/publishing-books-errors.html.

Anguiano, Dani. "Robert Durst Charged with 1982 Murder of Wife Katherine Durst." *Guardian*, October 22, 2021. https://www.theguardian.com/us-news/2021/oct/22/robert-durst-charged-murder-1982-wife-kathie-durst.

Arratoon, Adrian. Interview with author, February 3, 2015.

Associated Press. "Robert Durst Has Been Indicted in the 1982 Murder of his Wife, Kathie Durst." NPR, November 1, 2021. https://www.npr.org/2021/11 /01/1051278966/robert-durst-indicted-1982-murder-wife-kathie.

Attar, Robert. Interview with author, February 13, 2015.

Bagley, Katherine. Interview with author, January 6, 2015.

Bagli, Charles. "As Durst Murder Case Goes Forward, HBO's Film Will Also Be on Trial." *New York Times*, April 24, 2019. https://www.nytimes.com /2019/04/24/arts/television/robert-durst-the-jinx.html.

Bagli, Charles. "Robert Durst Charged with 2nd-Degree Murder in His Wife's Disappearance." *New York Times*, November 1, 2021. https://www .nytimes.com/2021/11/01/nyregion/robert-durst-murder-charge.html.

Banta, John. Interview with author, March 19, 2015.

BBC News. "Covid: Twitter Suspends Naomi Wolf after Tweeting Anti-Vaccine Misinformation." June 6, 2021. https://www.bbc.com/news /world-us-canada-57374241.

Berger, Michele. Email message to author, March 18, 2015.

Bertsche, Rob. Email message to author, March 31, 2022.

Bertsche, Rob. Interview with author, March 25, 2015.

Borel, Brooke, Knvul Sheikh, Fatima Husain, Ashley Junger, Erin Biba, and Deborah Blum, and Bettina Urcuioli. "The State of Fact-Checking in Journalism." Knight Science Journalism Program at MIT, June 2018.

Bhatia, Rahul. Interview with author, February 3, 2015.

Blanton, Riley. Interview with author, March 5, 2015.

Bodin, Madeline. Interview with author, February 5, 2015.

Brooks, Jillian. Interview with author, February 4, 2015.

Canby, Peter, and Carolyn Kormann. Interview with author, November 3, 2014.

Cantwell, Maria. "Smith-Cantwell Amendment Lifting Abaya Requirement on American Servicewomen in Saudi Arabia Expected to Pass Senate Today." June 24, 2002. http://www.cantwell.senate.gov/public/index.cfm /press-releases?ID=f3a35aff-4283-4793-8372-3e777e882d42&.

CBSNews.com Staff. "Female Pilot Sues over Muslim Garb." *60 Minutes*, January 17, 2002.

Casarez, Jean. "New York Grand Jury Indicts Robert Durst on Murder Charge." CNN, November 1, 2021. https://www.cnn.com/2021/11/01/us /robert-durst-indicted-wife-murder-charge-new-york/index.html.

Chicago Manual of Style Online. "Manuscript Preparation, Copyediting, and Proofreading." Accessed June 22, 2015. http://www.chicagomanualofstyle .org/qanda/data/faq/topics/ManuscriptPreparation/faq0006.html.

Ciarrocca, Michelle. Email message to author, August 13, 2021.

Ciarrocca, Michelle. Interview with author, February 9, 2015.

Collazo, Julie Schwietert. Email message to author, February 8, 2015.

Condon, Emily. Interview with author, February 18, 2015.

Connett, David. "Naomi Wolf Banned from Twitter for Spreading Vaccine Myths." *Guardian*, June 5, 2021. https://www.theguardian.com/books/2021/jun/05/naomi-wolf-banned-twitter-spreading-vaccine-myths.

Conrad, Jennifer. Email message to author, February 18, 2015.

Cosier, Susan. Interview with author, January 15, 2015.

Cotts, Cynthia. Interview with author, March 22, 2015.

Cummings, Corinne. Interview with author, March 13, 2015.

D'Anastasio, Cecilia. Interview with author, March 9, 2015.

Dazell, Becky. Interview with author, February 3, 2015.

Dillow, Clay. Interview with author, January 6, 2015.

Discover Fact-Checking Guide (unpublished).

Dost, Stephen. Interview with author, March 10, 2015.

Economic Research Institute. "Editorial Fact Checker Salary." Accessed March 24, 2022. https://www.erieri.com/salary/job/editorial-fact-checker/united-states.

Editorial Freelancers Association. "Editorial Rates." Accessed January 3, 2022. https://www.the-efa.org/rates/.

Emig, Danielle. Interview with author, February 9, 2015.

Esteves, Bernando. Interview with author, February 4, 2015.

Finkbeiner, Ann. Interview with author, January 12, 2015.

Fishman, Boris. Interview with author, November 8, 2014.

Flood, Alison. "Naomi Wolf Accused of Confusing Child Abuse with Gay Persecution in Outrages." *Guardian*, February 8, 2021. https://www.theguardian.com/books/2021/feb/08/naomi-wolf-accused-of-confusing-child-abuse-with-gay-persecution-in-outrages.

George, Rose. Interview with author, February 17, 2015.

Giridharadas, Anand. "What to Do When You're a Country in Crisis." *New York Times*, May 17, 2019. https://www.nytimes.com/2019/05/17/books/review/upheaval-jared-diamond.html.

Greenberg, Julia. Interview with author, January 6, 2015.

Grotto, Jason. Interview with author, January 12, 2022.

Grunbaum, Mara. Interview with author, February 16, 2015.

Habte, Bethel. Interview with author, September 3, 2021.

Harris, Michelle. Interview with author, March 12, 2015.

Harris, Michelle. Interview with author, September 16, 2021.

Hermann, Todd, Paul Durbin, and Scott Wyerman. Interview with author, April 7, 2015.

Hogan, Beatrice. Interview with author, February 20, 2015.

Hunger, Bertolt. Email message to author, February 17, 2015.

International Documentary Association. "31st Annual IDA Documentary Awards Nominees & Winners" (2015). Accessed September 7, 2021. https://www.documentary.org/awards2015.

Jameson, Daniel. Interview with author, January 20, 2015.

Jones, Alice. Interview with author, February 3, 2015.

Kachka, Boris. "Will Book Publishers Ever Start Fact-Checking? They're Already Starting." *Vulture*, June 23, 2015. http://www.vulture.com/2015/06/will-book-publishers-ever-start-fact-checking.html#.

Kaufman, Dan. Interview with author, November 21, 2014.

Kiernan, Lousie. "Calculating the Work behind Our Work," ProPublica, December 29, 2017. https://www.propublica.org/article/calculating-the-work-behind-our-work.

Kormann, Carolyn. Email message to author, December 2, 2021.

Kralyevich, Vinnie. Interview with author, March 11, 2015.

Krieger, Emily. Email message to author, August 26, 2021.

Krieger, Emily. Interview with author, February 13, 2015.

Krieger, Emily. Interview with author, September 30, 2021.

Krogh, Ryan. Interview with author, March 5, 2015.

LaFrance, Adrienne. Interview with author, November 7, 2014.

Lee, Edmund, and Alexandra Alter. "After Plagiarism Claims, Ex-Times Editor Says Her Book ''Will Be Fixed.'" *New York Times*, February 7, 2019. https://www.nytimes.com/2019/02/07/business/media/jill-abramson-book-plagiarism.html.

Levitt, Aimee. Interview with author, February 4, 2015.

Li, David K., and Tim Fitzsimons. "Robert Durst Sentenced to Prison for 2000 Murder of Friend Susan Berman." *NBC News*, October 14, 2021. https://www.nbcnews.com/news/us-news/robert-durst-sentenced-life-prison-2000-murder-friend-susan-berman-n1281512.

Liguori, Rob. Interview with author, November 16, 2015.

Los Angeles County District Attorney's Office. "Robert Durst Convicted of Murdering Friend in 2000." September 17, 2021. https://da.lacounty.gov/media/news/robert-durst-convicted-murdering-friend-2000.

Maldonado, Cristina. Interview with author, February 6, 2015.

"Matthew Sweet Questions Key Evidence in Naomi Wolf's New Book." *BBC News*, June 14, 2019. https://www.bbc.com/news/av/world-us-canada-48639663.

McClusky, Mark. Interview with author, March 10, 2015.

McManus, Emily. Interview with author, February 18, 2015.

Mercado, Mia. "Naomi Wolf's Anti-Vaxx Tweets Just Got Her Account Suspended." *The Cut*, June 7, 2021. https://www.thecut.com/2021/06/naomi -wolfs-anti-vaxx-tweets-just-got-her-account-suspended.html.

Miguez, Luiza Machado. Interview with author, March 6, 2015.

Murano, Edgard. Interview with author, February 4, 2015.

Murphy, Kate. Interview with author, March 4, 2015.

Muselmann, Jacob. Interview with author, March 3, 2015.

Neary, Lynn. "Checking Facts in Nonfiction." *Weekend Edition*, June 8, 2019. https://www.npr.org/2019/06/08/730898366/checking-facts-in -nonfiction.

O'Donnell, Nora. Interview with author, April 1, 2015.

Oprah Winfrey Show. "Moment #18: Oprah Confronts James Frey" (2006). Accessed January 2, 2016. http://www.oprah.com/own-tv-guide -magazines-top-25-best-oprah-show-moments/Moment-18-Oprah -Confronts-James-Frey-Video.

Ornes, Stephen. Interview with author, February 5, 2015.

Palmer, Katie. Interview with author, January 9, 2015.

Palus, Shannon. Interview with author, January 6, 2015.

Pandell, Lexi. Interview with author, February 6, 2015.

Parker, Ashley. "Pioneering Combat Pilot Persists in Rise from Arizona." *New York Times*, March 30, 2015.

Parmar, Tekendra. Interview with author, March 16, 2021.

People v. Robert Durst (SA089983).

Poe, Charles. Interview with author, March 12, 2015.

Popular Science Fact-Checking Guide (unpublished).

Queally, James. "Robert Durst Indicted in New York in Death of His First Wife, Kathie." *Los Angeles Times*, November 1, 2021. https://www.latimes .com/california/story/2021-11-01/robert-durst-indicted-in-new-york-in -death-of-his-first-wife-kathie.

Rausch, Katherine. Interview with author, January 21, 2015.

Redden, Molly. Interview with author, January 27, 2015.

Reed, Jordan. Interview with author, February 20, 2015.

Reed, Susan. Interview with author, February 17, 2015.

Robb, Amanda. "A Fighter Pilot Takes the Fight to D.C." *More*, April 2015.

Rojas-Burke, Joe. Interview with author, February 11, 2015.

Rolzhausen, Yvonne. Interview with author, March 3, 2015.

Rolzhausen, Yvonne. Interview with author, January 13, 2022.

Rosolie, Paul. *Eaten Alive*. Discovery Channel, 2014.

Rubin, Deborah. Interview with author, February 17, 2015.

Ruiz, Matthew. Interview with author, January 26, 2015.

Schaefer, Maximilian. Interview with author, February 2, 2015.

Sehgal, Parul. "Naomi Wolf's Career of Blunders Continues in 'Outrages.'" *New York Times*, June 5, 2019. https://www.nytimes.com/2019/06/05/books/review-outrages-naomi-wolf.html.

Silverman, Craig. Interview with author, September 30, 2014.

Smoking Gun. "A Million Little Lies." January 8, 2006. http://www.thesmokinggun.com/documents/celebrity/million-little-lies.

Smusiak, Cara. Interview with author, February 10, 2015.

Southorn, Graham. Interview with author, January 28, 2015.

Stieb, Matt. "The Latest Bizarre Twists in the Robert Durst Murder Trial." *New York Magazine*, August 24, 2021. https://nymag.com/intelligencer/article/robert-durst-murder-trial-the-jinx.html.

Sweet, Matthew (@DrMatthewSweet). "Because my thoughts on @naomirwolf's @ViragoBooks Outrages are scattered in threads, and I'm being asked about details, I thought I would put them all in one place. Hope everyone thinks this is okay. You'll find our @BBCFreeThinking interview here." Twitter, May 23, 2019, 2:31 p.m. https://twitter.com/DrMatthewSweet/status/1131628734279294981.

Sweet, Matthew. "Blind to Bestiality and Pedophilia: Why Naomi Wolf's Latest Book Is Its Own Outrage." *Telegraph*, February 5, 2021. https://www.telegraph.co.uk/books/non-fiction/blind-bestiality-paedophilia-naomi-wolfs-latest-book-outrage/.

Television Academy. "The Jinx: The Life and Deaths of Robert Durst: Awards and Nominations" (2015). Accessed September 7, 2021. https://www.emmys.com/shows/jinx-life-and-deaths-robert-durst.

Peabody Awards. "The Jinx: The Life and Deaths of Robert Durst" (2015). Accessed September 7, 2021. https://peabodyawards.com/award-profile/the-jinx-the-life-and-deaths-of-robert-durst/.

Villani, Erika. Interview with author, February 10, 2015.

Voosen, Paul. Interview with author, February 2, 2015.

Wade, Lizzie. Interview with author, January 15, 2015.

Waldman, Jonathan. Interview with author, January 22, 2015.

Wiebe, Jamie. Interview with author, January 15, 2015.

Williams, Stacie. Interview with author, January 9, 2015.

Wojcicki, Ester. Interview with author, March 5, 2015.

Zaleski, Luke. Interview with author, March 4, 2015.

Zielinski, Sarah. Interview with author, February 3, 2015.

Zimmer, Carl. Email message to author, February 9, 2015.

Zorich, Zach. Interview with author, January 21, 2015.

Zweig, David. Interview with author, February 9, 2015.

CHAPTER FOUR

Abdoh, Salar. Interview with author, November 13, 2014.

Agish, Meral. Interview with author, February 10, 2015.

Aikins, Ross. Interview with author, February 2, 2015.

Alkon, Cheryl. Interview with author, January 22, 2015.

American Association for Public Opinion Research. "Survey Disclosure Checklist." Accessed March 23, 2022. https://www.aapor.org/Standards -Ethics/AAPOR-Code-of-Ethics/Survey-Disclosure-Checklist.aspx.

Arratoon, Adrian. Interview with author, February 3, 2015.

Associated Press. *Manual de Estilo.* http://www.manualdeestiloap.com/.

Attar, Robert. Interview with author, February 13, 2015.

Bagley, Katherine. Interview with author, January 6, 2015.

Baker, Allison. Interview with author, March 31, 2022.

Banta, John. Interview with author, March 19, 2015.

Berger, Michele. Email message to author, March 18, 2015.

Bertsche, Rob. Email message to author, March 31, 2022.

Bertsche, Rob. Interview with author, March 25, 2015.

Bhatia, Rahul. Interview with author, February 3, 2015.

Bissinger, Buzz. "Shattered Glass." *Vanity Fair,* September 1998.

Blanton, Riley. Email message to author, September 20, 2021.

Blanton, Riley. Interview with author, March 5, 2015.

Bodin, Madeline. Interview with author, February 5, 2015.

Borel, Brooke, Knvul Sheikh, Fatima Husain, Ashley Junger, Erin Biba, and Deborah Blum, and Bettina Urcuioli. "The State of Fact-Checking in Journalism." Knight Science Journalism Program at MIT, June 2018.

Boseley, Sarah. "Processed Meats Rank Alongside Smoking as Cancer Causes—WHO. " *Guardian,* October 26, 2015.

Brooks, Jillian. Interview with author, February 4, 2015.

Brookshire, Bethany. Email message to author, October 10, 2016.

Canby, Peter, and Carolyn Kormann. Interview with author, November 3, 2014.

Carman, Ashley. "Artificial Intelligence Might Eventually Write This Article. " *The Verge,* September 28, 2021. https://www.theverge.com/2021/9/28 /22696041/artificial-intelligence-ai-gpt-3-writer-podcast-vergecast.

Carpenter & Zuckermann. "Steve Glass." Accessed September 16, 2021. https://czrlaw.com/legal-team/steve-glass/.

Chokshi, Niraj. "As Amazon Fires Spread, So Do the Misleading Photos." *New York Times,* August 23, 2019. https://www.nytimes.com/2019/08/23 /world/americas/amazon-rainforest-fire-photos.html.

Ciarrocca, Michelle. Interview with author, February 9, 2015.

Collazo, Julie Schwietert. Email message to author, February 8, 2015.

Condon, Emily. Interview with author, February 18, 2015.

Conrad, Jennifer. Email message to author, February 18, 2015.

Cosier, Susan. Interview with author, January 15, 2015.

Cotts, Cynthia. Interview with author, March 22, 2015.

Cummings, Corinne. Interview with author, March 13, 2015.

D'Anastasio, Cecilia. Interview with author, March 9, 2015.

Dazell, Becky. Interview with author, February 3, 2015.

Der Spiegel. "The Relotius Case: Final Report of the Investigation Commission." [In German.] May 25, 2019. https://cdn.prod.www.spiegel.de/media/67c2c416-0001-0014-0000-000000044564/media-44564.pdf.

Dillow, Clay. Interview with author, January 6, 2015.

Discover Fact-Checking Guide (unpublished).

Dost, Stephen. Interview with author, March 10, 2015.

Editorial Freelancers Association. "Editorial Rates." Accessed December 3, 2021. https://www.the-efa.org/rates/.

Emig, Danielle. Interview with author, February 9, 2015.

Epstein, Reid. "Alaska Election Offers Two Chances to Vote for Dan Sullivan." *Wall Street Journal*, August 12, 2014.

Esteves, Bernando. Interview with author, February 4, 2015.

Fairbank, Viviane. Interview with author, March 31, 2022.

Farid, Hany. Interview with author, November 16, 2021.

Fichtner, Ullrich, "Der Spiegel Reveals Internal Fraud." *Spiegel International*, December 12, 2018. https://www.spiegel.de/international/zeitgeist/claas-relotius-reporter-forgery-scandal-a-1244755.html.

Finkbeiner, Ann. Interview with author, January 12, 2015.

Fishman, Boris. Interview with author, November 8, 2014.

FiveThirtyEight. "FiveThirtyEight's Pollster Ratings." March 25, 2021. https://projects.fivethirtyeight.com/pollster-ratings/.

Fortenbaugh, Robert. *The Nine Capitals of the United States*. New York: Maple Press, 1948. Available at http://www.senate.gov/reference/reference_item/Nine_Capitals_of_the_United_States.htm.

Franklin, Tim, and Bill Adair. Interview with author, October 30, 2015.

George, Rose. Interview with author, February 17, 2015.

Gholipour, Bahar. "New AI Tech Can Mimic Any Voice." *Scientific American*, May 2, 2017. https://www.scientificamerican.com/article/new-ai-tech-can-mimic-any-voice/.

Glass, Ira. "Mr. Daisey and the Apple Factory." *This American Life*, January 6, 2012. http://www.thisamericanlife.org/radio-archives/episode/454/mr-daisey-and-the-apple-factory.

Greenberg, Julia. Interview with author, January 6, 2015.

Grunbaum, Mara. Interview with author, February 16, 2015.

Harris, Michelle. Interview with author, March 12, 2015.

Harwell, Drew. "An Artificial-Intelligence First: Voice-Mimicking Software Reportedly Used in a Major Theft." *Washington Post*, September 4, 2019. https://www.washingtonpost.com/technology/2019/09/04/an-artificial -intelligence-first-voice-mimicking-software-reportedly-used-major -theft/.

Hermann, Todd, Paul Durbin, and Scott Wyerman. Interview with author, April 7, 2015.

Hogan, Beatrice. Interview with author, February 20, 2015.

Hough, Andrew. "CNN Sorry over Graphic Blunder That Uprooted London to Norfolk." *Telegraph*, February 3, 2012.

World Atlas. "How Many Countries Are in the World?" Accessed September 12, 2021. http://www.worldatlas.com/nations.htm.

Hunger, Bertolt. Email message to author, February 17, 2015.

Hunger, Bertolt. Email message to author, September 30, 2021.

Hurst, Phoebe. "Sorry Everyone, Bacon Could Be as Bad for You as Cigarettes." *Munchies*, October 23, 2015. http://munchies.vice.com/articles /sorry-everyone-bacon-could-be-as-bad-for-you-as-cigarettes.

In re Stephen Randall Glass on Admission, S196374 State Bar Ct., No. 09-M-11736 (Cal. Jan. 27, 2014).

International Agency for Research on Cancer. "Agents Classified by the IARC Monographs, Volumes 1–114." Accessed November 5, 2015. http:// monographs.iarc.fr/ENG/Classification/.

Irwig, Les, Judy Irwig, Lyndal Trevena, and Melissa Sweet. "Relative Risk, Relative and Absolute Risk Reduction, Number Needed to Treat and Confidence Intervals." In *Smart Health Choices: Making Sense of Health Advice*, 213–16. London: Hammersmith Press, 2008.

Jameson, Daniel. Interview with author, January 20, 2015.

Jones, Alice. Interview with author, February 3, 2015.

Jones-Rooy, Andrea. Interview with author, October 14, 2021.

Karras, Tero, Samuli Laine, and Timo Aila. "A Style-Based Generator Architecture for Generative Adversarial Networks." arXiv, March 29, 2019.

Kaufman, Dan. Interview with author, November 21, 2014.

Kennedy, Courtney. "What Are Non-Probability Surveys?" Pew Research Center, August 6, 2018. https://www.pewresearch.org/fact-tank/2018/08 /06/what-are-nonprobability-surveys/.

Kralyevich, Vinnie. Interview with author, March 11, 2015.

Krieger, Emily. Interview with author, February 13, 2015.

Krieger, Emily. Interview with author, September 30, 2021.

Krogh, Ryan. Interview with author, March 5, 2015.

Knight Science Journalism Program at MIT. KSJ Fact-Checking Project. Accessed December 3, 2021. https://ksjfactcheck.org/.

LaFrance, Adrienne. Interview with author, November 7, 2014.

Levitt, Aimee. Interview with author, February 4, 2015.

Liguori, Rob. Interview with author, November 16, 2015.

Lutz, Sebastian. Email message to author, November 16, 2021.

Macron, Emmanuel (@EmmanuelMacron). "Our house is burning. Literally. The Amazon rain forest - the lungs which produces 20% of our planet's oxygen - is on fire. It is an international crisis. Members of the G7 Summit, let's discuss this emergency first order in two days! #ActForTheAmazon." Twitter, August 22, 2019, 3:15 p.m. https://twitter .com/EmmanuelMacron/status/1164617008962527232.

Maldonado, Cristina. Interview with author, February 6, 2015.

Marchionni, Doreen, and Vinny Green. "Apology from Members of Snopes Senior Management." Snopes, August 13, 2021. https://www.snopes.com /2021/08/13/apology-from-senior-management/.

McClusky, Mark. Interview with author, March 10, 2015.

McIntyre, Loren. *Amazon Rain Forest Afire* (2003). Accessed September 20, 2021. https://www.alamy.com/stock-photo-amazon-rain-forest-afire -30695050.html.

McManus, Emily. Interview with author, February 18, 2015.

Mehta, Dhrumil. Interview with author, December 7, 2021.

Miguez, Luiza Machado. Interview with author, March 6, 2015.

Murano, Edgard. Interview with author, February 4, 2015.

Murphy, Kate. Interview with author, March 4, 2015.

Murphy, Mekado. "Werner Herzog Is Still Breaking the Rules." *New York Times*, July 1, 2007.

Muselmann, Jacob. Interview with author, March 3, 2015.

New York State Department of Environmental Conservation. "Freshwater Eel." Accessed June 22, 2015. http://www.dec.ny.gov/animals/85760.html.

Nightingale, Sophie, and Hany Farid. "AI-Synthesized Faces Are Indistin-guishable from Real Faces and More Trustworthy." *PNAS* 119, no. 8 (2022): e2120481119. https://www.pnas.org/doi/10.1073/pnas.2120481119.

O'Donnell, Nora. Interview with author, April 1, 2015.

Ornes, Stephen. Interview with author, February 5, 2015.

Palmer, Katie. Email message to author, November 30, 2021.

Palmer, Katie. Interview with author, January 9, 2015.

Palus, Shannon. Interview with author, January 6, 2015.

Pandell, Lexi. Interview with author, February 6, 2015.

Peiser, Jaclyn. "The Rise of the Robot Reporter." *New York Times*, February 5, 2019. https://www.nytimes.com/2019/02/05/business/media/artificial-intelligence-journalism-robots.html.

Pew Research Center. "Methods 101." Accessed December 29, 2021. https://www.youtube.com/playlist?list=PLZ9z-Af5ISavJpPlvdMU4T-etIDOUmldk.

Poe, Charles. Interview with author, March 12, 2015.

Popular Science Fact-Checking Guide (unpublished).

Rausch, Katherine. Interview with author, January 21, 2015.

Redden, Molly. Interview with author, January 27, 2015.

Reed, Jordan. Interview with author, February 20, 2015.

Reed, Susan. Interview with author, February 17, 2015.

Rennert. "Regional Variations in Spanish Words Translated from English." Accessed April 3, 2015. http://www.rennert.com/translations/resources/spanishvariations.htm.

Rojas-Burke, Joe. Interview with author, February 11, 2015.

Rolzhausen, Yvonne. Interview with author, March 3, 2015.

Rolzhausen, Yvonne. Interview with author, January 13, 2022.

Ronaldo, Cristiano (@Cristiano). "The Amazon Rainforest produces more than 20% of the world's oxygen and its been burning for the past 3 weeks. It's our responsibility to help to save our planet. #prayforamazonia." Twitter, August 22, 2019, 1:22 p.m. https://twitter.com/Cristiano/status/1164588606436106240.

Rosin, Hanna. "Hello, My Name Is Stephen Glass, and I'm Sorry." *New Republic*, November 10, 2014.

Rosin, Hanna. Interview with author, November 17, 2015.

Rubin, Deborah. Interview with author, February 17, 2015.

Ruiz, Matthew. Interview with author, January 26, 2015.

Salary Expert. "Editorial Fact-Checker." Economic Research Institute. Accessed December 3, 2021. https://www.salaryexpert.com/salary/job/editorial-fact-checker/united-states.

Sample, Ian. "What Are Deepfakes—and How Can You Spot Them?" *Guardian*. January 13, 2020. https://www.theguardian.com/technology/2020/jan/13/what-are-deepfakes-and-how-can-you-spot-them.

Schaefer, Maximilian. Interview with author, February 2, 2015.

Scriber, Brad. "Fact-Checking: How to Get Everything Perfectly Right Always." Presentation at the National Association of Science Writers, Cambridge, MA, October 2015.

Schroeck, Eric. "Fox News *Again* Mislabels Vermont as New Hampshire."
Media Matters, January 7, 2012.

Seabrook, John. "The Next Word: Where Will Predictive Language Take Us?"
New Yorker, October 14, 2019. https://www.newyorker.com/magazine
/2019/10/14/can-a-machine-learn-to-write-for-the-new-yorker.

Silverman, Craig. Interview with author, September 30, 2014.

Smusiak, Cara. Interview with author, February 10, 2015.

Somaiya, Ravi. "Stephen Glass Repays Harper's $10,000 for His Discredited
Work." *New York Times*, October 16, 2015.

Southorn, Graham. Interview with author, January 28, 2015.

Spiegelhalter, David. Email message to author, February 28, 2022.

Sterling Jones, Dean. "The Co-founder of Snopes Wrote Dozens of Plagiarized Articles for the Fact-Checking Site." *BuzzFeed News*, August 27,
2021. https://www.buzzfeednews.com/article/deansterlingjones/snopes
-cofounder-plagiarism-mikkelson.

This Person Does Not Exist. Accessed November 24, 2021. https://
thispersondoesnotexist.com/.

United Nations. "Who Are the Current Members of the United Nations?"
Accessed September 13, 2021. https://ask.un.org/faq/14345.

U. S. Census Bureau. "U.S. and World Population Clock." Accessed January 6,
2022. https://www.census.gov/popclock/.

U.S. Department of State. "Fact Sheet: Independent States in the World."
January 29, 2021. http://www.state.gov/s/inr/rls/4250.htm.

U.S. Fish and Wildlife Service. "American Eel." Accessed August 5, 2022.
https://ecos.fws.gov/ecp/species/7759.

U.S. Diplomatic Mission to Germany. "The Nation's Capital." Accessed July 1,
2022. https://usa.usembassy.de/government-capital.htm.

Vigen, Tyler. *Spurious Correlations*. Accessed July 1, 2022. http://www
.tylervigen.com/spurious-correlations.

Villani, Erika. Interview with author, February 10, 2015.

Vincent, James. "Tom Cruise Deepfake Creator Says Public Shouldn't Be
Worried about 'One-Click Fakes.'" *The Verge*, March 5, 2021. https://www
.theverge.com/2021/3/5/22314980/tom-cruise-deepfake-tiktok-videos-ai
-impersonator-chris-ume-miles-fisher.

Voosen, Paul. Interview with author, February 2, 2015.

Wade, Lizzie. Interview with author, January 15, 2015.

Waldman, Jonathan. Interview with author, January 22, 2015.

Warzel, Charlie. "I Used AI to Clone My Voice and Trick My Mom into
Thinking It Was Me." *BuzzFeed News*, August 27, 2018. https://www

.buzzfeednews.com/article/charliewarzel/i-used-ai-to-clone-my-voice -and-trick-my-mom-into-thinking.

Weinberg, Abigail. "The Three Most Viral Photos of the Amazon Fire Are Fake. Here Are Some Real Ones to Share." *Mother Jones*, August 26, 2019. https://www.motherjones.com/politics/2019/08/amazon-viral-fire -photos-fake-misleading-leonardo-dicaprio/.

Wiebe, Jamie. Interview with author, January 15, 2015.

Williams, Stacie. Interview with author, January 9, 2015.

Wohlsen, Marcus. "Inside Dropbox's Quest to Bury the Hard Drive." *Wired*, September 17, 2013.

Wojcicki, Ester. Interview with author, March 5, 2015.

Yong, Ed. "Beefing with the World Health Organization's Cancer Warnings." *Atlantic*, October 26, 2015.

"You Won't Believe What Obama Says in This Video!" *BuzzFeedVideo*, April 17, 2018. https://www.youtube.com/watch?v=cQ54GDm1eLo.

Zaleski, Luke. Interview with author, March 4, 2015.

Zerofsky, Elisabeth. "The Deep Pathology at the Heart of a Scandal at Der Spiegel." *New Yorker*, January 30, 2019. https://www.newyorker.com /news/dispatch/the-deep-pathology-at-the-heart-of-the-scandal-at-der -spiegel.

Zielinski, Sarah. Interview with author, February 3, 2015.

Zimmer, Carl. Email message to author, February 9, 2015.

Zorich, Zach. Interview with author, January 21, 2015.

Zweig, David. Interview with author, February 9, 2015.

CHAPTER FIVE

ABC Media Watch (Australia). "Fury at the Mail." November 5, 2018. https:// www.abc.net.au/mediawatch/episodes/daily-mail/10465244.

arXiv. Accessed September 20, 2021. https://arxiv.org/.

Bartholomew, Robert. "Science for Sale: The Rise of Predatory Journals." *Journal of the Royal Society of Medicine* 107, no. 10 (October 2014): 384–85.

Beall, Jeffrey. "Beall's List: Potential, Possible, or Probable Predatory Scholarly Open-Access Publishers." *Scholarly Open Access*, November 5, 2015.

Beall, Jeffrey. Email message to author, September 24, 2021.

Beall's List of Potential Predatory Journals and Publishers. Accessed September 20, 2021. https://beallslist.net/.

Benedikt, Allison, and Hanna Rosin. "The Missing Men," *Slate*, December 2, 2014. http://www.slate.com/articles/double_x/doublex/2014/12/sabrina _rubin_erdely_uva_why_didn_t_a_rolling_stone_writer_talk_to_the _alleged.html.

Benker, Christian, Richard P. Langford, and Terry L. Pavlis. "Positional Accuracy of the Google Earth Terrain Model Derived from Stratigraphic Unconformities in the Big Bend Region, Texas, USA." *Geocarto International* 26, no 4. (2011): 291–303.

bioRxiv. "What Is an Unrefereed Preprint?" Accessed September 20, 2021. https://www.biorxiv.org/content/what-unrefereed-preprint.

Blanton, Riley. Email message to author, August 16, 2021.

Blanton, Riley. Interview with author, March 5, 2015.

Brezgov, Stef. "List of Publishers." *Scholarly Open Access*, May 27, 2019. http://scholarlyoa.com/publishers/.

Burri, Margaret. Email message to author, February 23, 2022.

Canby, Peter. Interview with author, November 3, 2014.

Clark, Jocalyn. "How to Avoid Predatory Journals—a Five Point Plan." *BMJ*, January 19, 2015. http://blogs.bmj.com/bmj/2015/01/19/jocalyn-clark-how-to-avoid-predatory-journals-a-five-point-plan/.

Cornell University Library. "Evaluating Web Pages: Questions to Consider: Categories." Accessed June 23, 2015. http://guides.library.cornell.edu/evaluating_Web_pages.

Cornell University Library. "Fake News, Propaganda, and Disinformation: Learning to Critically Evaluate Media Sources: What is Fake News?" Accessed September 20, 2021. https://guides.library.cornell.edu/evaluate_news.

Coronel, Sheila, Steve Coll, and Derek Kravitz. "How Columbia Journalism School Conducted This Investigation." *Columbia Journalism Review*, April 5, 2015.

Coronel, Sheila, Steve Coll, and Derek Kravitz. "*Rolling Stone* and UVA: The Columbia University Graduate School of Journalism Report." *Rolling Stone*, April 5, 2015.

Coronel, Sheila, Steve Coll, and Derek Kravitz. "*Rolling Stone*'s Investigation: 'A Failure That Was Avoidable.'" *Columbia Journalism Review*, April 5, 2015.

Cotts, Cynthia. Interview with author, March 22, 2015.

Duke University Writing Studio. "How to Read and Review a Scientific Journal Article: Writing Summaries and Critiques." Accessed June 23, 2015. http://twp.duke.edu/uploads/media_items/scientificarticlereview.original.pdf.

Editors. "How to Survive 10 Nightmare Scenarios." *Outside*, November 6, 2007.

Elias et al. v. Rolling Stone, LLC et al., Case No. 15-CV-5953 (P.K.C.) United States District Court, S.D. New York (decided June 28, 2016).

Elias v. Rolling Stone LLC, No. 16–2465 (2d Cir. 2017).

Ember, Sydney. "Rolling Stone to Pay $1.65 Million to Fraternity Over Discredited Rape Story." *New York Times*, June 13, 2017. https://www.nytimes.com/2017/06/13/business/media/rape-uva-rolling-stone-frat.html.

Emig, Danielle. Interview with author, February 9, 2015.

Finkel, Michael. "Is Youssouf Malé a Slave?" *New York Times Magazine*, November 18, 2001.

Finkel, Michael. "The Strange and Curious Tale of the Last True Hermit." *GQ*, September 2014.

Gardner, Eriq. "Rolling Stone Settles Last Remaining Lawsuit over UVA Rape Story." *Hollywood Reporter*, December 21, 2017. https://www.hollywoodreporter.com/business/business-news/rolling-stone-settles-last-remaining-lawsuit-uva-rape-story-1069880/.

Getty Research Institute. Accessed July 1, 2022. getty.edu/research.

Google Maps Help. "Find & Improve Your Location's Accuracy." Accessed July 1, 2022. https://support.google.com/maps/answer/2839911?hl=en&co=GENIE.Platform%3DAndroid#:~:text=GPS%3A%20Maps%20uses%20satellites%20to,to%20a%20few%20thousand%20meters.

Google Scholar. Accessed July 1, 2022. https://scholar.google.com/.

Google Search Help. "How to Search on Google." Accessed June 23, 2015. https://support.google.com/websearch/answer/134479?hl=en.

Grudniewicz, Agnes. "Predatory Journals: No Definition, No Defense." *Nature*, December 11, 2019. https://www.nature.com/articles/d41586-019-03759-y.

Grunbaum, Mara. Interview with author, February 16, 2015.

Haag, Matthew. "Rolling Stone Settles Lawsuit over Debunked Campus Rape Article." *New York Times*, April 11, 2017. https://www.nytimes.com/2017/04/11/business/media/rolling-stone-university-virginia-rape-story-settlement.html.

Hermann, Todd. Email message to author, August 31, 2021.

Hermann, Todd, Paul Durbin, and Scott Wyerman. Interview with author, April 7, 2015.

Jones, Tom. "What Does 'Off the Record' Mean? The Latest Journalism Controversy." *Poynter*. September 20, 2021. https://www.poynter.org/commentary/2021/what-does-off-the-record-mean-the-latest-journalism-controversy/.

JSTOR. Accessed July 1, 2022. http://www.jstor.org/.

Kapoun, Jim. "Teaching Undergrads WEB Evaluation: A Guide for Library Instruction." *College & Research Libraries News*, July/August 1998.

Kinkela, David. *DDT and the American Century: Global Health, Environ-*

mental Politics, and the Pesticide That Changed the World. Chapel Hill: University of North Carolina Press, 2011.

Kolata, Gina. "For Scientists, an Exploding World of Pseudo-Academia." *New York Times*, April 7, 2013.

Krogh, Ryan. Interview with author, March 5, 2015.

Lurie, Peter, Harinder S. Chahal, Daniel W. Sigelman, Sylvie Stacy, Joshua Sclar, and Barbara Ddamulira. "Comparison of Content of FDA Letters Not Approving Applications for New Drugs and Associated Public Announcements from Sponsors: Cross Sectional Study." *BMJ*, April 8, 2015. http://www.bmj.com/content/350/bmj.h2758.

Merriam-Webster. "The Real Story of 'Fake News.'" Words We're Watching. Accessed September 20, 2021. https://www.merriam-webster.com/words -at-play/the-real-story-of-fake-news.

Merriam-Webster's Geographical Dictionary. 3rd ed. Springfield, MA: Merriam-Webster, 2007.

Miller, Greg. "The Secret of Google Maps' Accuracy Revealed." *Wired*, September 12, 2014. https://www.wired.co.uk/article/google-maps.

Mohammed, Nagi Zomrawi, Ahmed Ghazi, and Hussam Eldin Mustafa. "Positional Accuracy Testing of Google Earth." *International Journal of Multidisciplinary Sciences and Engineering* 4, no. 6 (2013): 6–9.

Nicole P. Eramo v. Rolling Stone, LLC, et al., Civil Action No. 3:15-CV-00023, United States District Court, W.D. Virginia, Charlottesville Division (Partial Summary Judgment decided Sept. 22, 2016).

Nijhuis, Michelle. "The Pocket Guide to Bullshit Prevention." *The Last Word on Nothing*, April 29, 2014. http://lastwordonnothing.com/2014/04/29 /the-pocket-guide-to-bullshit-prevention.

NPR. "Anonymous Sourcing." In *NPR Ethics Handbook.* Accessed June 23, 2015. http://ethics.npr.org/tag/anonymity/.

Open Access at Manchester. "Advice on Predatory Journals and Publishers." Accessed June 23, 2015. http://www.openaccess.manchester.ac.uk /checkjournal/predatoryjournals/.

Ornes, Stephen. Email message to author, September 27, 2021.

Ornes, Stephen. Interview with author, February 5, 2015.

Ornes, Stephen. "The Nobel Thieves." *Discover*, June 2007.

Penenberg, Adam. *NYU Journalism Handbook for Students: Ethics, Law and Good Practice.* Accessed April 9, 2015. http://journalism.nyu.edu /publishing/ethics-handbook/human-sources/.

Phi Kappa Psi v. Rolling Stone, et al., Demurrer. Virginia Circuit, Sixteenth Judicial Court File No. CL15-479; Hearing May 17, 2016, Letter Decision by Judge Richard E. Moore, issued August 31, 2016.

PLOS. "Preprints." Accessed September 20, 2021. https://plos.org/open-science/preprints/.

Potere, David. "Horizontal Positional Accuracy of Google Earth's High-Resolution Imagery Archive." *Sensors* (Basel) 8, no. 12. (2008): 7973–7981.

PubMed Help. Accessed September 20, 2021. http://www.ncbi.nlm.nih.gov/books/NBK3827/#pubmedhelp.PubMed_Quick_Start.

PubMed. Accessed September 20, 2021. http://www.ncbi.nlm.nih.gov/pubmed.

Purdue University Libraries. "How to Read a Scientific Paper." Accessed June 23, 2015. https://www.lib.purdue.edu/help/tutorials/scientific-paper.

Purugganan, Mary, and Jan Hewitt. "How to Read a Scientific Article." Cain Project in Engineering and Professional Communication. Accessed June 3, 2015. http://www.owlnet.rice.edu/~cainproj/courses/HowToReadSciArticle.pdf.

Rezzouqi, Hajar, Ihsane Gryech, Nada Sbihi, Mounir Ghogho, and Houda Benbrahim. "Analyzing the Accuracy of Historical Average for Urban Traffic Forecasting Using Google Maps." *Proceedings of SAI Intelligent Systems Conference* (2018): 1145–56.

Roberts, Donald, and Richard Tren. *The Excellent Powder: DDT's Political and Scientific History.* Indianapolis: Dog Ear Publishing, 2010.

Rolling Stone. "A Note to Our Readers." December 5, 2014.

Shapiro, T. Rees. "Jury Awards $3 million in Damages to U-Va. Deal for Rolling Stone Defamation." *Washington Post*, November 7, 2016. https://www.washingtonpost.com/local/education/jury-to-deliberate-damages-to-u-va-dean-in-rolling-stone-defamation-lawsuit/2016/11/07/e2aa2eb0-a506-11e6-ba59-a7d93165c6d4_story.html?utm_term=.5eed76a2f6d8.

Shapiro, T. Rees. "Federal Judge Dismisses U-Va. Fraternity Members' Defamation Lawsuit against Rolling Stone." *New York Times*, June 29, 2016. https://www.washingtonpost.com/news/grade-point/wp/2016/06/29/federal-judge-dismisses-u-va-fraternity-members-defamation-lawsuit-against-rolling-stone/.

Shapiro, T. Rees, and Emma Brown. "Rolling Stone Settles with Former U-Va. Dean in Defamation Case." *Washington Post*, April 11, 2017. https://www.washingtonpost.com/local/education/rolling-stone-settles-with-u-va-dean-in-defamation-case/2017/04/11/5a564532-1f02-11e7-be2a-3a1fb24d4671_story.html.

Sheldon, Tom. "Preprints Could Promote Confusion and Distortion." *Nature*, July 24, 2018. https://www.nature.com/articles/d41586-018-05789-4.

Siegel, Robert. "Reading Scientific Papers." The Vaccine Revolutions (course of study). Accessed June 23, 2015. http://web.stanford.edu/~siegelr /readingsci.htm.

Spencer, Hawes, and Ben Sisario. "In Rolling Stone Defamation Case, Magazine and Reporter Ordered to Pay $3 million." *New York Times*, November 7, 2016. https://www.nytimes.com/2016/11/08/business/media/in -rolling-stone-defamation-case-magazine-and-reporter-ordered-to-pay -3-million.html.

Stanford Graduate School of Education. "Sam Wineburg." Accessed May 3, 2022. https://ed.stanford.edu/faculty/wineburg.

Statista. "Leading Daily Newspapers in the United States in September 2017 and January 2019, by Circulation." Accessed September 20, 2021. https://www.statista.com/statistics/184682/us-daily-newspapers-by -circulation/.

Sumner, Petroc, Solveiga Vivian-Griffiths, Jacky Boivin, Andy Williams, Christos A. Venetis, Aimée Davies, Jack Ogden et al. "The Association between Exaggeration in Health Related Science News and Academic Press Releases: Retrospective Observational Study," *BMJ*, December 10, 2014. http://www.bmj.com/content/349/bmj.g7015.

Sutherland, William, Solveiga Vivian-Griffiths, Jacky Boivin, Andy Williams, Christos A. Venetis, Aimée Davies, Jack Ogden et al. "Policy: Twenty Tips for Interpreting Scientific Claims." *Nature*, November 20, 2013.

Tennant, Jonathan, Laurent Gatto, Corina Logan. "Preprints Help Journalism, Not Hinder It." *Nature*, August 29, 2018. https://www.nature.com /articles/d41586-018-06055-3.

Muck Rack. "Top 50 Newspapers in the U.S." Accessed September 20, 2021. https://muckrack.com/rankings/top-50-us-newspapers.

University of Maryland Libraries. "Evaluating Web Sites: A Checklist." Accessed June 23, 2015. http://www.lib.umd.edu/binaries/content/assets /public/usereducation/evaluating-web-sites-checklist-form.pdf.

University of Michigan Library. "What Is 'Fake News'?" Accessed September 20, 2021. https://guides.lib.umich.edu/fakenews.

University of Washington Information School. "Mike Caulfield." Accessed May 3, 2022. https://ischool.uw.edu/people/faculty/profile/mica42.

U.S. Board on Geographic Names. Accessed June 23, 2015. http://geonames .usgs.gov/.

Victor, Daniel. "Former University of Virginia Fraternity Members Sue Rolling Stone." *New York Times*, July 29, 2015.

Virginia Magazine. "Rolling Stone Settles with Phi Kappa Psi." Accessed September 20, 2021. https://uvamagazine.org/articles/rolling_stone_settles _with_phi_kappa_psi.

Warzel, Charlie. "Don't Go Down the Rabbit Hole." *New York Times*, February 18, 2022. https://www.nytimes.com/2021/02/18/opinion/fake-news-media-attention.html.

Wemple, Erik. "The Full Demise of Rolling Stone's Rape Story." *Washington Post*, December 11, 2014.

Writing@CSU. "Writing the Scientific Paper." Colorado State University. Accessed June 23, 2015. https://writing.colostate.edu/guides/guide.cfm?guideid=83.

Wurster, Charles F. *DDT Wars: Rescuing Our National Bird, Preventing Cancer, and Creating the Environmental Defense Fund.* New York: Oxford University Press, 2015.

CHAPTER SIX

Dropbox. Accessed July 1, 2022. https://www.dropbox.com/.

Fact-checker and researcher interviews with author.

Google Search Help. "View Web Pages Cached in Google Search Results." Accessed January 7, 2022. https://support.google.com/websearch/answer/1687222?hl=en.

Hightail. Accessed July 1, 2022. https://www.hightail.com/.

Internet Archive Wayback Machine. Accessed July 1, 2022. https://archive.org/web/.

Overview Docs. Accessed July 1, 2022. https://help.overviewdocs.com/.

Oxford Dictionaries. S.v. "stet." Accessed June 23, 2015. https://www.lexico.com/en/definition/stet.

CHAPTER SEVEN AND APPENDIX ONE ANSWER KEY

Borel, Brooke. "The Scientist Pot Farmer: On the Hunt for Safe Cannabis Agriculture." *Undark*, April 7, 2016.

KSJ Fact-Checking Project. "Teaching Materials." Accessed September 22, 2021. https://ksjfactcheck.org/fact-checking-101.

CONCLUSION

Adair, Bill, and Mark Stencel. "A Lesson in Automated Journalism: Bring Back the Humans." Nieman Lab, July 29, 2020. https://www.niemanlab.org/2020/07/a-lesson-in-automated-journalism-bring-back-the-humans/.

Alcindor, Yamiche. "Anti-Vaccine Movement Is Giving Diseases a 2nd Life." *USA Today*, April 6, 2014. https://www.usatoday.com/story/news/nation/2014/04/06/anti-vaccine-movement-is-giving-diseases-a-2nd-life/7007955/.

Alexa Report on Snopes.com. Accessed June 24, 2015. http://www.alexa.com/siteinfo/snopes.com (site discontinued).

Anderson, Janna, and Lee Rainie. "The Metaverse in 2040." Pew Research Center, June 30, 2022. https://www.pewresearch.org/internet/2022/06/30/the-metaverse-in-2040/.

Antiviral: Here Is What's Bullshit on the Internet This Week (column). *Gawker*. Accessed July 1, 2022. https://www.gawker.com/antiviral-here-is-whats-bullshit-on-the-internet-this-1505902054.

Basu, Tanya. "Meta Is Desperately Trying to Make the Metaverse Happen." *MIT Technology Review*, October 11, 2022. https://www.technologyreview.com/2022/10/11/1061144/metaverse-announcements-meta-connect-legs/.

Bilton, Nick. "Social Media Bots Offer Phony Friends and Real Profit." *New York Times*, November 19, 2014. https://www.nytimes.com/2014/11/20/fashion/social-media-bots-offer-phony-friends-and-real-profit.html.

Bock Clark, Doug. "The Bot Bubble." *New Republic*, April 20, 2015. https://newrepublic.com/article/121551/bot-bubble-click-farms-have-inflated-social-media-currency.

Borel, Brooke. "Can AI Solve the Internet's Fake News Problem? A Fact-Checker Investigates." *Popular Science*, March 20, 2018. https://www.popsci.com/can-artificial-intelligence-solve-internets-fake-news-problem/.

Chen, Adrian. "The Agency." *New York Times*, June 2, 2015. https://www.nytimes.com/2015/06/07/magazine/the-agency.html.

Civil. Accessed July 1, 2022. https://civil.co/ (site discontinued).

Coalition for Content Provenance and Authenticity. Accessed July 1, 2022. https://c2pa.org/.

Cosentino, Gabriele. "From Pizzagate to the Great Replacement: The Globalization of Conspiracy Theories." In *Social Media and the Post-Truth World Order*, 59–86. Cham, Switzerland: Palgrave Pivot, 2020. Available at https://link.springer.com/chapter/10.1007/978-3-030-43005-4_3.

@deeptomcruise. TikTok. Accessed July 1, 2022. https://www.tiktok.com/@deeptomcruise?.

Dewey, Caitlin. What Was Fake on the Internet This Week. WashingtonPost.com (column discontinued).

DiMaggio, Anthony R. "Conspiracy Theories and the Manufacture of Dissent: QAnon, the 'Big Lie,' Covid-19, and the Rise of Rightwing Propaganda." *Critical Sociology* (January 2022). https://journals.sagepub.com/doi/abs/10.1177/08969205211073669.

Emergent. Accessed July 1, 2022. http://www.emergent.info/.

Eordogh, Fruzsina. "Inside an Instagram Bot Farm." *Motherboard*, August 10, 2015. https://www.vice.com/en/article/4x3zy9/inside-an-instagram-bot-farm.

FactCheck.org. Accessed July 1, 2022. http://www.factcheck.org/.

Factmata. Accessed July 1, 2022. https://factmata.com/.

Farid, Hany. Interview with author, November 16, 2021.

Franklin, Tim, and Bill Adair. Interview with author, October 30, 2015.

Frenkel, Sheera, and Kellen Browning. "The Metaverse's Dark Side: Here Comes Harassment and Assaults." *New York Times*, December 30, 2021. https://www.nytimes.com/2021/12/30/technology/metaverse-harassment-assaults.html.

Haberman, Maggie, and Jonathan Martin. "Trump Once Said the 'Access Hollywood' Tape Was Real. Now He's Not Sure." *New York Times*, November 28, 2017. https://www.nytimes.com/2017/11/28/us/politics/trump-access-hollywood-tape.html.

Hare, Kristen. "Poynter Names Director and Editor for New International Fact-Checking Network." *Poynter*, September 21, 2015. https://www.poynter.org/reporting-editing/2015/poynter-names-director-and-editor-for-new-international-fact-checking-network/.

Harrison, Ellie. "Shockingly Realistic Tom Cruise Deepfakes Go Viral on TikTok." *Independent*, February 26, 2021. https://www.independent.co.uk/arts-entertainment/films/news/tom-cruise-deepfake-tiktok-video-b1808000.html.

Hill, Kashmir. "This Is Life in the Metaverse." *New York Times*, October 7, 2022. https://www.nytimes.com/2022/10/07/technology/metaverse-facebook-horizon-worlds.html.

Imhoff, Roland, Felix Zimmer, Olivier Klein, João H. C. António, Maria Babinska, Adrian Bangerter, Michal Bilewicz et al. "Conspiracy Mentality and Political Orientation Across 26 Countries." *Nature* 6 (2022): 392–403. https://www.nature.com/articles/s41562-021-01258-7.

Ivancsics, Bernat. "Blockchain in Journalism." Tow Center for Digital Journalism, January 25, 2019. https://www.cjr.org/tow_center_reports/blockchain-in-journalism.php.

Kollipara, Puneet. "How the Anti-Vaccine Movement Is Endangering Lives." *Washington Post*, May 5, 2014. https://www.washingtonpost.com/news/wonk/wp/2014/05/05/how-the-anti-vaccine-movement-is-endangering-lives/.

LaFrance, Adrienne. Interview with author, December 1, 2021.

Lee, Dave. "The Tactics of a Russian Troll Farm" *BBC News*, February 16, 2018. https://www.bbc.com/news/technology-43093390.

Levin, Sam. "Facebook Promised to Tackle Fake News. But the Evidence Shows It's Not Working." *Guardian*, May 16, 2017. https://www.theguardian.com/technology/2017/may/16/facebook-fake-news-tools-not-working.

Marchionni, Doreen, and Vinny Green. Apology from Members of Snopes Senior Management." Snopes, August 13, 2021. https://www.snopes.com/2021/08/13/apology-from-senior-management/.

Makuch, Ben. "How Those Viral Tom Cruise Deepfakes Were Made." *Vice*, March 19, 2021. https://www.vice.com/en/article/xgzb9d/how-those-viral-tom-cruise-deepfakes-were-made.

McCammon, Sarah. "How Religion, Education, Race and Media Consumption Shape Conspiracy Theory Beliefts." NPR, May 27, 2021. https://www.npr.org/2021/05/27/1000865185/how-religion-education-race-and-media-consumption-shape-conspiracy-theory-belief.

McDonough, Meghan. "Artificial Intelligence Is Now Shockingly Good at Sounding Human." *Scientific American*, December 9, 2020. https://www.scientificamerican.com/video/artificial-intelligence-is-now-shockingly-good-at-sounding-human/.

Meta. Accessed July 1, 2022. https://about.facebook.com/meta/.

Metaphysic (AI creators). Accessed July 1, 2022. https://metaphysic.ai/.

Metz, Cade. "Everybody into the Metaverse! Virtual Reality Beckons Big Tech." *New York Times*, December 30, 2021. https://www.nytimes.com/2021/12/30/technology/metaverse-virtual-reality-big-tech.html.

Metz, Rachel. "How a Deepfake Tom Cruise on TikTok Turned into a Very Real AI Company." CNN, August 6, 2021. https://www.cnn.com/2021/08/06/tech/tom-cruise-deepfake-tiktok-company/index.html.

Meyer, Robinson. "Only You Can Stop Facebook Hoaxes." *Atlantic*, January 22, 2015.

Mikkelson, David. Interview with author, March 5, 2015.

Mooney, Chris. "The Huge Implications of Google's Idea to Rank Sites Based on Their Accuracy." *Washington Post*, March 11, 2015.

Ohlheiser, Abby. "Twitter's Ban Almost Doubled Attention for Biden Story." *MIT Technology Review*, October 16, 2020. https://www.technologyreview.com/2020/10/16/1010644/twitter-ban-hunter-biden-emails-backfires/.

Oremus, Will. "Facebook Is Cracking Down on Viral Hoaxes. Really." *Slate*, January 20, 2015. http://www.slate.com/blogs/future_tense/2015/01/20/facebook_hoaxes_news_feed_changes_will_limit_false_news_stories.html.

Ovis. Accessed July 1, 2022. https://www.ovisnews.com/.

Owens, Erich, and Udi Weinsberg. "Showing Fewer Hoaxes." Facebook

Newsroom, January 20, 2015. http://newsroom.fb.com/news/2015/01 /news-feed-fyi-showing-fewer-hoaxes/.

Park, Sunkyu, Jaime Yejean Park, Jeong-Han Kang, and Meeyoung Cha. "The Presence of Unexpected Bias in Online Fact-Checking." *HKS Misinformation Review*, January 27, 2021. https://misinforeview.hks.harvard.edu /article/the-presence-of-unexpected-biases-in-online-fact-checking/.

Perez, Chris. "Justin Bieber Saves Man from Bear Attack." *New York Post*, August 5, 2014. https://nypost.com/2014/08/05/justin-bieber-saves-man -from-bear-attack/.

PolitiFact. Accessed July 1, 2022. http://www.politifact.com/.

Ravenscraft, Eric. "What Is the Metaverse, Exactly?" *Wired*, November 25, 2021. https://www.wired.com/story/what-is-the-metaverse/.

Roy, Jessica. "Rapper B.o.B. says the Earth Is Flat; Neil deGrasse Tyson Drops Diss Track in Response." *Los Angeles Times*, January 26, 2016. https://www.latimes.com/science/sciencenow/la-sci-sn-flat-earth-bob -diss-track-20160126-story.html.

SciCheck. Accessed July 1, 2022. http://www.factcheck.org/scicheck/.

Silverman, Craig. "Bear Attack Foiled by Justin Bieber's Music: A Story Too Good to Check." *Poynter*, August 8, 2014. https://www.poynter.org /reporting-editing/2014/bear-attack-foiled-by-justin-biebers-music-a -story-too-good-to-check/.

Silverman, Craig. Interview with author, September 30, 2014.

Silverman, Craig, Craig Timberg, Jeff Kao, and Jeremy B. Merrill. "Facebook Hosted Surge of Misinformation and Insurrection Threats in Months Leading Up to Jan. 6 Attack, Records Show." ProPublica and the *Washington Post*, January 4, 2022. https://www.propublica.org/article/facebook -hosted-surge-of-misinformation-and-insurrection-threats-in-months -leading-up-to-jan-6-attack-records-show.

Snopes. Accessed July 1, 2022. http://snopes.com/.

Stecula, Dominik, and Mark Pickup. "How Populism and Conservative Media Fuel Conspiracy Beliefs about COVID-19 and What It Means for COVID-19 Behaviors." *Research & Politics* 8, no. 1 (2021). https://journals .sagepub.com/doi/full/10.1177/2053168021993979.

Sterling Jones, Dean. "The Co-founder of Snopes Wrote Dozens of Plagiarized Articles for the Fact-Checking Site." *BuzzFeed News*, August 27, 2021. https://www.buzzfeednews.com/article/deansterlingjones/snopes -cofounder-plagiarism-mikkelson.

Tech & Check Cooperative. Duke Reporter's Lab. Accessed July 1, 2022. https://reporterslab.org/tech-and-check/.

Thornhill, Ted. "Finally, Proof that Justin Bieber IS Unbearable: Russian Fisherman Saved from Bear Attack When Ringtone Featuring One of the Pop Brat's Songs Scares It Away." *Daily Mail*, August 5, 2014. https://www.dailymail.co.uk/news/article-2716479/Fisherman-saved-bear-attack-Justin-Bieber-ringtone-went-mauled-scared-bear-away.html.

YouTube. "Very Realistic Tom Cruise Deepfake | AI Tom Cruise." Uploaded February 28, 2021. https://www.youtube.com/watch?v=iyiOVUbsPcM.

Vingiano, Ali. "A Russian Guy Says His Justin Bieber Ringtone Saved Him from a Bear Attack." *BuzzFeed News*, August 6, 2014. https://www.buzzfeednews.com/article/alisonvingiano/this-man-says-his-justin-bieber-ringtone-saved-him-from-a-be.

Wakefield, Jane. "Facebook's Fake News Experiment Backfires." *BBC News*. November 7, 2017. https://www.bbc.com/news/technology-41900877.

Walker, John. "Justin Bieber Basically Saves a Russian Man from a Bear." MTV, August 6, 2014. https://www.mtv.com/news/1890283/justin-bieber-baby-bear-attack/.

Wall Street Journal Editorial Board. "Fact-Checking Facebook's Fact Checkers." March 5, 2021. https://www.wsj.com/articles/fact-checking-facebooks-fact-checkers-11614987375.

White, Alan, Tom Phillips, and Craig Silverman. "The King of Bullsh*t News." *BuzzFeed News*, April 24, 2015. http://www.buzzfeed.com/alanwhite/central-european-news#.gw6Qkm6op.

Wohlsen, Marcus. "Stop the Lies: Facebook Will Soon Let You Flag Hoax Stories." *Wired*, January 1, 2015.

Index

Page numbers in italics refer to illustrations